More God

More God

Seeing The Blessings Through The Pain

NATE LYTLE WITH JAMES H. PENCE

WESTBOW
PRESS
A DIVISION OF THOMAS NELSON

Scripture taken from the HOLY BIBLE, NEW INTERNATIONAL VERSION®. Copyright © 1973, 1978, 1984 Biblica. Used by permission of Zondervan. All rights reserved.

Photographs courtesy of Danny Vivian, G Scott Imaging, Joe Vulgamore and Michael Boyd

WestBow Press books may be ordered through booksellers or by contacting:

WestBow Press
A Division of Thomas Nelson
1663 Liberty Drive
Bloomington, IN 47403
www.westbowpress.com
1-(866) 928-1240

Because of the dynamic nature of the Internet, any web addresses or links contained in this book may have changed since publication and may no longer be valid. The views expressed in this work are solely those of the author and do not necessarily reflect the views of the publisher, and the publisher hereby disclaims any responsibility for them.

Certain stock imagery © Thinkstock.
Any people depicted in stock imagery provided by Thinkstock are models, and such images are being used for illustrative purposes only.

ISBN: 978-1-4497-3189-2 (hc)
ISBN: 978-1-4497-3188-5 (sc)
ISBN: 978-1-4497-3187-8 (e)

Library of Congress Control Number: 2011960787

Printed in the United States of America

WestBow Press rev. date: 12/5/2011

"Nate's journey highlights the realities of life with a brain injury, balanced with a message of optimism and hope. Through Nate's eyes we realize that different can be good. Different can be a gift in itself. Different can ignite a passion or skill or talent individuals have yet to discover.

Nate's experience teaches us that the real danger is to be emotionally paralyzed, not physically paralyzed. Once we get into the mindset that we are in control of our destiny, we get our power back. We find a way to stay productive, enjoy our family and community, and participate in meaningful activity.

This book is a testimony to his ability to see beyond his personal situation, take advantage of a life changing moment and create a lasting legacy to inspire others whose lives have been interrupted by disability. Nate reminds us that a disabling accident or injury can be a new beginning. His words challenge us to take back our lives - the world depends on our contributions and to never bury our gifts or silence our voice."

Carl E. Josehart
CEO, TIRR Memorial Hermann

"Nate is a walking miracle. His story reminds us of how God uses difficulties as an opportunity to glorify His name. This book will inspire you to trust God in your hardest of days."

David Nasser
Pastor/Author

"When I think of Nate Lytle's story I am reminded how God's ways are not our ways. If God is going to use a man in great ways, he usually first leads him through the deepest valleys. These valleys and trials prune us and prepare us for the battles that await us as we step out in faith on the front lines of spiritual battle. When the trials of life come your way I encourage you to draw close to Jesus Christ and his promises like Nate did. This story will encourage and inspire you!"

Bryan Jennings
Founder & Executive Director
Walking On Water

"Nate's story is one more amazing reminder that God is in the details of our lives and our surfing. Even in the darkest times God's goodness is still there."

Dean Plumlee
National Director Christian Surfers United States

"Nate is an inspiration for everyone. He has a remarkable story that inspires anyone that they too can overcome the difficult challenges we sometimes face in life. I recommend anyone who needs some inspiration to read Nate's story and learnhow they too can overcome the impossible."

Todd Huston, M.A.
Author, Speaker, leg-amputee world-record mountain climber

Dedication

For my loving wife, parents, family, and awesome friends that
have endured this struggle with me. Without you, there would
be no story to tell.
For those struggling with the effects of a brain injury,
may you see the blessings through the pain.

—Nate Lytle

For my lovely wife Laurel. You are my constant source of inspiration
and encouragement.

—James H. Pence

Acknowledgements

This book could never have been written without the contributions of many others. From the moment of Nate's injury forward, a host of family, friends, church family members, fellow surfers, doctors, nurses, therapists, and case workers all played a part in the story of Nate Lytle's amazing recovery.

The authors want to express their gratitude to all those who have allowed their own stories to be shared as part of this book. We also wish to thank those who wrote down their thoughts, recollections, prayers, and experiences for inclusion in Nate's story.

Special thanks goes to the members of El Ride, who told a good portion of this story through their PFN posts, and to Tammy Lytle, who kept a detailed journal from the day of Nate's accident to shortly before he left TIRR Memorial Hermann for TLC.

—Nate Lytle and James H. Pence

Prologue

They're going to make him jump. Are they crazy?

Nate Lytle's eyes remained fixed on three boys standing at the railing of Horace Caldwell Pier. He'd been watching them for several minutes. Even over the roar of the waves, he could hear them arguing. It had apparently started as a dare then moved to a challenge. Now the oldest of the three boys was ordering the youngest—he couldn't be older than eight—to climb onto the pier railing.

It was a good fifteen-foot drop to the water below.

Nate sat on his surfboard, about twenty-five feet away from the pier, watching the drama unfolding above him.

"You'd better get up there," the oldest of the three ordered.

"I don't want to," the little boy shouted back.

"Get up on the railing. Now!"

"No!" screamed the boy.

They won't really do it, Nate thought. *They won't make him jump.*

Nate and about fifteen other surfers were catching waves out near the end of the pier, but Nate had forgotten all about surfing for the moment. He couldn't take his eyes off the three boys.

The shouting continued. The boys shoved each other. More angry shouts.

Finally, the little boy climbed up onto the railing and jumped.

Oh, this is going to be bad.

The boy hit the water and came up screaming. His arms flailed as he tried to swim. In mere seconds, the boy's fear exploded into hysteria.

He was going down.

Nate looked around. There were surfers all around, but nobody was trying to help the boy. Nate was only fifteen—not even old enough to drive to the beach by himself—but he knew that if he didn't act quickly, the little boy would drown.

Nate started paddling. He was only about twenty-five feet away, but on a short board it would take precious extra seconds to get over there.

"Man, hey! Stop! Stop!" Nate called out, trying to get the boy to calm down.

It didn't do any good.

A wave pushed the boy over toward one of the pilings. He grabbed hold and held on for dear life, but as he did, razor-sharp barnacles shredded the skin of his chest and legs. The water all around him began to turn red.

As Nate saw the blood wash through the waves, he shouted, "Let go. Let go of the piling. You're getting cut up." But the boy, frozen with terror, only wrapped his arms and legs tighter around it.

The other two boys leaned over the railing and yelled at their companion, but neither jumped in to help him.

Nate reached the boy but couldn't get him to let go of the piling. Even though the barnacles were slicing him to ribbons, the panic-stricken child clung to the piling and wailed. Nate got off his board, then he wedged his hand under the boy's arm and across his chest and tried to pull him back off the piling, but the boy held on with his legs.

"I promise I'll paddle you in, but you've got to let go."

Nate reached down and pulled the boy's legs free, cutting his own hand in the process. The skin on the boy's chest and legs looked like it had been chewed up by a cheese grater, but he didn't appear to be feeling any pain.

"This is going to hurt, but I've got to get you up on my board. Then I can paddle you in," Nate shouted above the roar of the surf. He hoisted the little boy onto his board, taking the leash from his own ankle and putting it around the boy's. Then Nate pulled himself partway onto the board, just behind the terrified boy and they began the nearly one-hundred-yard journey back to shore.

The boy's breaths came in rapid gasps. He was dangerously close to hyperventilating and losing consciousness.

"Slow your breathing," Nate said. "You've got to pace yourself. We've got a long paddle back to shore."

It took almost ten minutes for Nate to paddle the injured boy to shore, but in a way that was good. The EMTs had already arrived and were waiting for them when Nate's surfboard hit the beach.

Nate stood by as the paramedics took charge of the boy and put him on a gurney.

"You're a hero," one of the EMTs told him. "If you hadn't brought him in, he'd have drowned."

A crowd was quickly gathering and, uncomfortable with the spotlight, Nate slipped away and went back to Brian's truck. He wanted the focus to be on the boy, not on himself.

In the next few days when people tried to call Nate a hero and bring attention to him for what he'd done, he blew it off.

"Anybody would have done it," Nate said, even though nobody else had made any attempt to help the boy.

That was Nate.

Always thinking of others.

Part One

Crisis

Chapter 1

Decision Time

"God, I'm torn up. Can you please give me some kind of direction or discernment? Tell me yes or no, hot or cold? Something?"

Nate Lytle sat in his truck at Riverside Park in Victoria, Texas, with his Bible in his lap. It was a good place to connect with God, particularly at this time of night. Everyone had gone home and Nate pretty much had the park to himself. That was good, because he had a decision to make, and it wasn't an easy one.

Nate had been wrestling with himself and God for a couple of months, yet he didn't feel any closer to knowing what to do than he had when he'd first started.

The decision should have been a no-brainer. It was the ministry opportunity of a lifetime. At least that's what everybody was telling Nate.

Scott Weatherford and Brian Brown, the pastors from Parkway Church, where Nate and his family were members, were leaving to plant a church in Tallahassee, Florida. A key part of that new church's outreach would be to the students at Florida State University. It was an awesome mission field: three campuses and more than 100,000 students. Nate already had a vital ministry with the high school and college students at his own church. He led small groups and shared the Word of God with sixty to eighty students every Sunday. Now Brian had invited him to come to Tallahassee to help spearhead the college outreach.

Nate was a natural. He had a laid-back style and related well to college students. And he loved to speak truth into people's lives. And on

3

the plus side, the surfing would be great in Florida. Of course, that wasn't and never would be Nate's primary motivation for choosing a ministry. But it certainly was a perk.

So why didn't he have any peace about it?

Brian had picked up on Nate's uncertainty and invited him over to his house that night to discuss it. Brian was like a wise older brother to Nate; he was also one of Nate's best friends. After they'd had dinner and Brian's boys were off riding their skateboards, Brian brought up the subject of the move.

"So, what's God telling you?" he asked.

"I don't know, man. I'm kinda' scared," said Nate.

"What are you scared about? Money? A place to live? You know you can stay with us. The boys love you and look up to you like an older brother."

"No, dude," replied Nate. "I don't worry about stuff like that. I just want to make sure this is God's call for my life. I don't want to get caught up in your vision. I think it's awesome what God is doing in you, but maybe it's not the best thing for me."

That was the problem in a nutshell.

Everybody was excited about this new ministry. Nate knew that it would be easy to get caught up in the excitement and just assume that it was part of God's call on his life. But how could he be sure one way or the other?

"There's no pressure, man," Brian told him. "You're a great asset to the ministry here, and you'll be awesome wherever you go. But pray about it and let me know."

Nate stayed at Brian's well into the evening, and when he left he knew he needed time to be alone and pray. Brian and Scott were going to take an exploratory trip to Florida and they had invited Nate to come along.

And now here he sat in Riverside Park, desperately seeking God's direction.

God, what do you want me to do?

Nate knew it would be very easy to jump on board and go to Florida with Brian and Scott, and there was no doubt he could accomplish a lot for God's Kingdom if he did. But Nate believed that every person has his or her own call from God. What if he moved to Florida and found that he had relied on his own wisdom and not God's call?

As Nate sat in his truck asking God for wisdom, he opened up his Bible to the book of Jeremiah and saw a passage he'd never read before.

> *The LORD replied, "Don't say, 'I'm too young,' for you must go wherever I send you and say whatever I tell you. And don't be afraid of the people, for I will be with you and will protect you. I, the LORD, have spoken!" Then the LORD reached out and touched my mouth and said, "Look, I have put my words in your mouth! Today I appoint you to stand up against nations and kingdoms. Some you must uproot and tear down, destroy and overthrow. Others you must build up and plant," (Jeremiah 1:7-10, NLT).*

Was this God's confirmation? Was it God's way of telling Nate that he had been called to speak truth into college students' lives in Florida? It certainly seemed that way. So Nate agreed to travel to Tallahassee with Brian and Scott on their exploratory trip. But Nate took his surfboard and drove his own truck. He wanted to be by himself so he could think and pray during the long road trip.

This was an important decision and he was determined not to get caught up in all the excitement.

More than anything, Nate wanted to do God's will.

❖   ❖   ❖

The trip to Florida was a success, at least in confirming that a huge door of ministry stood open before Nate. Along with Brian and Scott, Nate spent the week meeting pastors, learning what other churches were doing, and networking with people who could help establish this new ministry. They also investigated the possibility of sponsorships, funding sources, and the other things they would need to successfully launch a church.

All the lights appeared to be green, but still it wasn't a simple decision.

Nate's home church was without a youth pastor and many people in the congregation wanted him to step into that role. It would be a natural move for Nate, since he was already spending a lot of his time doing volunteer youth work in the church.

God, move me. Use me. Do whatever it takes to bring glory to Christ. Whatever it takes to encourage people and bring them to Christ.

By mid-May, 2007, Brian and Scott had moved to Florida. Nate was still struggling with his decision. Even though it seemed like an awesome opportunity, he had no peace. He was being pulled in several different directions, and he knew that the only solution to his dilemma was to pursue deeper intimacy with God.

But Nate realized that seeking that intimacy with God might involve laying aside his other great passion: surfing.

In an online prayer journal that he started on May seventeenth, the first question was: "What will pursuing intimacy with God cost you?"

Nate's answer: "At this point . . . layin' surfing on the altar."

Surfing and Sacrifice

Nate began surfing when he was fourteen years old. He'd been skateboarding for some time, but the city of Victoria had started issuing tickets to skateboarders and there were no public skateboard parks. About that time, Nate's church hosted a surfing clinic for the youth of the community. His pastors, Brian and Scott, invited him to come along. Now that he no longer had skateboarding, Nate needed a new outlet. He attended the clinic and instantly fell in love with the sport.

So great was Nate's passion for surfing that he was known to go out even when there weren't any good waves.

There is a purity—almost a spirituality—to surfing that Nate finds difficult to explain.

"It's an adrenaline rush, but it's peaceful at the same time. You're out there and there's so much adrenaline going down the line, but it's like glass, like you're walking on water."

Surfing also provided a supremely quiet place for Nate to be alone with God. When he was out there in the water, there were no distractions. Just Nate, the Lord, and the waves.

And surfing had become a ministry in its own right. Nate ministered to the surfers he met when he was at the beach through his quiet testimony, his involvement with the Christian Surfers group, and his willingness to love and pray for people. Nate's witness was not an "in your face" confrontational style. Rather, he lived his faith and spoke about it unashamedly. The quality of his life added the stamp of authenticity to his words.

But although surfing was a passion and a ministry to Nate, he was becoming concerned that perhaps it had also become an idol. Whenever he wanted to go surfing, Nate had to make a three-hour round trip to Corpus Christi. When he compared the time spent on his frequent trips to the beach with the amount of time he needed to spend preparing for his student ministry and for Sunday services, Nate realized that his passion was taking up a large amount of his time.

Maybe too much of his time.

Even though he still was uncertain of God's will regarding Florida, Nate knew what God was calling him to do about surfing.

On May 18, 2007, Nate wrote in his online prayer journal:

> *I want your presence felt with me always. Not just on Sunday mornings or Wednesday nights. Not just in my quiet time. Always. I want my day to begin and recur with you. To know that a day with you never truly ends, because you never leave me.*
>
> *So will I sacrifice? You've called me to amazing works for you and you alone. I believe you call us all to serve. Whether or not that service is part-time volunteer or full-time lifestyle is answered only through your call for each of our lives. I know you've asked and tugged and wrestled with me to be the one who leads a life all for you. You've given me physical gifts that I have put priority in over you because I've tried to use them for your glory. Maybe the reason you gave me these great gifts is to truly test my devotion to you. To see if I was really willing to give up my all. I'll tell you with all my heart that this will be the hardest thing I've ever been asked to give away. Even though you've asked me to lay it aside for so long, this will be the first time I've been willing to cooperate.*

God was calling Nate to lay down the one thing he loved more than anything else in the world, his single passion. God was calling Nate to lay down the one thing that could potentially take God's place in his heart: surfing.

He knew it from the time he'd started his online prayer journal, but every passing day his resolve became stronger. Nate decided to lay aside surfing for one year so that he could focus on further developing his relationship with God.

The year would begin on June fourth, the day after his first and last surfing competition.

❖   ❖   ❖

Nate told his family about his plans to lay aside surfing for a year. But even though it was the middle of May, he couldn't follow through right away because he had committed himself to participating in a longboard competition in Galveston on Sunday, June 3rd.

Nate wasn't at all interested in competitive surfing, but back in April, when a longboard competition was announced for early June in Galveston, his friend Dustin encouraged him to register.

"I don't want to glorify myself," Nate said, but Dustin wouldn't take no for an answer.

"Dude, you're a longboarder. You've got great skills. You'll do great. You've got to at least try it one time."

Nate finally agreed and signed up for the competition, and on Friday, June 1st he drove to Galveston to stay with J. P., another one of his surfing buddies. Nate was glad to have the opportunity to be with J. P. for another reason. He wanted to get his feedback about the possible move to Florida.

J. P. saw how torn up Nate was about the decision.

"Dude," he said. "You don't need to go to Florida to touch people's lives. You touch people's lives in the water all the time. Do you really want to be a pastor?"

That was another question that had nagged at Nate for a while.

Nate's decision wasn't only about whether to be a college pastor in Florida or a youth pastor in Texas. The truth was, he didn't feel called to be a pastor or to go into full-time ministry at all. Nate just wanted to share Christ with people. Did he have to go to Florida or become a youth pastor to do that? Or was J. P. right? Could he touch more lives just being down at the beach?

Those questions were in the back of Nate's mind as he went down to the Flagship in Galveston early on Sunday morning to help the Christian Surfers group set up the tents for the competition. He came to the contest, but his mind was back at home, thinking about ministry. He replayed J. P.'s words: "You can touch lives anywhere. You don't have to go to Florida or be a youth pastor."

When Nate paddled out for his first heat, he knew that it would be a short competition for him. He would be competing against Morgan Faulkner, the best professional surfer to come out of Texas.

Nate laughed and relaxed.

Surfers don't normally talk much when they're competing against each other, but Nate called out, "What's up, Morgan?"

"What's up, dude?" Faulkner replied.

"Looks like it's going to be a short event for me," Nate said.

"Dude, you're crazy," said Faulkner, shaking his head.

But Nate knew that he'd never make it out of his heat. So instead he cheered on Morgan. Whenever a good wave came along, Nate yelled, "That's a good one! Go! Go! Go!" Faulkner just kept looking back at Nate as if he really were crazy. Nate was probably one of the few surfers who ever cheered him on when he was supposed to be competing against him.

After the heat, Nate sat on the beach for a while, and then he walked down to another jetty and surfed by himself. For Nate, that's what surfing was all about: having time alone with God and nature. Having time to think, to worship, to pray.

Later, J. P. and some other Christian surfing buddies found Nate sitting on the beach.

"You didn't make it out of your heat, did you?" they asked.

Nate looked up at them and smiled. "What do you think?"

They just nodded and laughed. "Morgan." But they also knew that competition wasn't what Nate was all about. He was interested in impacting others for the Kingdom of God.

After the competition, Nate told J. P. and the others, "I've got to get back to Victoria. I have to work early tomorrow."

Nate said goodbye to his friends and began the three-hour-drive home. The competition was a wash, but it had been a good time. His conversation with J. P. had helped clarify in his mind what he needed to do. Tomorrow, June fourth, Nate would do the most difficult thing he'd ever done. He would lay aside surfing for a whole year and concentrate on his relationship with God. His all-consuming desire was for God to use him, and Nate would do whatever was necessary for that to happen. If being used by God meant that he would have to embrace sacrifice, then that was exactly what he would do. Nate knew it would be tough, but he liked a challenge.

He had no idea how great a challenge he was about to face.

Chapter 2

Emergency

Nate had a great time at the surf competition, especially hanging with J. P. and his other surfing buddies, but it was time to change focus. Even though he had misgivings about moving to Florida, Nate had decided to go. With the decision made, Nate planned to make the move on Saturday, June ninth.

On Sunday evening after returning from the competition, Nate told his mother, Tammy, that he just couldn't get peace about going to Florida. He didn't understand why he couldn't hear God telling him whether to stay or go. Nate then went to bed so he would be refreshed for work the next morning. Nate had been helping his father Billy at his business, Engenco, after finishing his four and a half years in the Coast Guard.

Engenco, short for Engine Generator Company, was the fulfillment of one of Billy Lytle's lifelong dreams: owning his own business. On the Engenco Web site, Billy writes: "God has 'given me one of the desires of my heart . . . Psalm 37:4.' Thus I will never cease to give Him the praise and thanks He so rightly deserves!"

Engenco provides engines, generators, and parts to the oil and gas industry. Most of the engine parts were housed in a large warehouse about fifty yards behind the main office building. Engenco's warehouse was a claustrophobic maze of twelve-foot shelves, loaded with heavy engine and generator parts. In addition to the well-stocked shelves, additional inventory was kept on pallets and in boxes in the aisles between the shelves.

Monday, June 4, 2007

Early Monday morning, Nate was in the warehouse attempting to retrieve a diesel exhaust manifold that a customer had requested. After several attempts to retrieve the manifold on his own, Nate called the front office and asked Billy if he would give him some help.

"I'll come out and help you with that in a few minutes," Billy said.

The diesel exhaust manifold was on top of a twelve-foot shelf and weighed three hundred pounds. There was no way that Nate could carry it down. It was too heavy and too high up. He normally would use a forklift, but the pallet on which the manifold rested had broken, so a forklift wouldn't work. Nate wheeled over a hand-crank lift. Although it wasn't the best choice for such a load, the hand-operated lift was rated to hold heavy items such as the manifold. Nate raised the lift and positioned it in front of the manifold; he then brought over a ten-foot A-frame ladder and placed it next to the lift. About that time, Billy arrived.

The shelf was deep and sturdy, and Nate knew it would hold his weight. All he had to do was scoot the manifold into the lift's waiting arms. Nate climbed the ladder. When he was nearing the top Nate tried to get onto the shelf where the manifold was, but was having some difficulty. He then said, "I can't do this," so Billy suggested they trade places. Nate agreed and came down the ladder. Billy proceeded up the ladder and climbed onto the shelf. Nate positioned himself near the top on the ladder. The two began to manhandle the exhaust manifold, slowly shoving and pulling it toward the edge of the shelf and onto the forks of the waiting lift. But once the manifold was halfway onto the forks, it became stuck. Seeing where the manifold was hung up, Nate said, "I'll move it." He reached over and pushed on the fork of the lift. When he did, the manifold slid off the forks. On the way down the heavy hunk of iron struck the bottom rung of the ladder.

The next thing Nate knew, he was airborne.

For Nate, the scene unfolded almost as if he were watching it in slow motion. Nate looked up and saw the warehouse ceiling, then looked down and saw the concrete floor and steel parts rushing toward him.

"Oh, this is gonna suck," Nate thought.

Nate put his left hand out to brace his fall. His left wrist shattered the instant he hit the ground.

Next, he heard a high-pitched ringing, like an electronic beep that wouldn't shut off.

❈   ❈   ❈

For Billy, the accident happened so quickly, it was as if Nate had simply vanished. One second, he was on the ladder only a few feet away, and the next he was gone. Billy looked over the edge of the shelf and saw Nate lying on the floor cradling his hand. He quickly clambered down the ladder and went to his son.

"Are you all right? Did you hit your head?"

Nate lay there groaning, "Oh Dad. My hand. My hand."

"Don't worry about your hand. Did you hit your head?"

"No. My hand. I hurt my hand."

Nate's left hand and wrist were a sickening sight. If it weren't for the skin and muscle still holding Nate's hand onto his arm, the hand could simply have dropped off. It hung there grotesquely.

Billy knew they needed to get to the hospital immediately.

"Don't move. Hang in there," he told his son. "I'll go get the truck and take you to the hospital."

Billy had no intention of dialing 911.

The property on which Engenco resides had recently been annexed into the city, but the address had not been updated in the city's 911 files. Several months back, there had been a grass fire at their place, and the fire department got lost trying to find them. Billy knew Nate's wrist was badly hurt and they couldn't waste time waiting for the EMTs to find them.

On his way up to the front office, Billy pulled out his cell phone and called his wife Tammy.

"Nate fell and hurt his wrist," Billy said. "I'm taking him to the hospital."

Billy jumped into his Ford F-250 pickup truck and drove back to the warehouse. He helped Nate walk out to the cab of the truck and lie down in the back seat. Then he got in front and drove as fast as he could to the emergency room.

In the back seat of the F-250 cab, Nate managed to get out his cell phone. With his one good hand, he sent off a quick text to J. P. that said simply, "I fell and busted my wrist. Pray for me." Next, he tried to call Shawn, a friend from church, but by mistake he dialed a different friend named Shad.

"Shawn, Shawn. I'm hurt. I'm hurt."

As Billy drove and heard Nate trying to talk on the phone, he noticed something very strange and disturbing. As Nate tried to talk, a mixture of gibberish and Coast Guard commands came out.

Billy drove faster.

❋   ❋   ❋

Tammy Lytle was Engenco's bookkeeper and also worked at a medical uniform shop. She was on her way to work at the uniform shop when she got her husband's call. She knew that whatever Nate's injury was, it was serious. Billy and Nate were both the kind of men who blew off injuries. If they were going to the hospital, Nate was really hurt. She drove straight to the hospital and was walking toward the emergency room when she met Billy, on his way out to park the truck.

"Where's Nate?" She asked.

"He's inside, sitting in a wheelchair, waiting to be signed in," replied Billy.

Tammy went into the ER waiting room. She noticed immediately that the sign-in nurse was not at her desk. Tammy went over and stood behind Nate and tried to encourage him. When she saw his hand dangling from his wrist, it was all she could do not to look away.

"Mom, my hand." Nate said, trying to lift his hand.

"It's okay Nate," said Tammy. "Just be calm and wait for the sign-in nurse to come to the window."

Like most hospitals, this one had a registration procedure for walk-in emergency patients. First, a patient has to sign in at the reception window and fill out the necessary paperwork. Then, the walk-in patients must sit in the lobby and wait until the nurse calls them. The nurse then checks the patient's vitals, and after that the patient returns to the lobby to wait until called back to a treatment room.

If you don't come in by ambulance, it can be a long wait.

As Tammy and Nate waited for the sign-in nurse to return to her window, Nate tried to say something, but it came out as gibberish.

"What did you say?" Tammy asked Nate.

Nate tried to speak, but only meaningless syllables came out. Seconds later his head began to loll to one side and his body began to go limp.

Concerned that Nate might slip out of the wheelchair, Tammy called out to a nearby security guard, "Can you please come help me hold him in the chair?"

The security guard came over to help, but quickly realized that Nate was in trouble.

"Let's get him to the back," he said.

They tried to roll the chair, but Nate's feet were in the way.

"Nate," said Tammy, "can you lift up your feet so we can wheel you?"

Nate was barely able to lift his feet up and put them on the foot rests. Tammy and the security guard wheeled him to the back, toward the treatment rooms. As they rolled down the hall they met Dr. John McNeill, the ER doctor who was on-call that day.

"What are you doing back here?" he asked.

"My son fell and hurt his wrist," Tammy replied. "But he started talking weird."

"What do you mean he's talking weird?" Dr. McNeill said.

"I don't know," Tammy said. "He's trying to talk, but it's just gibberish."

A look of concern came over Dr. McNeill's face. He knew that if Nate was talking funny, his injury could be far more serious than a broken wrist.

"Let's get him back to the trauma room," Dr. McNeill said.

Billy caught up with them as they wheeled Nate back into the trauma room. As Tammy and Billy watched the trauma team get Nate onto the bed, Nate kept apologizing for all the trouble he was putting everyone through. Then he began talking in gibberish again. When the trauma team began to ask Nate his name, he began to call out his name and Coast Guard ranks and orders.

Dr. McNeill asked Tammy and Billy to wait in a small waiting area near the trauma room door. As the door swung closed, they heard Nate say, "I'm gonna puke."

❈   ❈   ❈

As Tammy and Billy sat outside Trauma One, waiting for Dr. McNeill's report, Billy asked Tammy how they got him back so fast.

"Nate started talking really weird and he couldn't sit up."

"That's weird," Billy said, recalling how Nate was talking gibberish in the truck.

"What happened at the shop?" Tammy asked.

"Nate was on the ten-foot ladder and I was on the other side of the rack. We were trying to lower the manifold with straps, but it slipped and fell. Then next thing I knew, Nate was gone. He was trying to sit up by the time I got off the ladder. The manifold hit the last rung of the ladder and propelled Nate off of it. I asked him if he'd hit his head, but he just kept saying, "My hand, my hand.""

As Billy recounted for Tammy the story of their rush to the hospital, the door to Trauma One opened and Dr. McNeill came out.

Something about the expression on his face told Tammy and Billy that the news was not going to be good.

"We think your son has a severe head injury," Dr. McNeill said.

Tammy and Billy were puzzled.

"What?" asked Tammy.

"We lost him. We lost vitals. We lost everything. He's been intubated and sedated, and he's on life support."

Tammy couldn't believe what she was hearing. "No, he just hurt his hand," she kept repeating.

"When we got his cap off," said Dr. McNeill, "there was a soft spot on the left side of his head. If there's been head trauma, it's very serious and he will require surgery, but we need to do a CAT scan first. We're waiting on a room to become available now."

Dr. McNeill paused and said, "You need to come in and talk to your son."

"Will he understand us?" Tammy asked.

"Well . . ." Dr McNeill hesitated.

"Why do we need to talk to him?"

"You need to talk to your son," the doctor repeated. "We're waiting on a CAT scan, but we don't know . . ." Dr. McNeill's voice trailed off and he looked down toward the floor.

A horrible realization swept over Tammy and Billy.

"You don't think he's going to make it through the CAT scan. Is that what you're telling me?"

"Mrs. Lytle, you need to come talk to your son."

Tammy and Billy Lytle followed Dr. McNeill through the door into trauma room one. They learned later that, without surgery, Nate would have had less than fifteen minutes left to live.

Chapter Three

Surgery

Billy and Tammy Lytle were in shock. In only a few minutes, their son had gone from what they thought was a severe wrist injury to being on life support. They were waiting on a CAT scan room to become available so the doctors could assess the damage. In the meantime, Dr. McNeill had told them that they should come in and talk to Nate and tell him whatever they needed to tell him.

He was telling them that they needed to say goodbye.

Nate was hooked up to a respirator when Billy and Tammy entered the trauma room. He looked peaceful, like he was sleeping.

"Nate," said Tammy, "You're going to be okay. We love you, and whatever happens, you're going to be okay." Tammy didn't know whether Nate could hear or understand what she was saying, but she wanted, first and foremost, to console him. "You're going to be with people that love you and will take care of you and support you. No matter what happens. You listen to God and do what you need to do so that you'll be okay. And everyone else will be okay if you're okay. You're a wonderful son, and we love you."

Billy told Nate how much he loved him, and then he prayed for his son.

For a few moments longer Tammy and Billy stood there looking at Nate, a loving, caring, and giving young man who always tried to help everyone he came in contact with. Tammy was trying to be strong for

Nate, but she was also wondering how she would live without him if he didn't make it.

Finally, the nurses told them that they needed space to work on Nate and get him ready for the CAT scan. Billy and Tammy went back to the little waiting area.

As they left the trauma room, they began to wonder how long it would be before they would get Nate into the CAT scan. Dr. McNeill had essentially told them that he didn't think Nate would live long enough to get through the scan. But for some reason, it was taking a while to get him back there. Tammy and Billy knew that every second counted, and the seconds were flying by.

They had barely gotten into the hallway when Justin, a young man who lived across the street from the Lytles and who had grown up with Nate, came around the corner.

"Mrs. Lytle, what are y'all doing here?"

"Nathan's in the trauma room"

"Nate? What are they doing?"

"Well," she said, "they need a CAT scan. But there's not a room open or something. I don't know what's going on, but they need it now!"

Justin didn't miss a beat. "I run that area. I can take him back there now."

Justin went into the trauma room and seconds later, they rushed Nate off to do the CAT scan.

As they waited for the CAT scan report to come in, Billy and Tammy sat back down in the conference room and began to make phone calls to family members, friends, and a few of Nate's friends as well. Tammy called a friend to bring Nate's younger sister Elissa to the hospital.

In a very short time, people began to show up at the main ER waiting room. Dr McNeill hadn't reported in yet, so Billy helped Tammy walk out to greet the family and friends who were arriving. Tammy was overwhelmed. She felt like she was in the middle of a nightmare; she couldn't believe this was all happening. Many of the people remarked about how strong she was. Tammy realized later that it was more shock than strength. The full implications of what had happened to Nate still hadn't hit her.

As they waited for word, the ER waiting room continued to fill up until there were nearly thirty people there, praying and waiting. When Nate's younger sister Elissa arrived, Billy and Tammy took her aside and broke the news to her. Elissa cried and sat down to join the vigil.

Tammy had been keeping a watchful eye on the glass doors that led back to the treatment area and finally she saw Dr. McNeill making his way down the hall. She and Billy went back into the ER and asked him what the news was.

Dr. McNeill's face told much of the story.

The news was not good.

"Your son has a severe head injury," Dr. McNeill said. "He has shattered his skull. The CAT scan shows that there are pieces of his skull sticking into his brain. We've called in a neurosurgeon and he's on his way over."

Tammy couldn't believe what she was hearing. "No! This cannot be happening!" she said. "He hurt his hand, not his head!" Tammy's thoughts flashed back to thirty-four years earlier when her uncle suffered a head injury and didn't survive.

It was all Tammy could do to hold herself together, but she wanted to be strong for the others who were out in the waiting room. She and Billy went out to pass along the news about Nate's condition.

As Tammy was sharing with the now more than fifty people who had assembled in the ER waiting room, she glanced through the glass doors into the ER and saw Dr. Keith Norvill coming down the corridor. Dr. Norvill had gone to their church in the past and they had been in a small group together a year earlier. Tammy decided to go say hi and tell him about Nate.

As Tammy and Billy approached, Dr. Norvill looked down and, as he did, Tammy realized that he must be the neurosurgeon.

Dr. Norvill said, "Tammy. Billy. You guys, I've looked at Nate's CAT scan, and he needs emergency surgery. A large portion of his skull has been shattered into pieces and has pierced his brain."[1]

---

[1] Tammy and Billy would later learn that Nate's CT showed early herniation, which usually causes death, and that he had a midline shift of 1.7 centimeters. A midline shift of just one to two millimeters doubles the

Tammy and Billy nodded. "Okay. Let's do it."

Dr. Norvill shook his head and looked away. "No, I need you to understand something. I do not think I can fix this."

"What do you mean, you don't think you can fix this?" asked Tammy.

"I've never seen an injury so severe. I just don't think this can be fixed."

"God can fix it if it's His will," Tammy said.

"Well . . ." Dr. Norvill replied, his face showing his doubt.

"Can we pray before you do the surgery?"

The neurosurgeon nodded. "Yes, but I've got to hurry."

Billy Lytle prayed a quick prayer that God would guide the doctor's hands as he performed the surgery.

"Keith," said Tammy, "If you and God cannot fix this to where Nate can talk and share God with people, he needs to go home. He can go without walking. He can manage to live in a wheelchair if he has to. But Nate can't be Nate if he can't tell people about God."

"I'll do what I can," he said. "But time is of the essence and I need to do the surgery now."

As they were getting Nate ready to move to the surgical floor, Dr. McNeill came over to talk to Tammy and Billy. "How could he have shattered his skull?" she asked. "There wasn't any blood, and he didn't feel any pain."

"He had a cap on," replied the doctor. "That probably cushioned the impact and kept his skin from breaking so that the injury was not outwardly visible. And his brain is bleeding and swelling. Sometimes that can buffer the pain." Dr. McNeill paused for a moment, then added, "Nate's very lucky; there hasn't been a neurosurgeon on call here for over three months. Dr. Norvill is a friend of mine, so I called him and asked him to come over to the hospital to see Nate."

The implications of Dr. McNeill's statement were staggering. If he had not been working the ER that morning, there would have been no

---

chances of non-survival. With Nate's being 1.7 centimeters (or seventeen millimeters), Dr. McNeill did not think he would survive.

neurosurgeon to see Nate. With the severity of the injuries, they usually would have tried to CareFlight him to Houston, but Nate would never have survived the flight. As this sank in, so did a small sense of calm. Tammy was thankful that God had not only sent a surgeon they knew personally, but one they could pray with. They knew that, whatever the outcome, God would be directing Dr. Norvill's hands.

Still dealing with the shock of learning how serious Nate's condition was, Tammy and Billy went back out to the ER waiting room to tell the small crowd assembled there about the CAT scan results.

The group of friends and family waiting for news continued to grow, and now their pastor and other church staff members had arrived as well. Tammy explained Nate's situation and asked the pastor to pray. She loved Nate and couldn't conceive of what life without him would be like. But she also knew her son's heart. She asked pastor Cole, "Please just pray that God will heal Nate at least to where he can talk and share his life and God with people. But if He can't do that, then I don't think he would want to live."

The pastor led them in prayer, and when he finished, a nurse came out and told them that they were taking Nate upstairs for surgery. The Lytles followed along to the surgical waiting room. A few minutes later, friends and family followed. Before long, the waiting room was so full that it was difficult to move around in. All the chairs were full; people were sitting all over the floor and standing against the walls. A lot of the visitors were teenagers from Nate's youth group at church.

Tammy looked around at the diverse group of people, now numbering nearly fifty. She knew that Nate had touched many people's lives in his twenty-three years, but it was overwhelming to see so many here before her eyes. He touched those from two years old to eighty years old; some of his closest friends were in their thirties, forties, and fifties.

Is his ministry time on earth over?

Tammy's chest felt heavy and it was hard to breathe, but at the same time, her body felt light. She rubbed her arm, trying to wake herself up, hoping that this was all a bad dream. Tammy began to think about Nate telling her the night before that he couldn't get a peace about whether he should go to Florida or stay in Victoria. She began to realize that it might have been because he wouldn't be alive to do either. Or that he would be so injured that he wouldn't be able to leave on the ninth to go to Florida.

Dr. Norvill had told Tammy and Billy that Nate would probably not make it through the surgery. So as the hours in the waiting room passed, they didn't know whether it was a good thing or bad. On the one hand, as long as the surgery was still going on, it meant that Nate was still alive; on the other hand, every minute he spent in the operating room meant that there was one more injury they were trying to fix.

As they waited for news, Tammy's cell phone kept ringing. Friends, family, surfers, and even men that Nate had served with in the Coast Guard were all calling in, asking for news. The phone calls and activity were a welcome distraction for Tammy during the long wait, helping her to focus on something other than the amount of time the surgery was taking. Many of the people in the waiting room remarked about how strong Tammy was being and how well she was handling everything. What they didn't know is that Tammy was in shock, still trying to figure out if all of this was real.

Finally, after several hours, Dr. Norvill came into the waiting room and asked Tammy and Billy to accompany him to a nearby conference room.

"Nate made it through the surgery," he said. "His pupil dilation is a lot worse than when he went in, and he's about a five on the Glasgow Coma Scale."

Tammy knew that Dr. Norvill was not giving them good news. She'd had a friend whose daughter had suffered a brain injury a while back. Tammy had learned about the Glasgow Coma Scale from her friend.[2] The scale is a means for measuring the severity of a brain injury. A score lower than eight on the scale is critical. Upwards of fifty percent of patients with that kind of score will die within the first six hours.

"There were several hematomas," Dr. Norvill continued. "Pieces of his skull have pierced and cut his brain, and I had to carefully remove each of those fragments. I couldn't put those fragments back together, so he has a large hole in his skull.

---

[2]   For more information about the *Glasgow Coma Scale*, see Appendix 2.

"I had to remove three large hematomas, and when I removed the last one, it was so deep that the left side of Nate's brain collapsed. Then it started filling with blood and began swelling. The good thing is that, because there's a large piece of his skull missing, the brain has room to swell. If Nate survives this, I'll go in later and put in a plate to fill the hole."

"What does all this mean?" Tammy and Billy asked.

"What it means," replied Dr. Norvill, "is that I don't see how Nate can survive this kind of a blow to his head. If he does survive, medically I don't see how he'll ever walk, talk, or even communicate again. If I were you, I'd begin looking into arrangements."

Tammy and Billy were afraid to ask what kind of arrangements he meant.

Dr. Norvill's words hung in the air like a prophecy of doom. The one thing that Billy and Tammy were most concerned about—Nate's ability to communicate—was the very thing the surgeon said would probably never return. Tammy knew this was not only going to be a physical battle, but also a spiritual one.

Tammy and Billy thanked Dr. Norvill for trying to help Nate. "We know you did everything you could," they said.

They went back out to the surgical waiting room and passed on the discouraging news. Many of the people gathered there began to cry. A few tried to look on the positive side—at least Nate had made it through the surgery. Others sat in stunned silence. Several kept saying, "How could this be happening to someone who is so young and such a servant of God?"

Once Nate was out of recovery, they put him in the surgical ICU.

Tammy and Billy spent the rest of the day visiting Nate when they could, praying and watching for any sign of responsiveness. When they weren't in the ICU, they sat with others in the waiting room talking, praying, and wondering how this could have happened.

Tammy's mind raced with thoughts and concerns.

This can't be real!

I need to wake up.

How am I supposed to act? What does everyone expect from me?

I have to be strong for my daughter and my husband.

How can I be strong for them when I feel like I'm dying myself?

Will Nate live? Will he ever wake up?

Will he ever walk or talk again?

I can't do this.

God's in control. He can fix this. But is it his will to fix it?

How can this be happening?

She was surrounded by people who cared about her and Nate, yet she felt alone. Her heart was breaking and it felt like it was going to beat out of her chest.

How could her twenty-three-year-old son, a young man who had saved so many lives physically, mentally, emotionally, and spiritually now be facing the end of his own life on earth? Why was it being taken from him so early?

Tammy cried out to the Lord in her heart.

God, please help him! And please help me to get through this!

Chapter Four

El Ride

Word of Nate's condition spread like a south Texas grass fire. Soon, the ICU waiting room overflowed with family, friends, surfing buddies, church members, and youth. The news spread quickly via phone calls, texts, and Internet.

El Ride International is an online surfing community and discussion board that is populated primarily, though not exclusively, by surfers from the Texas Gulf Coast. Many of Nate's surfing buddies frequented the message board, and as soon as news about Nate's accident was posted, prayers and comments began to roll in. Eventually, the thread grew to become the longest single discussion thread in El Ride's history. It also launched a juggernaut prayer outreach that quickly became identified as Pray for Nate (PFN).

J. P., one of Nate's best surfing buddies, whom he met when he was stationed with the Coast Guard in Galveston, got the ball rolling. Nate had texted him from Billy's truck as he was on the way to the hospital, and told him that he had hurt his wrist. Later, Tammy called him and alerted him to how serious Nate's condition was.

J. P. immediately called another member on the board and asked him to post a message requesting prayer for Nate.

"Just got a call from JP1 and he said Nate (texasboy) fell from a ladder this morning. He messed up some ribs but he also hit his head and is going into emergency surgery to relieve some pressure on the brain. Lift him up."

That post went out at 10:50 a.m. on June fourth. Within minutes, replies began to come in.

"He's got 'em. Get well soon, Nate."—surfnsail[3]

"Prayers here."—Surfncpa

"Praying hard for you Nate."—nip

"Prayin hard for my fellow Walden rider."—jsh

"Prayers sent. Just saw and talked to him yesterday at the LB pro. What an awesome guy."—surfsesh

"Surfed with Nate, Saturday. Always a big smile and a positive attitude. Definitely thinking about you bro. Please update."—Bones

Throughout the day on June fourth, the updates would come. As far away as Tallahassee, Florida, Nate's friend and former pastor, Brian, relayed information that he was receiving from Tammy and others.

"Nate's in surgery right now; the doctor told his parents before he went in that it really didn't look good. Right before they took him in there was a good sign, they said his eyes would follow light. Keep praying."—brianb8888

A few hours later, Brian reported the initial results from Nate's surgery:

"He's out of surgery. He has movement on his right side, but not his left at this point. His pupil movement is good, so that is a good sign. They are leaving his skull open at this point to relieve pressure and drainage, they'll have to go back and put in a metal plate in about three weeks. From what I understand he will be in ICU for at least three weeks and then possibly stay in the hospital for a month or two if all things go well. If not, this will be a long process. He can't have any visitors for the next few weeks; they don't want him to get excited.

"The best thing you can do is pray for him and his family. If you know Nate well, you know all he wants is for God to use his life for

---

[3] Author's Note: In the interest of preserving the integrity of the El Ride posts, they have been included "as is" with little or no editing. The members' screen names are printed exactly as they occurred on the bulletin board (e.g. many are not capitalized). Occasionally, minor edits have been made for the sake of clarity.

His glory. Pray that God will be glorified in all of this, even if we don't understand it."—brianb8888

One of Nate's surfing buddies who is also a pediatrician posted a physician's perspective on Nate's condition after talking with Tammy:

"I spoke with Nate's mom. They happen to know his neurosurgeon personally and feel very comfortable with him. It sounds like the care he's getting is top notch and very appropriate.

"I think that the potential for recovery is much greater for a traumatic brain injury in comparison to an anoxic insult (such as lack of oxygen due to a near drowning) and I'm praying that Nate makes a full recovery.

"They are able to monitor and control his intracranial pressure through his open skull as well as being heavily sedated and intubated. He has not been moving his left arm yet, but he does have a fractured left wrist. He moves his left foot a little with stimulation. He is able to move his right side; I think he tried to reach for his tubes.

"Continue to pray for Nate and his family."—nip

Nate was in a coma and the movements on his right side were involuntary movements, but it was still movement, and thus encouraging.

After Nate was out of surgery, his friend, Danny Vivian, posted this to El Ride:

"I just left the hospital. Brian just about covered it. The doctors told Nate's family that they will know more in a week or so about any potential loss of speech, motor function, etc. Nate's mom, dad, and sister are really in a state of shock, but they have lots of friends around them. We filled up the entire ICU waiting room.

"God has big plans for Nate, no matter the end result of his recovery."—wavehound

If anyone knew that God's hand was on Nate in a special way, Danny Vivian did. Indeed, Danny was instrumental in introducing Nate to surfing.

In the past, Danny worked with the youth at Nate's church. A lifelong surfer, Danny loved to introduce others to the sport. So one Saturday, he and some of the other men in the church held a surf clinic for the young people. It wasn't anything fancy, just a trip to the beach at Port Aransas, but nearly fifty kids attended. A local surf shop loaned the group some surfboards and they had a great day together.

Danny didn't realize it at the time, but that day had a powerful impact on Nate.

A few weeks later, as Danny and his family were about to sit down to eat dinner, their telephone rang. It was Nate, and he wanted to talk about surfing. Danny didn't know Nate particularly well at the time. He remembered him mostly for his unusual hairstyle—the sides of his head were shaved and on top his hair was long and standing straight up. Danny talked to him for almost a half-hour before he finally got back to his supper.

Soon, Nate was calling Danny two and three times a week to talk about surfing. "He was just so gung ho about surfing," Danny said. "Everything was surfing, surfing, surfing." Eventually, Nate started going along when Danny, Brian, and Scott went to the beach.

As time passed, Danny got to know Nate better through church and the youth group, and as Nate grew to high school age and to adulthood, they became good friends. Even after Nate enlisted in the Coast Guard, they kept in touch.

Danny was on his way to Corpus Christi when Tammy called him and told him about Nate's accident. He turned his car around immediately and headed back to Victoria. When he got to the waiting room, he was overwhelmed by the number of people there.

Over fifty people had crammed into the surgical ICU waiting room.

According to Danny, the atmosphere in the room was almost surreal. Everyone was standing around in shock. It felt almost like the aftermath of a hurricane. No one could believe what was happening.

As Danny stood there in the crowded room waiting to hear whether Nate would live or die, he knew one thing for certain: God had great things planned for Nate.

Nevertheless, the waiting was almost unbearable.

Shad Estes, another of Nate's buddies, also spent the day in that waiting room. On the way to the hospital, Nate had accidentally called Shad from Billy's truck. Shad had been on the phone with a customer when Nate's frantic call came through. Shad couldn't understand what his friend was saying. All he could make out was that Nate was saying something about Shawn.

He was trying to talk to Nate when Billy took the phone and also said "Shawn," but then he lost the connection.

Shad didn't know what was wrong, but he had a sick feeling in his stomach.

A few minutes later, he got a call from Tammy, telling him that Nate was in the emergency room. Shad went to the hospital immediately and spent most of the rest of the day there, waiting and supporting Tammy, Billy, and Elissa.

Shad later wrote down the agonizing emotions of that day in a journal/letter to Nate:

"I walked up and down the hall and just asked God to please not take you from me like this. I prayed and prayed for God to let you be okay. I was there when they wheeled you out to go to surgery. Your mom told me to talk to you . . . . I told you that I love you and you're going to be okay.

"They wheeled you into surgery and we waited and waited. A couple of times I left the surgery waiting area and walked down the hall and got on my knees to talk to God. I cried and cried and asked God please let you be okay and that you wouldn't be taken from me like this. I remember telling you that God told me that he was going to take you away from me and that kept coming up in my head. I didn't want God to take you away like this. I kept praying and praying for God to let you live. I tried to hold it all in like I do with everything else and not cry around people. But when I was alone I just busted out, asking God to spare your life.

"We all gathered together and prayed, all forty or fifty people in a circle in the waiting room, praying God to use Norvill's hands in surgery as HIS hands.

"There were friends of yours everywhere. It was powerful to see forty people in the waiting room praying for one of our brothers . . . ."

Leigh Goris, who had been in Nate's small group was one of those people who waited and prayed:

"I remember our small group hanging out in the ICU waiting room. There were so many people there that we had to sit on the floor.

The mood in the room wasn't doom and gloom as one might expect. With so many of Nate's family and friends there, many of which were his church family, the mood of the room seemed calm and hopeful. Nate's sister sang a song for Nate as everyone in the waiting room joined hands and prayed for Nate's recovery. People couldn't keep a dry eye when she sang, but I don't think it was in sadness. I think the sense of community and the love we all shared for Nate was the motivation behind the tears."

Stephen Infanger, another of Nate's friends, observed that while Nate was fighting for his life in ICU, God was at work in a special way in the waiting room:

"Looking back at those in the waiting room with me, I remember your family and friends taking up most of the space in there. It wasn't only how many people that were there that impressed me, but the faith and the support that was in the room. I'm not sure if I've seen firsthand a more genuine account of community support before or since then. The faith of the people there was equally impressive. It was the type of faith that could be felt in my heart. Matthew 18:20 comes to mind when remembering the waiting room—'For where two or three are gathered together in my name, there am I in the midst of them.' And God was definitely there with us."

As the day wound down, Shad Estes took time to reflect on his relationship with Nate and the events of the day:

"I thought back about the day and what all went on. I realized life is too short not to tell people how you feel about them. Something can change in a split second for you. I got to talk to your dad today about our friendship and I know that it is a God-ordained friendship. I told him how you have friends in life that are just surface deep but with Nate I have a friendship that is truly built from Christ. I told him how I could pray with you and how we challenged each other spiritually.

"I miss you man and I love you a lot. God is going to take care of you and I know he has a big plan for you. Sleep well, Dude, and I will see you tomorrow. God is all around you. I have set my alarm for five o'clock. I am going to try to make it to the six o'clock visitation. Goodnight, Bub."

Everyone who knew Nate was quick to point out his passion for encouraging people in their walk with God. Nate didn't know it at the time, but God had just begun to use him in an amazing way. Over the next six weeks, even though he was in a coma, Nate's impact on those around him increased exponentially.

Chapter 5

Waiting, Praying, and Watching

Tuesday, June 5, 2007

Nate lay in a coma in the surgical ICU surrounded by machines, monitors, and equipment. He was attached to a respirator that breathed for him, and IV tubes fed fluids and medication into his body. Although he looked like he was sleeping peacefully, he was quietly fighting the battle of his life. His brain was swelling, a common occurrence after a traumatic brain injury.

Ironically, the softball-size hole in Nate's skull now allowed room for his brain to swell, helping to relieve potentially deadly pressure inside his skull. But Nate faced a host of other potential problems. He had begun to run a fever, another common but dangerous complication. Over the next few days, Nate, along with the doctors, nurses, and his family and friends, would be engaged in a life-or-death war against those and other life-threatening complications.

If that weren't enough, Nate's left arm was tied down. Because his left wrist was completely shattered in the fall, the doctors didn't want him to injure it further by moving it. He would still need surgery to repair the wrist but was much too weak to go through it at the moment. Surgery would have to wait.

Nate was allowed to have visitors six times a day, but for only 30 minutes at a time. The first visiting time was at 6:00 a.m., and Tammy and Billy were there, praying for Nate and checking on how he was doing. Tammy looked at the medical equipment that surrounded Nate, watching and praying that his vital signs would improve and that he would show some sign of recovery.

Tammy felt led to start a journal because Nate would want to know everything that happened. She also knew that Nate, if he made it through this, would want to write a book about this journey. She also began to keep a prayer journal.

Tammy wrote in her journal: "So many machines, monitors, and tubes. I keep reading the numbers on all the machines hoping the ones that need to go up will go up and the ones that need to go down will go down, but they don't."

Still, as the hours passed, there were some scattered reports with good, or at least hopeful, news. Danny Vivian posted an update to the El Ride board at about three p.m.:

"Got to see Nate (from a distance) a little while ago. His family is able to go to his bedside. The latest is that another CT scan was done today, which showed some improvement. When moving him to do the CT scan, the nurses say he made attempts to take his ventilator tube out. He has also opened his eyes briefly, and moved his limbs some. All these are good signs. There is still some bleeding from the brain, but apparently no more swelling. Originally the doctors were talking about keeping him in an induced coma for 4–5 days, but now are talking about reducing the meds some for brief periods to see what type of reaction they get as far as movement, etc."—wavehound

As the first day after Nate's accident wore on, even Nate's nurses noticed that there was something special about this young man. One of his nurses, Selena, came to Billy and Tammy with a somewhat unusual request.

"Is it okay if I pray over Nate?"

"Sure," Tammy and Billy told her.

"I pray over him every time I work with him," she said. "There's something special about this kid."

Billy and Tammy nodded. "Yeah, there is."

"He's in a coma, but he's so at peace. He almost glows from the inside out. You can tell that God is in him."

According to Selena, even the nurses who didn't profess a belief in God saw something different about Nate.

Throughout the day, many friends and family members came by the ICU to visit and pray over Nate. The waiting room remained packed with a standing room only crowd. Tammy and Billy remained at the hospital all day, visiting Nate every time they were allowed. Each time they left the room, Tammy would pray that it wouldn't be the last time they saw their son alive.

Nate, keep resting and take all the time you need to heal. We are all here and love you. God, please help us through this.

Wednesday, June 6, 2007

If the Lytles were not on enough of a roller-coaster ride with Nate's injury, the next day brought more stress. As Tammy waited to go in and see Nate, a hospital volunteer found her and told her that she had a telephone call—from their veterinarian. Their daughter Elissa's dachshund got out and was hit by a car. Thankfully, the little dog survived, but it had suffered a bad head injury and might possibly lose its eyesight in one eye.

It seemed as though the Lytle family was besieged by accidents involving head injuries. Less than a week before Nate's injury, their oldest son, Will, had totaled his car and had suffered a head injury as well. The avalanche of accidents was overwhelming, and it made Tammy wish she could somehow put a protective bubble around their youngest child, Elissa.

When would it all stop?

The vigil continued through Wednesday without much change in Nate's condition. Nate loved to listen to Christian music, so Billy brought Nate's iPod from home, and the nurses allowed him to put earphones on him. It made Tammy and Billy feel better knowing that he would have some form of comfort when they couldn't be with him. They had no idea whether or not Nate could hear the songs, but later that day, something happened that gave everyone a ray of hope.

Nate's younger sister, Elissa, was nineteen at the time of his accident, and she kept watch at the ICU along with her parents. Elissa had a beautiful singing voice, and Nate loved to listen to her, so during one of the visitation periods, Tammy suggested that Elissa sing to Nate.

Elissa stood by Nate's bedside, took his hand, and began to sing a song titled "It'll Be Alright".[4]

Forget the worries of this life and let His love shine through,
And it'll be alright, everything'll be alright,
Jump over all the obstacles that stand in front of you,
And it'll be alright, everything'll be alright.
When the winds of change start to blow in your direction,
Listen to what He has to say.
When you can't deny the power of the resurrection,
Give your heart to Jesus; He'll carry you away, carry you away.
Forget the worries of this life and let His love shine through,
And it'll be alright, everything'll be alright,
Jump over all the obstacles that stand in front of you,
And it'll be alright, everything'll be alright.

All attention in the ICU was focused on Elissa and Nate. Most of those who were listening were quietly weeping. Then Elissa felt something unexpected.

Nate gently squeezed her hand.

Tears began to flow down Elissa's cheeks, and she struggled to finish the song.

Seconds later, Nate began moving his head, along with his right arm and leg.

Danny Vivian passed the news on in a post to the El Ride forum:

"[Nate] was quiet tonight, temp was up a little, sleeping soundly. Right before we left, his sister leaned down and sang a song to him. The girl's got pipes, and even the nurses stopped to listen. As soon as she began to sing, Nate started moving his head, arm and leg. It was a good way to end the day."—wavehound

This wasn't the first time that Nate had moved since his accident. Indeed, he'd been moving his head and his right arm and leg off and on throughout the day. Whenever the Lytles saw Nate move, they were

---

[4]   "It'll Be Alright", John Elefante, Used by permission.

hopeful that these were signs that he was recovering. But every time they pointed these movements out to the doctors and nurses, they got the same response: Nate's movements were not "purposeful." In other words, when Nate moved his head, arm, or leg, it was just his body reacting to the conditions around it, but the movements were not conscious actions on Nate's part.

Nate's prognosis was still very poor.

In the midst of the discouraging atmosphere, Tammy and Billy found comfort in reading the supportive text messages coming in on Nate's phone and also in monitoring the posts that continually were streaming in to the El Ride board. On this day, she found a particularly encouraging post from one of the many people whose lives Nate had touched:

> "Praying for you bro. II Peter 1:5-7 says we should make every effort to have faith, goodness, knowledge, self-control, perseverance, godliness, and brotherly kindness. You display all the characteristics. What a blessing you are to those who know you. I pray that God will fully restore your body and mind to continue the good work that he's already started in you. I am so touched by the sweetness and kindness of his words. I again start to think that surely, God would not take you from this world, knowing how you touch others, but then also realize that He is God and that He could use you whether he lets you live or takes you home."—Joey

Tammy and Billy knew that what Joey had written was true. God was using Nate and, no matter whether he was with them or in heaven, Nate would touch people's lives for God.

Late on Wednesday, Billy and Tammy were exhausted. The medical staff encouraged them to go home and try to get some sleep. Tammy didn't want to leave for fear that Nate might take a turn for the worse when they weren't there, but the nurses told her that she and Billy needed to rest if they were going to be able to be strong for Nate. They promised to call them if there was any change in Nate's condition.

Reluctantly, Tammy and Billy agreed to go home, even though it would only be a few hours. It was already midnight and the first visitation time would be at six a.m.

It would be a short night, and when they arrived the next morning they would learn that Nate's condition had indeed changed—for the worse.

Thursday, June 7, 2007

Tammy had difficulty sleeping that night because she kept waking up, thinking that the phone was ringing. All in all, she only got about two hours of sleep.

When they got to the hospital, they learned that Nate's temperature had gone up during the night and the medical staff was taking aggressive measures to reduce his fever. Nate was on a cooling blanket that circulated cool water under his body. The nurses were also using ice and fans to keep Nate's temperature from becoming dangerously high.

The ICU felt frigid, and it appeared that Nate was noticing the change in temperature.

He kept trying to move to one side, away from the cold. He appeared fidgety and restless.

Tammy and Billy pointed out their son's movements to the nurse, hoping again that this was a sign that Nate was still there, that he was coming back from his injury. But again the nurse told them that Nate's movements were not purposeful but rather his body's way of reacting to the cold.

"His facial expressions are still the same," she said. "Sometimes the body just moves or reacts to things on its own, involuntarily."

There was other discouraging news. Some of Nate's other vital signs had changed as well. Unfortunately, the changes were for the worse.

After their six a.m. visit with Nate, Billy and Tammy returned to the waiting room where other family and friends had already begun to assemble for the day's vigil.

As they waited, Billy brought up something to Tammy that had been bothering him.

"Do you think I should close down the business?" he asked. "I keep thinking, what if the pallet hadn't broken, or what if we'd tried to get the manifold down another way? What if Nate had left sooner for Florida? What if the ladder had been a few inches farther away so that the manifold would have missed it?"

Before the accident, Engenco was a place that Billy took pleasure in. It was a dream fulfilled. Now it was the place where Nate was hurt and, if he didn't survive, maybe killed. Billy wasn't sure if he could face working there day after day with that knowledge.

Tammy reassured him that she, Nate, Will, and Elissa would understand if he couldn't bear to work there anymore, but she also reminded him that they needed him to continue to earn an income while the family went through this crisis.

"You worked hard to start that company and you love your work," Tammy told him. "Nate's accident isn't your fault or the business's fault. It's up to you what you decide to do and, whatever you decide, we will all support you."

Billy hated leaving Tammy and Elissa there at the hospital and especially not being there with Nate, but he understood that one of them had to work, and he made more money than Tammy did. Billy decided that he would try going back to his shop. He went back home, changed clothes, and went back to work.

But he returned to the ICU for every scheduled visitation time.

As for Tammy, she was never alone. A steady stream of family, fellow church members, and other friends kept the surgical ICU waiting room full. Nevertheless, her heart still ached for Nate. She hated to see him moving back and forth on the cooling blanket, so obviously uncomfortable. Then it dawned on her that, if what the nurses were saying was true, Nate might not even know that he was uncomfortable.

She didn't like to dwell on that thought.

That night, she wrote in her journal:

Nate, I am so sorry you are going through this and feel so helpless to be your mom and unable to help you. I would trade places with you in a heartbeat if I could. I am terrified to leave you, but I will be back in a few hours to spend the day here again. I love you, my son.

God, please help me. I feel like I can't breathe. I trust You and love You and want what is best for Nate, but my heart feels like it is about to burst. Please give me comfort and peace. I trust Your Word and know that You are the Great Healer. Where I am confused is that I don't know if it is Your will to heal Nate, or to bring him home to You. You are the only one that can bring me through this journey we are on. I don't know how people without You go through something like this. I thank You for each day You have brought us through. Without You, I have no hope. I love You, Father.

After the last visitation of the day, Tammy and Billy went home to try to catch a few hours sleep.

Friday, June 8, 2007

Tammy had a burning question, and she had held it in long enough. She decided to put Dr. Norvill on the spot.

"If nothing gets worse, do you think [Nate] might at least live through this, maybe not walk or talk, but live through this?"

Dr. Norvill gave Tammy a weary glance, and then looked toward the floor, as though he was carefully weighing his words. "If not one thing changes for the worse, he might be able to at least live through it."

It wasn't much, only the smallest ray of hope, but Tammy clung to it.

Nevertheless, the day was filled with ups and downs.

On the positive side, Nate's brain had finally stopped bleeding, so they were able to remove the drain tube. They had also turned down the respirator, and it appeared that Nate was partially breathing on his own. Dr. Norvill also told her that Nate's brain was realigning itself, another good sign. He even conceded that some of Nate's movements could be purposeful, although he didn't sound convinced and said it was still too early to tell. Others, however, were beginning to think that some of Nate's movements, at least, were very purposeful.

Earlier, a fan that was pointed at Nate to keep him cool had caused his gown to blow up. Nate reached down with his right hand and pushed the gown back down. That one movement caused many of the nurses who had previously been skeptical to consider that there was more than simply reflex involved.

Still, there were also negatives that caused concern. Nate's temperature was still very high, as were his blood pressure and heart rate. And the nurses were having difficulty with Nate's IVs. The doctor finally decided that Nate would need a central line—a surgically-implanted catheter—to make sure they could give him his medications. They explained to Tammy and Billy that this could be a dangerous procedure, and even more so if there was any infection.

Tammy and Billy prayed before they signed the consent form, but they knew that they didn't have a choice in the matter. If Nate was to have any chance at survival, they had to get his medications into him, and this was the only way.

When they went to meet the doctor who would insert the central line they were again amazed at God's provision. Again, the doctor was someone they were familiar with—the father of one of Nate's best friend's (Michelle) boyfriend. They were comforted and encouraged that God appeared to be providing the right people at the right time to give Nate the best care possible.

Not only was God providing good care for Nate, but He had been apparently preparing Nate for the battle he was now fighting. Tammy found out just how much God had been working in her son's life when she made a surprising discovery at home.

On Friday afternoon, Dr. Dean McDaniel, another friend of Nate's, paid a visit. He suggested that Tammy bring things in that would stimulate Nate's brain, such as pictures of family and friends, pictures of Nate surfing, photos of his youth group, and put them up in the ICU where Nate could see them.

Tammy asked one of her best friends, Connie—who had been coming to the hospital every day since Nate's accident—to take her home to get some pictures. As Tammy sorted through photos and papers, looking for things to put on Nate's wall, she found a red folder. It appeared to be some type of Bible study or journal. As Tammy read through it, she was amazed at the depth and the insight of the comments in the journal.

Later, she showed it to Jaime, who was previously Parkway Church's youth director and another one of Nate's best friends. Tammy told Jaime that whoever wrote all the entries was an amazing person and had an awesome relationship with God. Jaime immediately recognized it.

"Do you know what this is?" Jaime asked.

"No," Tammy replied.

"This is an online prayer journal. This is Nate's prayer journal."

Tears filled Tammy's eyes as she leafed through that red folder. She had always known that Nate had a great relationship with God, but she hadn't realized how deep it was. As she read the journal entries, she saw Nate's willingness to sacrifice—to do anything God wanted him to do—even to the point of laying down his life.

The journal stirred up conflicting emotions in Tammy.

On the one hand, she was deeply proud of Nate and his walk with God; on the other hand, she was worried about how God might choose to use Nate. Would He take him home or leave him trapped in a severely disabled body?

Ironically, only two weeks earlier, Nate had written in his prayer journal: "I want to seek and praise you, not only in the good times, for any of us can do this. I want to seek and praise you when thrown through the valley. To look at each roadblock as a challenge and an encouragement instead of discouragement. When you place roadblocks in front of me and I turn to you to conquer them, the glory and praise is brought to You alone. Could I maintain this attitude while in the valley? I believe You will give us the strength and courage to [do this]."

Her son's words were speaking to her and others around her as he lay in a coma.

Friday evening was another incredible display of God's love and provision. Over forty people showed up at the ICU waiting room. Some brought food for the Lytles, and others came to encourage, sing, and pray for Nate. Among the visitors were Tammy's brother Robby and his wife Jennifer. Her sister Terri was also there and they all went in as a family to visit Nate. Billy and Robby prayed over Nate. Tammy watched her son, hoping that he might open his eyes as he heard his family praying.

Nate moved around a little bit, but he didn't open his eyes.

After the last visitation period, Tammy, Billy, and the others left for the night. She went away feeling the conflicting desire to see Nate wake up, but also knowing that his body needed rest if he was to recover. She also went home feeling the physical and emotional strain of five straight days of waiting in the ICU.

Nate, I want so badly for you to wake up, but also want so badly for you to get whatever rest you need.

Father God, I am so tired and beg You for strength.

Chapter 6

Serve God and Love People

As a young teenager, Nate knew that he was called to ministry. He didn't feel called to pastoral ministry or the kind of service that would keep him in an office or behind a desk. Nate would never feel comfortable in that type of situation. But Nate knew early on that he was a "people person," and God quickly directed his heart toward ministering to others.

He was only fourteen when his first ministry opportunity presented itself.

Nate was involved with the youth group at the Parkway Church in Victoria, Texas when Mike Hurt, his youth minister, asked him to help out one Wednesday evening.

"Hey Nate," Mike said, "Three of our youth volunteers are sick and we need someone to lead a small group. Would you step up, man?"

It didn't sound like it would be very difficult. All he had to do was read five or six questions related to the lesson and lead a small group of his friends in a discussion. While many kids his age would have been terrified at the prospect, Nate agreed to fill in.

Even at that young age, Nate knew he was different from many other teens. While most of his friends were focused on girls, sports, and just being kids, Nate was deeply interested in spiritual things and his relationship to Jesus Christ. Nate was a normal teenager, but he was far more mature than most of his friends. That maturity didn't happen by accident.

From the time Nate became involved in surfing, his pastors, Scott Weatherford and Brian Brown, took him with them when they went to Port Aransas or Corpus Christi to surf. They would pick up a sleepy and bleary-eyed Nate at six in the morning on Saturdays and take him along on the ninety-minute drive to the beach. Although the primary purpose of the trip was to have a great time surfing, Scott and Brian used the three-hour round trip to build into Nate's heart and life. As they drove down and back they discussed spiritual things and posed questions that caused Nate to consider his walk with the Lord; questions such as, "What's God telling you, Nate?" or "Where's God taking you in your life?"

Those long trips to the beach and back, spending the day with two men of God whom he highly respected, made a lifelong impression on Nate and helped cultivate in him a deep relationship to the Lord Jesus Christ. Brian and Scott continued to build into Nate's life over the years, even taking him with them to a pastors' conference at the Saddleback Church, pastored by Rick Warren, author of *The Purpose Driven Life*. Nate was only sixteen the first time he went, yet as he found himself surrounded by men who were committed to ministry and serving God, Nate was challenged to deepen his own relationship to God.

So when Mike asked Nate to lead a small group on that particular Wednesday, it seemed like the natural thing to do. Nate wasn't worried about what his friends would think or if they would laugh at him. He went to Parkway that night and led the group.

When he walked out, he felt like a different person. He sensed a deep honor in having the privilege of leading and teaching others. He also felt empowered. And he knew, almost instinctively, that this is what God was calling him to do: minister to people.

When Nate led the group that Wednesday evening, he figured it was just a one-time deal. He was just filling in for someone who was sick. But the next week Mike came to him again.

"You did a great job last week," Mike said. "Would you like to try it again?"

Nate didn't need to be asked twice. He began leading the group on a regular basis. The group was made up of all his best friends, but that didn't intimidate Nate in the least. As a matter of fact, he found that his friends respected and looked up to him. Nate felt humbled, empowered, and honored by his friends' respect, and he worked hard at leading them.

Nate continued leading the group until he graduated from high school—at age sixteen—and for the following two years, until he entered the Coast Guard when he was eighteen.

When Nate joined the Coast Guard, his ministry didn't skip a beat. Even before he had finished boot camp, he was asked to be the religious petty officer for his group. During his four years in the service, wherever Nate went, he found opportunities to lead others and minister to them in spiritual things.

At his duty stations, Nate became the "go to" guy when any of the other men had problems or needed prayer. For his first two years, he even became the designated driver for many of his fellow seamen. For his part, Nate was worried that when they went out drinking at night, they might be killed trying to drive home. Nate didn't want that on his conscience, so he let his buddies know that he would drive them back to the base if they got drunk. Soon, it became a common event for him to get a two a.m. phone call from one of his buddies: "Hey Nate, could you come pick me up?" Being the designated driver was a noble effort on Nate's part, but after two years, it began to wear on him. Finally, he realized that he couldn't be responsible for other people's lives and bad decisions. Even though he stopped making himself available as a middle-of-the-night taxi service, Nate's ministry to his fellow servicemen continued.

The other men knew that Nate cared about them and their problems, so some of them would come to him for prayer when they were struggling with a personal issue. Sometimes they came just to talk. Others knew which church service Nate attended and would often ask if they could go to church with him.

What was it about Nate that was so winsome, so attractive that military men would seek him out for spiritual counsel and comfort? It was an attitude that came to characterize Nate's entire life and ministry: serve God and love others.

At one point in his Coast Guard career, his superiors called Nate in for a meeting. Nate wondered what was going on. They began to ask him what it was that made him the person he was and what made him have the attitude he had at such a young age. Nate was quick to tell them that it was because of God and his relationship with Him.

Nate passionately loved God and desired to serve him with all his heart. His commitment to his God was unquestionable. But Nate also knew that the best way to reach people for God was to love them and meet them where they were. Nate didn't come to people wearing a suit and tie and carrying a big Bible. Nate just came as Nate, a guy who loved God and who cared about people's needs, their hurts, and their pain.

After Nate got out of the Coast Guard and returned to Victoria, he resumed his ministry to the junior high and high school students at Parkway. Some Sundays he prepared and brought a message to between sixty and ninety students. When he wasn't bringing the message, he helped in the youth ministry in other ways. As he poured into the lives of young teenagers, Scott and Brian continued to build into his life as well.

Not long after he returned to Victoria, he noticed an unmet need at the Parkway church. Even though the church was large—approximately 1800 members—they had no college ministry. This was mostly because young people tended to move away from Victoria to go to college, so the college-age population in the church wasn't very high. Nate was already actively involved working with the teens, and it would have been easy to ignore the need, but he wasn't the kind of guy who ignored a need when he was aware of it.

Nate talked to Brian, the associate pastor, and told him that he saw a gap—a need—that wasn't filled and asked permission to start a ministry to college students. Nate didn't plan on taking on this new ministry indefinitely. His goal was to get it started and then train someone else to carry it on.

With Brian's permission, Nate started a college group called "Truth," and before long, they had forty to sixty people in attendance every week. Nate also opened the group up to other churches and anyone of college age in Victoria that wanted to come. He trained six small group leaders and developed a weekly lesson plan for them to follow. After about four months, the small group leaders were ready to be on their own, and Nate turned the new ministry over to them. They wanted him to stay on, but that had never been his intention. Nate loved working with the junior high and high school students, and he wanted to get back to them.

The people at Parkway recognized Nate's giftedness for ministry, and when Scott, Brian, and Jeremy, the music pastor, announced their intention to go to Florida, they asked Nate to step in as the youth pastor. It was that need on the part of the church that Nate was struggling with just before his accident. He saw the open door of ministry in Florida, but he also saw a gap at his home church since the youth pastor had recently resigned. Even though he finally decided to join Brian and Scott in Florida, it was difficult for him to see such a great unmet need at Parkway.

Although Nate was gifted in teaching and leading teens in his church, nowhere was his love of people more evident than in the way Nate ministered outside the church walls.

Nate knew that an important part of showing God's love to people was in making them feel valued. When he reached out to homeless people—something Nate loved to do—he didn't just take them food and then leave them. Nate "hung out" with them. He helped them with housing. He spent time with them and got to know their names, their problems, their struggles. Nate showed God's love to them "up close and personal." He walked with them and made them feel like someone cared about them. It was this same attitude that enabled him to have an impact on surfers.

Many surfers are a tightly-knit and closed group. They don't always readily welcome outsiders—even if those outsiders are other surfers. Even though Nate was a surfer himself, if he had approached the surfing community with a confrontational, "in your face" style, he never would have had a chance to share life with them. But Nate treated the other surfers the same way he treated everybody. It didn't matter to Nate if someone had done drugs just before they came to surf. He knew that he wasn't perfect himself. He loved them as they were. Instead, Nate regularly traveled to Matagorda and Corpus, surfing and hanging out with the surfers. As time passed, they opened up to him and shared their problems and needs, and Nate would always pray with them and let them know that God loved them.

Now, as Nate lay in a coma, many of the people he had touched remembered him and his impact on their lives. Many of them made their thoughts and prayers public on the El Ride board. When Jammie Helzer (who had been Nate's boss when he was stationed in Saginaw Michigan), heard about Nate's accident, he got on El Ride and wrote this:

"We all know you are a fighter. Man, I still remember when I gave Nate a hard time on the Coast Guard boat in Michigan. Man, was he mad. But you know, as much as I rode him to do better, he always managed to come to me every morning with a hand shake and a 'GOOD MORNING.' I did a lot of thinking about him this morning and this stuff about him always stands out: His willingness to forgive and forget, even when you would think that he has had enough. I also thought back to the day I left Michigan to come to Texas. That guy gave me the biggest hug and shook my hand and said, 'I will see you back in Texas.' And as Nate always does, he kept his word. Nate knows me and I am not a real religious man, but I caught myself praying multiple times over the weekend for him. Just one more thing that Nate has managed to do for me. Nate, even when you are down and out, you are still doing things for people that need your help. I Love You man, and I am definitely praying for you.

"Please keep this [thread] going. You all [El Ride] are our only information source here in the Coast Guard. Thank you . . . I WILL DO ANYTHING AND EVERYTHING THAT I CAN FOR MY MAN 'NATE DAWG.'"—Jammie Helzer

Nate Lytle dramatically impacted people's lives for God by consistently living out his simple philosophy: serve God and love people. He served God with all his heart and loved people without judging them. His approach to ministry was remarkably similar to that of the Lord Jesus, who was frequently criticized for being "a friend to publicans and sinners." Nate was a friend to everyone he met. He embodied the words of the Apostle John: "Whoever claims to live in Him [Jesus], should walk as Jesus walked," (I John 2:6).

Nate had walked as Jesus walked.

Now he was fighting for his life.

Chapter 7

Complications

Saturday, June 9th, 2007

The first post to the El Ride board for June 9th came at 4:37 a.m. It was only two words long: "Prayers continue . . . ." That brief post summarized the need of the day. Saturday was a day of complications for Nate and his family, complications that were not only physical, but also financial and emotional.

Nate had been in need of prayer since the moment of the accident, but now that need became critical. After someone has survived a traumatic injury, often the greatest danger to survival is not the injury itself but complications that set in afterward. When Tammy and Billy arrived at the hospital on Saturday morning, they quickly learned that Nate was now fighting a battle on three fronts. In addition to the brain injury, Nate had developed pneumonia. He also apparently had developed a bacterial infection in his blood.

Doctor Norvill updated Tammy and Billy on Nate's condition and told them that he was putting Nate on antibiotics and would run some tests to learn what kind of bacteria was in his blood and how bad the pneumonia was.

For Tammy, the doctor's news only added to the strain she was feeling.

There were so many different directions this could go, so many things that could endanger Nate's life. On the one hand, Nate was a

50

strong young man whose lifestyle, physical condition, and faith certainly gave him an advantage in his battle. Even so, Tammy wondered if Nate would be able to survive. She wanted to believe that he would live and make a full recovery, but everywhere she turned, people were cautioning her not to expect very much.

One comfort was that across the country, people who knew Nate—and many who didn't—were offering prayers on his behalf.

From the El Ride board at 6:52 a.m.:

"As we proceed through our selfish self-centered day, I ask each of you to take 30 seconds every hour today to think and say a prayer for Nate and family. It is so easy to just go on with our daily lives without thinking of others. Now is the time to think of someone else.

"Dear Heavenly Father, I beg of you to create a miracle today. I pray that you touch Nate in such a way that his health turns for the better beyond belief. I pray for a complete recovery, Father God. In Jesus name I pray."—C.S.

As the day wore on, encouragement came in the form of many visitors who came to see Nate and his family. Especially encouraging was a visit from Dr. Lawrence Fan, one of Nate's surfing buddies from Sugar Land who also was a physician. Lawrence, whose El Ride name is "nip," later posted his assessment of Nate's condition on the El Ride board:

"Nate is pretty well sedated today, but is resting comfortably and looks peaceful. In the past day or two when they let up on the sedation, he would reach for his breathing tube and sometimes kick his legs, so they wanted to keep him sedated today. That [Nate's movement] definitely sounds purposeful. He has on occasion briefly opened his eyes, including his left eye, which he was not doing previously.

"He continues to run a fever and is on antibiotics for pneumonia. His blood culture is growing out bacteria also, which hopefully is a contaminant. He is on blood pressure medicine and his BP is improved. He is being fed Ensure-type stuff through an NG tube. And he has a central line in for IV access.

"I was able to see him and talk to his nurse and look at his X-ray, and maybe interpret some of the medical lingo. So basically his biggest problems now are of course his head injury and infection (pneumonia and possible bacteria in the blood).

"His family has a wonderful support system, but as you can imagine, they're under a great deal of stress with little sleep."—nip

Lawrence also pointed out to Tammy and Billy another complication of Nate's condition: medical bills. Nate's health insurance from the Coast Guard had expired. Nate had taken college courses since he had gotten out of the Coast Guard, so Tammy and Billy had added them to their health insurance as a student. College ended in May, so they had to drop him from their insurance only a few days before the accident and, because he was between jobs, he had no other health insurance. Billy had never taken out workmen's comp insurance at Engenco because until Nate began to help him out for a short time, he had no employees other than himself. In a word, Nate's medical bills were going to be astronomical. That knowledge, plus concern over Nate's condition—and sheer exhaustion—began to take its toll on Tammy in particular.

Although the visitors who constantly filled the ICU waiting room were a great encouragement to Tammy, they also became something of a strain. Tammy had to repeat news and developments in Nate's condition so many times that she began to wear down. She felt a need to be strong for all of the visitors, but it got to the point where it became overwhelming. Those who are close to Tammy saw the strain she was under and wondered if there was something they could do about it.

The answer came later that day when another visitor came by the ICU waiting room. This particular visitor—who worked in the hospital—came up to Tammy and said, "You know, your son is very special."

Tammy thanked her and asked how she knew Nate.

"My nephew came to live with me a while back," she said. "His parents were having problems with him, and they sent him down here in hopes that he might be able to turn around. Nate became his small group leader and took him under his wing and that made a huge difference in his life. Now he's back with his family, and he's doing great."

Another of Nate's friends, Jaime, who had also worked as a youth leader in their church, was standing by and listening during the conversation. Jaime asked the lady if there was somewhere that Tammy might be able to go to get some rest.

"Follow me," she said.

They walked down the corridor, and she unlocked the door to a conference room.

"This room is used for counseling. It's normally kept locked, but you can use it whenever you need it, even to stay overnight if you want."

The room was equipped with a couch that could be used as a bed. Tammy made use of the room when she needed a nap and some time alone with God. She didn't feel comfortable using the room a lot or staying overnight because there were other people with family members in ICU who didn't have access to a room. But she recognized it as a blessing from God and would often go in there after her early-morning visit with Nate.

In many little ways, God was showing how He could and would provide for their needs. When they got home that evening, they found that Danny Vivian and his son Travis had mowed their lawn for them. It was often those little things that kept encouraging them in the day-to-day vigil that they kept in the ICU.

Billy and Tammy finally went home about midnight, praying that God would deal with the latest complications that Nate was facing. She wrote in her journal, *Father God, I pray that You heal this pneumonia and bacteria in Nate's body. I just don't know how much more he can take, but You do, so I have to trust You. I know You are in control Father, but my heart still aches.*

Sunday, June 10ᵗʰ, 2007

Tammy and Billy arrived early on Sunday morning, bringing a collage of photos to hang at the end of Nate's bed so that when he began to wake up, he would see familiar faces and scenes. When they arrived at the ICU for the six a.m. visit, they were greeted with good news. Nate's temperature had come down and was now at about 100 degrees. There were still serious concerns about his pneumonia and the possible staph infection, but at least his temperature was moving in the right direction.

Tammy also noticed that during the night they had removed Nate's "bite block," a plastic device that was designed to keep him from biting down on his breathing tube.

They stood there, looking at their son. The only sound in the room was the periodic hiss of the respirator as it breathed for Nate. It was so hard to see him lying there, surrounded by machines and with so many tubes going into him. Tammy hung the collage at the foot of Nate's bed, right where he could see it when he opened his eyes. After that, they returned to the ICU waiting room to continue their daily vigil. But they were not alone. Even that early in the morning, as reflected on the El Ride board, prayers were going up for Nate all over the country.

5:17 a.m. "Praying hard."—brianb8888

5:29 a.m. "Continued prayers for a full recovery, bro!"—dubs

6:24 a.m. "In my thoughts today . . . . Praying the Lord will continue to reach down and touch our friend . . . ."—Kapuna

7:16 a.m. "More prayers for Nate!"—Surfncpa

7:38 a.m. "First thing I did this morning was log on and check how Nate is doing. Stable is good!!! I'd rather see 'improving quickly, running around the halls bothering nurses,' but considering the severity of the injuries, I'll take stable and holding!!!! Got you on my mind, kid, keep fightin!!!!!!"—seabass

By the time afternoon rolled around, Dr. Norvill brought the Lytles a "good news, bad news" report. The good news was that the staph infection that had so worried them was not an infection after all. It was a surface contaminant, probably introduced in the lab. Tammy and Billy were relieved to learn that Nate did not have a potentially life-threatening blood infection.

Dr. Norvill brought more good news that afternoon. The swelling in Nate's brain—another potentially life-threatening complication—had begun to subside, and his brain was realigning itself. However, not all the news that day was good. Nate's pneumonia had gotten worse, and Dr. Norvill had decided to call in a pulmonologist (a lung doctor) to see what could be done. Soon, even this "bad news" would turn for the good.

The pulmonologist examined Nate and reported that, although Nate did have pneumonia, it was a variety that responded well to treatment. He doubled Nate's antibiotics and recommended that they do a tracheotomy so that the breathing tube could be removed from

Nate's mouth. He also suggested that it was time to begin weaning Nate from the respirator.

Complications had darkened the mood on this first weekend since the accident, but now, one by one, those complications were being overcome. Throughout the day, a growing realization crept over Tammy: amazing things were happening. By that evening, there was no doubt in her mind that God was at work.

At eight p.m., a nurse called Billy and Tammy back to the ICU. It wasn't a normal visitation time, but the nurse wanted to show them something. When they got to Nate's bed, they saw what the nurse was so excited about. Nate was moving his right leg to the left and right, and bending his knee. At one point he crossed his legs and one of his surfing buddies laughed and said, "He's trying to do a switchfoot" (a surfing move). What was even more exciting was that Nate had started to open his eyes. They weren't open wide—just slits—but it was a step in the right direction.

Some of the nurses cautioned the Lytles not to be too excited about Nate's movements as they were still not "purposeful," but others weren't so sure.

One nurse said, "There's something different about Nate. It's like there's an aura around him. Whenever I'm around him, I feel at peace. I've never really had a relationship with God, but seeing Nate and everyone who visits him has convinced me that I really need to. I heard that Nate doesn't have any insurance, and I'd like to donate toward his medical expenses."

Tammy and Billy thanked her and tried to convince her that it wasn't necessary, but she wouldn't take no for an answer.

It was another sign that, even though he was in a coma and in a hospital bed, Nate was impacting the lives of people he'd never met before. One post to the El Ride board that Sunday evening highlighted this:

"I asked the Sunday school classes to pray for you this morning. One of my 11th grade students, Keith, lifted you and your family up this morning and got choked up while praying. He doesn't even know you and yet God filled him with emotion while praying. The entire surfing community and people you don't even know are praying for you right now."—jsh

That night, Tammy wrote in her journal: *God, I thank You for the miracles we have seen so far. I don't know what the outcome to all this is, but I know that You have already performed many miracles in this situation. I ask You to please continue to perform them. I feel guilty for continuing to ask for so much, but Your Word tells us that it is okay to ask, so I am asking. I love You, Lord, and thank You for always loving me and being there for me, even when I question what is going on.*

Tammy and Billy stayed at the hospital till midnight, and when they left it was with a deep sense that God was at work and that he was going to use Nate's injury to touch people's lives.

What they didn't realize was that they would begin to see God working in amazing ways the very next day.

Chapter 8

Coast Guard

"Are you serious?"

That was the general reaction of family and friends when Nate announced that he planned to join the Coast Guard. It wasn't that they thought he was making a bad decision; it just seemed like the last thing on earth that Nate would do.

But Nate didn't do anything without making it a matter of considerable thought and prayer. He knew exactly what he was doing—and why.

Nate was all about helping other people. He was doing it spiritually by working with the students at his church. But ever since he'd graduated high school—at sixteen—Nate had been thinking about what he would do with the rest of his life. And the more he thought about it, the more he decided that he'd like to be able to help people physically as well as spiritually.

When he rescued the young boy who'd jumped off the pier in Port Aransas a few years earlier, he'd gotten a taste of what it felt like to save someone's life, and he liked how it felt. And like many young men and women after the events of 9/11, Nate looked toward the military. He quickly ruled out the Army and Marines. Nate wasn't a "war" person. The Navy was appealing, at least in the sense that he'd get to be near water and see a lot of different places. But Nate wasn't interested in being on a ship for three to six months at a clip. Nate was a people person, and he wanted to be where he could meet people.

One thing that was characteristic of Nate was that he liked to do things that were different, off the usual path. He'd never heard people in Victoria talking about going into the Coast Guard. So the more he thought about it, the more it sounded like a good option. Most important, as Nate prayed about joining the Coast Guard, he became convinced that it was something that God was calling him to do.

Even though he knew what he wanted to do, Nate had to wait before he could enlist. He had braces on his teeth and the recruiter told him that he'd have to get the braces off before he could go to boot camp. The Coast Guard didn't have any orthodontists at boot camp, and the training was too rigorous for him to risk going through it while wearing braces.

Nate kept checking with his orthodontist, hoping to get the braces off early, but each time he went they told him that he needed to keep them on just a little longer. Finally, in April of 2002, the braces came off and Nate was cleared to go.

Boot camp was a different world, a world the recruiter had not prepared him for. He wasn't used to being in an environment where people were screaming at him all the time. Nevertheless, Nate had no fear. He knew he was where God wanted him to be, and that was all that mattered. Before long, his familiarity with the water began to show through. On one of his first water tests—swimming the length of a pool and back—out of eighty recruits, Nate was easily the first one back. It wasn't long before his water skills earned him the nickname "Little Fish."

Although his ability to swim and his comfort in the water were notable, Nate stood out in other, more important ways. Military boot camp, even Coast Guard boot camp, is not normally a place where people have fun. But even during the hardest parts of his training, Nate was upbeat, smiling, and laughing. He also quickly became known for his Christian testimony. Whenever Nate had spare time, he was reading his Bible and praying. It wasn't long before he caught the attention of his company commander (the Coast Guard equivalent of a drill sergeant).

The company commander came into the barracks and called, "Lytle!"

Nate didn't know what was going on. Was he in trouble?

"Yes, Sir?"

"I hear you're knowledgeable in the Word."

The company commander's statement took Nate by surprise.

"Uhhhh, Sir?"

"I heard you're good at reading the Bible."

"Oh, yes, Sir. Well, I like to read it and stuff." Nate began to explain how he worked in the church and taught students, but the commander cut him off.

"I don't need the details," he said. "Would you be interested in leading our crew?"

The commander went on to explain that Nate would be responsible for putting together a prayer for the graduation ceremony. Also during the remaining eight weeks of boot camp, he would serve in the role of religious petty officer for the forty men in his crew. If they had a spiritual question or need, they could come to him.

Right there at Cape May, a place of physical and mental discipline, Nate was reminded of the Apostle Paul's statement to Timothy, "For physical training is of some value, but godliness has value for all things, holding promise for both the present life and the life to come" (1 Timothy 4:8). And so, even though Nate had left behind his ministry at Parkway Church, God opened a door for him to serve people in Coast Guard boot camp.

First Duty Station

After Nate graduated from boot camp, he received his first assignment, and it was a disappointment. Recruits are allowed to give their superiors a "wish list" of four places they'd like to be stationed after graduation, but they are not guaranteed to receive their choice of assignments. Being a surfer, Nate assembled a dream list that included Hawaii, Southern California, Guam, and Puerto Rico.

He received orders to report to a station in Port Huron, Michigan.

Nate couldn't believe it. Of all the places the Coast Guard could have sent him, they sent him to Michigan—hardly a surfer's paradise. He wasn't happy at first, but he got over it. The Coast Guard was sending him where they needed him, and he would go with a servant's heart.

Nate came home for two weeks of leave, packed up his belongings—he wasn't sure he should even bother to bring a surfboard, but he finally decided to take it—and left for Michigan. He'd always wanted to see the country, so he decided to drive rather than fly.

The Port Huron station was small and the old, white buildings looked like leftovers from World War II. Nate would be there for at least six months. Before he could decide on a permanent job, he had to make "rate," which in his case meant he had to be promoted to E3 (Seaman). Until then, his duties included doing search and rescue, and law enforcement. For the most part, the work wasn't very exciting; it mostly involved towing disabled boats, rescuing boaters who had run out of gas and were drifting out to sea, saving drunken canoers, and the like. The rescue calls came night and day and eventually became so routine that Nate lost track of the number of people he had helped save.

What he didn't forget were the people he lost.

Nate found it difficult to put the failed rescues out of his mind. He often wondered, "What if we'd been there five or ten minutes sooner? Would it have made a difference?" Nate saw a man jump off a bridge and was helpless to stop him. "We were right there. We were so close." Another time, a group of four teens were drowning while their families watched from the shore. Nate's crew saved three of the young people but were unable to save the fourth. Nate couldn't believe that the local newspaper called them heroes when they had failed to save them all.

As time passed the failed rescues began to wear on Nate. "All I thought about were the people we lost. That's really what stuck in my mind."

Michigan was difficult for Nate in other ways. As the months passed and summer gave way to autumn and then winter, Nate began to struggle with depression. Nate had always been upbeat and happy; he wasn't used to being down all the time. While it was possible that the depression was growing out of his sadness over the people they'd lost, he thought something else might be going on. After a visit to the doctor, the diagnosis was Seasonal Affective Disorder (SAD). Having grown up in south Texas, where sun and warm weather are the norm, the gray skies and long nights of the Michigan winter were taking their toll on Nate.

The doctor recommended a "happy light," a device used to compensate for the lack of light experienced in the winter months.

Nate preferred a different solution; he wanted to get out of Michigan. However, until he made Seaman (E3), he was stuck there.

The seasonal depression notwithstanding, Michigan wasn't a total loss. Nate met some locals who tipped him off to a few nearby spots where he could surf. One of the best was across the Blue Water Bridge into Canada. In the town of Sarnia, Nate found a surfing spot that actually had big enough waves to make it fun.

Nate found Michigan to be a dark and cold place and he looked forward to the day when he would make Seaman and be able to choose a permanent job. When that happened, he would go off to school and then be reassigned.

Hopefully that assignment would be as far away from Michigan as possible.

Electrician's Mate

There are only twenty-two different jobs to choose from in the Coast Guard, and when Nate was promoted to Seaman, he had a difficult choice to make. His original plan was to go to AST (Aviation Survival Technician) school and become a rescue swimmer, someone who drops down out of a helicopter to assist people who are in trouble in the water. With his natural ease in the water and his passion for helping people, it seemed like a natural fit. However, the months Nate had spent doing search and rescue had changed his perspective. He loved rescuing people, but the emotional strain of losing them was just too great.

There was another reason that AST school no longer looked like a great option. There was a fifteen-month wait just to get in. That would mean nearly another year and a half of duty in Port Huron, Michigan before he even had the opportunity to go somewhere else. On top of that, he'd have several more months of training at AST school.

Greg, one of Nate's closest buddies, expressed an interest in going to Electrician's Mate "A" school, and Nate thought that it might be a good fit for him as well. The school would be challenging. Next to AST school, the Electrician's Mate training was the most difficult in the Coast Guard. Having worked with his dad in his engine and generator business,

Nate was comfortable around equipment and enjoyed the challenge of troubleshooting.

The best part was that there were immediate openings in the Electrician's Mate "A" school. He could go right away. So Nate and Greg signed up, and after enjoying a brief time of leave with Nate's family in Victoria, they drove together to Yorktown, Virginia to begin a rigorous period of training.

When Nate left Port Huron for the last time, he realized that it had been exactly eight months since he arrived there.

Electrician's Mate school was almost like being in college, except that there were a lot more rules at this school than any college would ever have. And it definitely lived up to its reputation as being difficult. The coursework was divided into several "blocks," the first of which was all math. Mathematics was not Nate's strongest subject, and he found himself challenged as he studied the various formulas he needed to know in order to be able to do his job safely and effectively. He worked hard to keep up because he knew that in this school, if he got behind, he'd be gone.

Even though the math was a struggle for him, Nate excelled with the hands-on troubleshooting, and as the training neared completion, he was sixteenth out of thirty in his class. The number was significant because choice of duty assignments was based on grade point average. A few weeks before the end of the school, a list of possible duty locations was distributed and everyone began thinking about where they wanted to go after the training was finished.

There was a slot in Hawaii that Nate wanted and could have chosen, but one of his buddies was from Hawaii and he wanted to go back there and be nearer to his family. So Nate passed on that choice. There weren't any openings in Texas, but there was one slot open in New Orleans. Nate thought about how nice it would be to get back down south where it was warm again, but being sixteenth in the class, he wondered whether or not a spot in New Orleans would still be open by the time he got to choose. Because the warm spots in the nice locations were the most desirable, they usually went first. So although Nate had his sight set on New Orleans, realistically he knew it probably wouldn't be available.

Unbeknownst to Nate, the fifteen students who had higher grade point averages had a private meeting. As was the case in boot camp and his previous duty station, Nate's attitude and his faith had made a strong impact on those around him. His friends knew he wanted to go back south, and they wanted to make it possible.

So the fifteen who were above him got together and said, "Let's figure out a way that we can all get assignments we want, but work it out so that Lytle can go to New Orleans."

The day before the choices were to be finalized Nate's friends told him what their plans were.

"We got together and discussed it," they told him. "And we worked it out so you can go to New Orleans."

Nate didn't know what to say. He was on the verge of tears.

"Y'all are crazy," Nate managed to say. "That's awesome. Are you sure?"

"It's all okay," they replied. "Everybody's getting to go where they want to go. Don't worry about it."

Nate went to bed that night rejoicing. It looked like God was going to make it possible for him to at least get closer to home. He was now dead-set on going to New Orleans.

But the next day, an unexpected turn of events would radically alter those plans.

Michigan—Again!

The next day, the entire class gathered together for a meeting with the chief. One by one in order of class ranking they selected their duty stations. Everything was going fine until the man in 15th place announced his choice.

"New Orleans."

Nate's face went white and he suddenly felt like he wanted to throw up. He couldn't believe what he had just heard.

Did he just say "New Orleans?"

Nate looked around and saw his buddies' shocked faces. This had taken them by surprise too. Later, Nate learned that the man's wife had persuaded him to change his choice and take New Orleans the night before the meeting.

Nate felt overwhelmed by a flood of emotion. He felt betrayed and angry. It was the first time in his life that he had ever wanted to fight someone, but at that moment he would have taken great pleasure in beating that guy down. But he didn't have time to voice or express his anger.

The Chief was calling his name.

"Sixteen, Lytle!"

It was time for Nate to make his choice, but the rug had just been pulled out from under him. Nate would not take someone else's choice away from them. He wouldn't do what had just been done to him. But that left him only one choice. He had to take the spot the man before him had vacated.

Nate spoke his choice quietly and without much enthusiasm.

"Saginaw, Michigan."

When Nate left Michigan several months earlier, he'd said, "I'm never going back there as long as I live." Now he was going back there and, what was worse, he could very well end up spending the rest of his enlistment there.

Nate's buddy, Greg, placed third in the class and had chosen to go to a station in Florida. He felt so bad about what happened that he went to the Chief after the meeting.

"I want to swap assignments with Lytle. Let him go to Florida and I'll go to Michigan."

The Chief shook his head. "I can't do that. I'll have to talk to the Senior Chief."

But before the Chief could take the matter any farther, Nate heard about it and went to Greg.

"Dude, don't do that," Nate told him. "You busted your butt to make third in the class. Just go down there and don't worry about it. I'll be okay."

Not getting assigned to New Orleans was a difficult pill to swallow, but Nate was not one to stay down long. If he had to go to Michigan again, he was going to make the best of it. Mark, a friend from Victoria, offered to move up there with him so he wouldn't have to go alone. So, after another brief period of leave, Seaman Electrician's Mate Lytle drove to Saginaw, Michigan.

All things considered, his new duty station was a distinct improvement over Port Huron. Saginaw was a newer station with nicer buildings. He made new friends, and his boss was from Dallas, so at least there was one person there who understood how much Nate missed Texas.

Unfortunately, Nate's friend Mark was no better suited for living in Michigan winters than Nate was. After about a month and a half, he told Nate, "I can't take it up here. I've got to go back home."

Nate couldn't help feeling disappointed, but deep down he understood.

"It's okay," he told his friend. "I wouldn't be up here either if I had a choice."

Not long after that, Nate discovered that he *might* have a choice, after all.

Nate discovered an online bulletin board, similar to Craigslist, but for the military only. It was possible to post your rank and assignment on the site and swap with someone else who had the same job and rank. Nate figured he didn't have anything to lose, so he posted his job and rate.

Months passed with no response, and Nate wasn't particularly surprised at that. From his perspective, he couldn't understand why anyone would want to leave a warm weather location and move to Michigan. And since Nate's billet in Michigan was for three more years, he figured that it probably wouldn't attract any takers.

He was about to give up hope when he got an email from Lee, a young man who was stationed in Galveston, Texas.

He was from Ohio and was interested in swapping with Nate.

Nate called him and said, "Are you serious? You really want to come up here?"

"Yeah, it's too hot down here."

Nate laughed. "Dude, I want to go back where it's hot."

As they talked, they realized that they had done law enforcement training together at Harbor Beach.

As far as they were concerned, the deal was done. But there was one problem. Lee was an EM3, but Nate was now an EM2. The rules specified that they had to be the same rate. One thing working in their favor was that Lee was doing the job of an EM2, even though he didn't have that rank.

Nate told him, "I'll talk to the Senior Chief and see what happens."

The Senior Chief had no problems with allowing Nate and Lee to swap jobs. He knew how badly Nate wanted and needed to get out of Michigan. "You're a good worker and you've got a good attitude. I'll process the paperwork and get you out of here."

Not long after that, Nate was on his way to Galveston.

"Thank you, Lord," Nate said as he left Michigan.

God had worked to bring him to a station that was six hours closer to home than if he'd been in New Orleans. Once again, God had confirmed to Nate that His way was best and that as long as Nate trusted in Him and followed His leading, God would indeed direct his path. What Nate didn't know then was that through this new assignment in Galveston, God was also preparing Nate for the biggest battle of his life.

Chapter 9

Chosen?

Monday, June 11, 2007

If there were any doubts that God was working through Nate's accident, the events of the next few days would begin to erase those doubts.

When Billy and Tammy arrived at five thirty on the morning of June eleventh, some of Nate's friends were already waiting. It was exactly a week since Nate had fallen, yet many people still came to encourage Tammy and Billy, to pray for Nate, and to watch and wait for news. When they went back to the ICU to see Nate that morning, two of Nate's friends, Danny and Dustin, accompanied them.

The report was good. The nurse told them that Nate had a quiet night, and that his temperature had stayed under 101.

As Nate lay there with earphones on his ears, listening to his iPod, Tammy stood over him. As she rubbed his forehead, she wondered what he might be dreaming about and if he could hear them. She wanted desperately to be able to hold him like she did when he was little, to wrap him in her arms and tell him everything would be all right. But right now that was not possible. Nevertheless, during her visits throughout the day, Tammy did everything she could to encourage Nate by praying over him, reading scripture to him, and keeping him updated on the El Ride posts. All day long, Nate's surfing buddies, and many people he didn't even know, were posting their prayers and words of encouragement, and

Tammy read every one to Nate. Tammy and Billy went in to see Nate during every visitation allowed. But they also realized that the others who were coming needed to have time with him. As hard as it was, Tammy and Billy would stay for a few minutes each time they visited, and then go back to the waiting area so others could visit and pray for him. So even though she tried to make the most of her brief visits with Nate, most of Tammy's day was spent in the surgical ICU waiting room.

It was there that she began to see God touch lives.

She was waiting for the three o'clock visitation when she noticed Carrie, someone she used to go to church with. Tammy went over to talk to her and found out that her father was in surgery. As they visited Tammy learned that her friend hadn't gone to church in a long time and most of her family with her didn't attend church. In the middle of the conversation, a nurse came in and told Carrie that they had found a blood clot during the surgery and that her father's condition was very serious. Tammy could see that Carrie was upset and she felt God nudging her to pray for them.

Tammy was reluctant, not because she didn't want to pray, but because she wondered how she could possibly be an encouragement to them when she was still struggling with her own trial. Nevertheless she felt very strongly that God wanted her to pray for them and so she asked, "Would you like me to pray with you and your family?"

She didn't really know what to say but trusted God to give her the right words, and when she finished they thanked her and asked her to keep them in her prayers. They also mentioned that they needed to get back in church and have a relationship with God. As Tammy was starting to go back to the other side of the waiting room, the doctor came out and told them that Carrie's father had come through the surgery and that his prognosis was good.

Tammy went back to her seat thankful that God was using Nate's accident to touch people's lives—but that was only the beginning.

By Monday afternoon, Nate had begun to move more and more, and to even open his eyes a little, though he didn't appear to be focusing on anything. But his increased activity was a great source of encouragement. After the 3:00 p.m. visitation, Danny Vivian posted to the El Ride forum:

"Just left the hospital. Wasn't able to stay long, but was there for the 3:00 visitation. It was abso-freakin-lutely amazing. I was standing outside the ICU doors when Nate's mom motioned me to hurry in. Nate's eyes were open and he was moving around a lot, like he was trying to climb out of bed. It looked like he was having trouble tracking and focusing, but he kept his eyes open a long time. Then he began to cry. He would squeeze his family's hands when they would talk to him. It looked like he was trying to talk, but the tubes prevented it. It was hard to watch, but yet a beautiful sight. After about five minutes, he began to fade off to sleep again. He went to sleep to the sound of his sister's voice as she sang to him. Like I said, abso-freaking-lutely amazing."—wavehound

On Monday evening, Nate's grandmother, nicknamed "Grammy," and his older brother Will came up from Corpus Christi for a visit. Will had been recovering from injuries he'd received in an auto accident, and so this was the first day he'd had a chance to visit since Nate fell. The visit had a deep emotional impact on Will and also brought a strong reaction from Nate himself.

When they went into the ICU, Tammy went over to Nate.

"Nate, Grammy's here. She'd sure like to see those beautiful eyes of yours for her birthday."

For a few seconds, Nate's eyelids fluttered, as if he were working hard to open them. He also looked like he was trying to move his right hand.

Then Will came up to the right side of the bed.

"Hey little bro. How are you doing? My hand's right over here."

Nate started moving his right arm as if he were trying to reach out to his brother. Then he started moving his right leg.

The joy that flooded through the room was palpable. There were those who kept saying that Nate's movements were not purposeful, but with every passing day it was becoming clear—at least to Nate's family and friends—that he was still "in there," and that he was going to come back.

Will held himself together for Nate when they were in the ICU, but after they left the room, the tears began to flow.

"It should have been me, not him. I'm the one who has gotten into trouble and made bad choices. He's never done anything wrong

69

to anyone. He's lived his whole life serving God. He does not deserve this."

Tammy, Billy, and the rest of the family tried to comfort Will. "God is in control, and he has a purpose for Nate's life," Tammy said. "We have to trust him." As Tammy spoke those words to her oldest son, she realized that she was speaking them to herself as well. That evening, she wrote in her journal:

Father God, thank You for what You have given us today. Thank You for the progress that Nate has made. I am still at times wondering if this is all a dream. I feel ashamed to be so upset about this. I get so confused with all the emotions and feelings that I have every day. At any given moment I am scared, numb, excited, happy, depressed, upset, hopeful, etc. Through it all, Lord, I am glad I have a relationship with You. I would never make it through one moment without You. I love You, Father.

Tuesday, June 12, 2007

Despite the apparent progress Nate made on Monday, by Tuesday morning, it looked as if he had taken several steps backward. When Billy and Tammy arrived for the 6:00 a.m. visitation, they were shocked at Nate's appearance. His lips were so swollen and bloody, he looked like a boxer who was on the losing end of a fight.

The nurses had reinserted Nate's bite block the previous day because he still was showing a tendency to bite down on his respirator tube. During the night, the bite block had slipped deeper into his mouth and was lodged behind his teeth. They were eventually able to pry his mouth open to remove the block, but by the time they did, Nate had bitten his lips badly several times.

How much more does he have to go through? Tammy wondered.

Then, that afternoon, Nate's doctors decided to proceed with the tracheotomy and to have a feeding tube inserted. God gave them another doctor that they knew and were comfortable with; Dr. McDaniel, who was the doctor that had suggested putting pictures above Nate's bed, was called in to do the trach and feeding tube. He was a friend of Nate's and had teenagers with whom Nate had invested his time and shared life.

Danny Vivian posted on El Ride about Nate's condition:

"Checked in at the hospital this morning. Nate had a restless night and apparently almost destroyed his hospital bed. They will be doing a tracheotomy at 1:30 and will also be placing a feeding tube directly into his stomach. That way he won't have all the tubes, lines, etc., in his mouth and nose. Hopefully the next tube he has in his face will be a chocolate Gorda one."

By 3:05 that afternoon, Nate was breathing through a trach tube, and the feeding tube had been inserted; there was no further need for a bite block.

But Nate's day—and the impact he would have on others—was far from over.

Scott and Brian, Nate's former pastors and the ones who had invited him to help plant a church in Florida, came to see him. Jeremy, the music pastor, was also with them. Like Nate's brother Will and many others before him, they weren't prepared for what they saw. They had heard about Nate's injury and condition through e-mail and texts and phone conversations. But the reality was far worse than anything they imagined.

When Brian saw Nate, he broke down in tears. Nate had practically been part of his family. Nate was like an older brother to Brian's boys. Now, the young man he had been so close to lay in a hospital ICU, still alive but shut away in a coma, surrounded by machines and monitors.

Brian went over to Nate's bed and whispered softly in Nate's ear. "Be a warrior. Fight. God has a plan for you."

Back in the waiting room, Scott said, "I didn't realize it was this bad until now." He wrote down his phone number. "Call me if you need anything at all."

After Brian, Scott, and Jeremy left, and as the evening wound down, Tammy made her first post on the El Ride board. Several days back, other El Ride members had suggested that she be given her own screen name and approved as a member so that she could keep the entire board updated on Nate's condition. Approval from the administrators had finally come through.

Nate's screen name was "texasboy," so Tammy's—naturally—was "texasboy's mom."

That evening she wrote:

"I cannot even begin to tell you all how awesome you all are. Your support and prayers for Nate are so overwhelming. I wish I could meet every one of you in person! This is probably the hardest thing our family has ever had to go through, but we know that God is in control. I don't know how anyone who doesn't believe that could make it through this. Even as Nate is going through this journey, so many lives are being touched.

"I miss Nate saying, 'Mom, look at this freakin' awesome day God has made' or 'hey Mamasita, I luv ya!' When I read this site and all the prayers that are being prayed and all the love that you are sending this way, it helps fill that void.

"I have printed out your comments and have been reading them to Nate when we go in to see him. I have told him each and every one of your names and that you are praying for him.

"I noticed some have asked about flowers, cards, etc. Flowers are not allowed in the ICU, but if you would like to send him a card or donation, I will make sure we read them to him until we know he is hearing us.

"Thanks again and love to all of you."—texasboy's mom

The first response to Tammy's post was not only encouraging, but also reflective of the prayer support that was coming in from the people on El Ride: "Lifting you up every morning and every night my friend. 'A righteous man may have many troubles but the Lord delivers him from them all,' Psalms 34:19."—jhs

Nate's sister Elissa sang again for him on the last visitation period of the evening. She held his hand and, as she sang, Nate's eyes fluttered and he squeezed her hand. Tears began to flow down Elissa's cheeks and she almost wasn't able to finish the song. Was it possible that Nate not only heard his sister's song, but was squeezing her hand and trying to open his eyes as well?

About midnight, it was time for everyone to go home to get at least a few hours of sleep. As Tammy looked around the nearly empty waiting room she noticed a woman sitting off in one corner. She had been there for several days. Tammy went over to her.

"Are you okay? Do you need anything?"

The woman began to cry.

"My husband is in ICU," she said. "He was working a temporary job here and had an accident at work. I had to leave my two small children to come here to be with him."

The woman looked frightened and exhausted.

"Where will you be sleeping tonight?" Tammy asked her.

"Here, in the waiting area. I've spent the last two nights sleeping on the chairs."

"I don't know if you will be comfortable with it or not, but my son is here in ICU, so we have an empty bed at my house. If you would like to, you can sleep in my son's bed this evening. You can take a shower and eat a bite, also."

The woman looked at Tammy like she was crazy.

"I understand if you don't feel comfortable going home with strangers," Tammy added.

The woman's expression softened. "I've been watching you and all the people up here. I've never seen or felt so much love before."

"God has blessed us," Tammy said. "And he has put a lot of loving and caring people in our lives.

"I'm not afraid to go with you," said the woman, "but I'd feel bad sleeping in your son's bed."

"If you knew my son," Tammy said, "you'd know that he would gladly give up his bed for you, even if he could sleep in it tonight."

Tears filled the woman's eyes as she gathered her things and followed Billy and Tammy home.

It had been a day of amazing things, as Tammy wrote in her journal that night:

Father God, this has been an emotional and exhausting day. Thank You for all that You have given us today. Thank You that Nate is still here with us and that You are working in so many people's lives. I know You have Nate in Your hands and pray that Your will be done, even though I am a little frightened of what it could be. Please continue to give me strength to go through this. I love You, Father.

Wednesday, June 13, 2007

The last few days had been a rollercoaster ride, but Wednesday, June thirteenth, was a day of good news. And that good news started the moment the Lytles and their new friend, JoAnn, arrived at the ICU.

The doctors told JoAnn that her husband was doing much better and would be transferred to their home town. She brought Billy and Tammy in to see him, and he thanked them when she explained how they had taken her into their home.

She also mentioned that maybe they should start going to church when they got home.

He agreed.

Again, even though he was in a coma, Nate was touching people's lives.

The good news didn't stop with JoAnn's husband. Nate seemed to be making great strides that day as well. By the 3:00 p.m. visitation, the nurses told them that even though Nate was still on the ventilator, he was mostly breathing on his own. His temperature was down to 99 and they had removed the cooling blankets. They had also stopped some of his medications. He was still fighting off the pneumonia, but even that was improving. By four that afternoon, the nurses had completely weaned Nate from the ventilator. He was breathing on his own for the first time since the accident. As encouraging as these developments were, they were small compared to what would happen that evening.

Billy and Tammy were in the waiting room when a nurse rushed out and called them to come back to the ICU. It wasn't visiting time, but the nurse told them they had to see what Nate was doing. When they got back there, they understood why the nurse was so excited.

Nate's eyes were open, and he appeared to be staring at the collage of pictures that Tammy had hung at the foot of his bed. "I don't know what he was thinking or seeing," Tammy wrote later. "But he was definitely looking up at it. It was so wonderful to see those beautiful hazel eyes, even if he had a blank stare in them."

At the 10 p.m. visitation, Nate gave even more evidence that he was still "in there." He began to cough and choke, but after he stopped, he rubbed his eye with his right arm and then put his arm behind his head.

From that moment on, no one was going to be able to tell Tammy and Billy that Nate's movements were simply "reflex" or "not purposeful."

A little later that evening, they called Billy and Tammy in to see Nate again. And again his eyes were open and he appeared to be staring at the collage. Billy and Tammy spoke to Nate, but when they did, he closed his eyes.

"He's just playing possum with you," one of the nurses joked. "His eyes are open, but when you talk to him, he closes them."

Everyone laughed.

"Seriously," the nurse said, "I think Nate might be trying to come out of his coma. When he opens his eyes, he might be wondering where he is. Then when he hears your voices, it comforts him and he rests easier."

As they went back to the waiting room, the stress of the previous week finally overwhelmed Tammy. She had been strong for everyone else, but conflicting thoughts about Nate's accident now began to spill out. And with those thoughts came the tears.

Has God abandoned Nate and us? Or has he chosen Nate for this because he is such a true servant of God. But if that's the case, why would anybody want to serve Him like Nate did?

Other, more frightening thoughts began to fill her mind. It was looking like Nate might survive now, but what kind of life would he have? Would he be condemned to spend the rest of his life in a hospital bed, hovering between life and death? That thought scared Tammy more than the thought of losing him.

Tammy was overwhelmed, and raced out of the hospital crying. When Tammy went home from the hospital that night, Tammy's sister Terri and three of Tammy's friends—Connie, Karen and Charlotte—came over to the house to encourage, support, and pray for her.

Tammy was thankful for their support—and it did help—but she went to bed feeling a mixture of confusion, fear, anger, awe, and complete exhaustion.

Most Heavenly Father, I thank You for today. I thank You for each and every positive thing we saw today, no matter how big or how small. You are an amazing God. I pray that You give me rest tonight, Father. I love You, Father, but I am angry right now also, Father. And though part of me is scared, I am also anxious to see all that You will do through this. I am so confused I don't even know how to pray or what to think. Please give me comfort.

Was Nate chosen to go through this horrible experience? Was it part of God's plan? Tammy didn't know. She only knew that there was no way she could get through the ordeal without God's help.

Chapter 10

TIRR Memorial Hermann[5]

Thursday, June 14th, 2007

"Nate has a chance of living through this now, but I'm not sure what kind of life it will be."

The neurosurgeon's words echoed in Tammy's mind. It was another "good news, bad news" moment. Everything seemed to point to Nate being on the road to recovery. He'd been moving his right arm and leg more, and had even given evidence of more "purposeful" movement. During the night, the nurses kept fans blowing on Nate to help keep his temperature down. At one point, one of the fans blew his gown up on his right side. Nate reached down, grabbed the gown, and pulled it over his knee.

All of the medical indicators were moving in the right direction, too. His white cell count was 11, almost back within the normal range of 6-10. His X-rays looked good and, although he was still fighting off pneumonia, even that seemed to be subsiding.

Only about a week and a half had passed since the doctors had told Billy and Tammy that they should start making "arrangements," which they had taken as meaning funeral arrangements. Now it looked like Nate

---

5   TIRR is part of the Memorial Hermann Healthcare System. The name of the hospital is officially TIRR Memorial Hermann, but will be referred to as TIRR MH throughout the book, except when used in a quotation.

was out of the woods. He had beaten unbelievable odds and survived an injury that most of the doctors had considered unsurvivable.

But what now? What would happen to Nate? Would he spend the rest of his life in a nursing home, living in a semi-conscious state and being fed through a tube? What kind of life was that?

God had walked with Billy and Tammy through every step of Nate's injury, and it seemed that even now he was preparing them for what they might face. In between visitation hours, Ruth, a friend from Tammy's church came and prayed with her.

"I prayed a lot about whether or not I should come," she said. "Are you prepared for whatever the outcome of this may be?"

They talked at length about the "what ifs."

What if things don't go the way Billy and I want?

What if Nate doesn't come back completely?

It was as if the Lord had sent this dear woman as His messenger, to encourage Tammy to begin preparing herself for the worst, while still praying for the best. Most of all, she was reminded to let God help her through whatever the outcome might be.

Even so, Tammy struggled to understand why God would put someone so vital, someone who loved Him so much, into a hospital bed, unable to communicate, unable to do the thing he loved the most—tell people about his Lord?

As if in answer to an unspoken prayer, Tammy found a post on El Ride that morning that spoke directly to her question. The post was by Brian Brown, Nate's dear friend and mentor, who had come all the way from Florida to see him two days earlier.

"I had the privilege of seeing my buddy for the first time on Tuesday. The emotions were all over the place from shock—of how fragile life can be, sadness—of not knowing if we will share a wave together in this lifetime again except in our memories, to ultimately joy.

"This may sound strange, but I know Nate, and more than anything he wants to reflect God's glory, no matter the cost.

"Nate, my buddy, God is using you—Be still! Suffering with Christ is not only the result of magnifying Him, but also the means. His beauty shines most brightly when treasured about health and wealth and life itself. He knew that suffering would be the path in this age for making him most visibly supreme. That is why He calls us to this. And, dude, you have never backed away from an opportunity or a challenge. He loves you, and that love does not mean making much of you or making life easy. It means making us able to enjoy making much of Him forever—no matter what it costs. We both know the hardest thing for you and I is to do nothing and be still, but, dude, God is using your life in an incredible way. Be still and sit in His presence today! Love you!"—brianb8888

Amazingly, Brian's post wasn't the only one that seemed specifically aimed at encouraging Tammy and Billy that day.

One member, who is also a doctor, posted:

"Just had a patient in whose husband was in a serious accident 2 yrs ago and had serious head injuries. He has made a significant recovery, albeit slow. I mentioned this case and she told me to let the family know that the healing of the brain takes time after trauma. The brain needs to rest, hence, the need sometimes to induce coma. He was . . . at TIRR in the med center for his rehab. He now walks, runs, fully speaks and the only residual effects are decreased strength in his hands."—seawalldoc

Another member, whose screen name was "Pearl," posted, "When I was 16 I was in a car wreck . . . and was in a coma for about 5 days . . . . Recovery was slow—I had lots of problems with short term memory, aphasia (knew the word I wanted to say but couldn't get it out of my mouth), difficulty reading, and anger . . . . It took about a year of some ups and downs but I went back to school part time, then full time, graduated, then went to college. I ended up getting my M.S. in Neuropsychology and working in cognitive rehab with brain injured folks.

IMHO [In my humble opinion] there really isn't a better chance for a good recovery than everything I've heard about Nate: A young, healthy, intelligent athlete with a ton of family and friends for support.

It may take longer than you think it will—but DO NOT lose your faith that he's going to be OK. I have no doubt that he will."—Pearl

After sharing about his mother's recovery from a severe head injury, Seabass offered this word of encouragement: "Nate, you'll be back in time for autumn swell, and if TX flat summers hold true, you may just be back in time for the NEXT swell. Good on ya, kid, good on ya."

Someone else wrote that they had just finished reading the book *90 Minutes in Heaven*, then commented, "The book helped me realize that Nate IS doing what he set out to do, just in a different way than he first intended. He's rallied people together and brought many of us that haven't been doing such a great job in praying lately to a standstill with a heart-pumping, adrenaline rush merciful prayer."—cinsdragonfly

Tammy had gone to bed the previous night wondering if God had chosen Nate to go through this fiery trial, if somehow God planned to use her son's injury to impact others.

Throughout the day, the answer that kept coming before her was *yes*.

Nevertheless, serious questions remained. How complete would Nate's recovery be? That afternoon, Cheri, one of Tammy's friends, came by to visit and brought along some information on traumatic brain injuries. Cheri's daughter had suffered a brain injury in an accident a few years back, and Tammy had been there to encourage Cheri and her family. Now Cheri was able to encourage Tammy through her own experience. As hard as it was to watch Cheri and her sweet family go through their own journey, God used it to help Tammy go through hers.

Tammy was thankful for the extra information, but she was also frightened. Reading the booklets and info Cheri had left with her brought her face to face with Nate's potential future. She wasn't eager to confront that. As Tammy read through the information Cheri had brought her, she found the Rancho Los Amigos Scale[6] to be particularly interesting.

The Rancho Los Amigos Scale describes brain function on a scale from 1 (No Response) through 8 (Purposeful, Appropriate) and measures "a person's reliance on assistance to carry out cognitive and physical functions." There is no set "pace" or "time" for a patient to pass through the eight levels of the scale. Indeed, some patients might spend long periods of time at a certain level while others moved through the same level quickly. Particularly unsettling was the possibility that a patient might become "locked in" on one level and never move past it.

When that happens, the solution is long-term care.

Nate's long-term prognosis was on Tammy's mind as she went in for the 3:00 p.m. visitation, and the signs were encouraging. Kevin, one

---

[6] For more information about the Rancho Los Amigos Scale, see Appendix 2.

of Nate's nurses, reported that the pneumonia was much improved and that he was amazed at Nate's progress. Nate's eyes were open, and he was staring at the collage Tammy had made. When she put his ear-buds in and turned on his iPod, he started moving his lips as if he were trying to sing along.

"Raise your arm, Nate," said Tammy.

Briefly, Nate lifted his right arm off the bed.

Was her son coming back?

If Nate was coming back, one thing was certain. He was going to need to go to rehab somewhere. Dr. Norvill had already mentioned that they needed to be thinking about getting him into a facility soon.

"What kind of rehab are we talking about?" Tammy asked

"Nate's at the point now where he might benefit from some regular rehab," the neurosurgeon had said. "I don't know how much it will help him, but it's worth a try."

"Where?" asked Tammy.

Dr. Norvill suggested a nearby rehab facility.

"Why there? Why can't we get him into a facility that specializes in brain injuries?"

"He doesn't have funding, Tammy. He has no insurance. There's no way he'd be able to go anywhere like that."

Tammy looked Dr. Norvill straight in the eye and said, "If you could send him anywhere, if he had all the money in the world, where would you send him?"

Dr. Norvill didn't even need to think about it. "If he had all the money in the world, I'd send him to a place called TIRR, The Institute for Rehabilitation and Research, in Houston."

As far as Tammy was concerned, Dr. Norvill's answer was a sign from God if there ever was one. Ever since Nate had been in ICU, she had heard about TIRR Memorial Hermann repeatedly from many different people—even one of the El Ride posters. Every one of them had said that when Nate was ready for rehab, he should go there.

Tammy had never heard of TIRR Memorial Hermann before Nate's accident—it had not yet received the national media attention that came with Congresswoman Gabrielle Giffords' treatment there—but she knew in her heart that this was the place her son needed to go.

"We're going to pray," she told the neurosurgeon, "and Nathan's going to TIRR."

Tammy wasted no time enlisting prayer support. She immediately put out the word, asking people to pray that God would somehow get Nate into TIRR MH. The request was sent by many people to many churches and prayer chains in the United States. In a post to El Ride, she told Nate's surfing buddies,

"The doctor that did his head surgery also said that Nate is almost to the point that he needs to be moved to a rehab facility. One of the doctor's first choices would be TIRR in Houston, but we have been told this would be difficult to do because of his financial situation. (We were in the process of trying to get him insurance since his Coast Guard insurance ran out, and he's not in school, but didn't make it in time.) It's unreal how many people have mentioned TIRR to us. I know that it might be hard humanly, but I know God can do all things . . . .

"Well, I know God can do this if it's His will. Every step of the way in this journey has already been a miracle. I have been keeping a journal of all of the events. In every step you can see God in this. I know He can take care of this too. Please continue praying."—texasboy's mom

God began to answer the prayers of Nate's family and friends sooner than anyone expected. Less than two hours after Tammy posted her prayer request, a brief, two-sentence reply showed up on El Ride: "The last thing I want to do is falsely raise your hopes, but I will see if the people I know have any pull at TIRR. I'm firing off some emails."

The poster's screen name was "Surfncpa".

Youth camp leaders in Colorado summer 2006 Steve,
Nate, Shad, Brian, and Steve

Saddleback Youth Leaders Training Conference spring 2007

Nate and the youth group praying for Brian before he
headed to Tallahasse, FL May 2007

Nate surfing Bob Hall Pier Corpus Christi, TX
December 20, 2006

Brian & Nate fall 2006

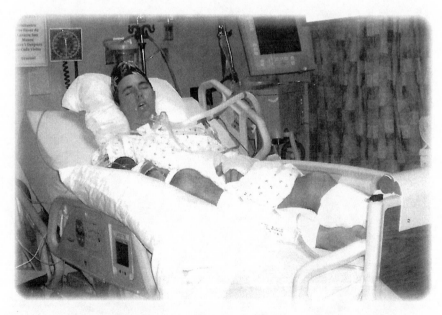

Nate in the intensive care unit at the local hospital in
Victoira, TX June 2007, in a comatose state

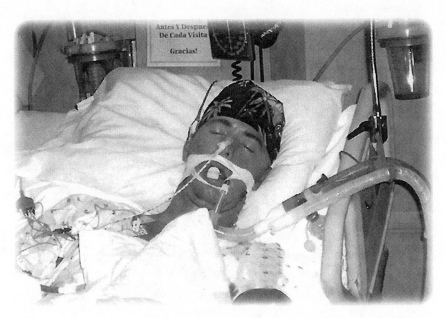

Nate in the intensive care unit at the local hospital in
Victoira, TX June 2007, in a comatose state

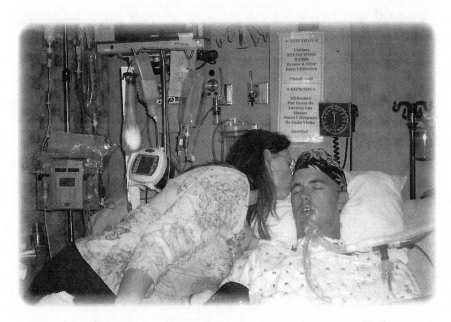

Nate with his mom, Tammy, in the intensive care unit at the
local hospital in Victoira, TX June 2007, in a comatose state

The exact mold of Nate's shattered skull

Nate at Coast Guard boot camp graduation with his
sister, Elissa, his Dad, Billy, and Mom, Tammy June 2002

The original El Ride Pray for Nate Thread

The complete El Ride Pray for Nate thread September 2007

Part Two

Long Journey Back

Chapter 11

PFN (Pray for Nate)

"Your life is screaming right now!"

Those words were the next-to-last line of an El Ride post from Brian Brown, Nate's dear friend and former pastor, and they summarized the miracle of Nate Lytle's life at that moment. Nate, a young man with a passion to talk to others about God, was now lying in an ICU bed, mute and comatose. Yet contrary to logic, Nate was speaking more loudly for God than he ever had. More than that, the reach of his message was expanding outward like ripples on a lake. Through his injury, Nate was touching people he'd never met with the love of God. And those who were close to him were being encouraged in their faith.

Brian's post came at 5:11 a.m.

"Dude, I could really use your help moving today . . . I understand you got other things going on, but if you decide to get up out of that bed, it's only a 14 hour drive. Come on, you've driven that to surf!

"My encouragement for you today . . . from Paul in Phil 1[7].

"'And I'm going to keep that celebration going because I know how it's going to turn out. Through your faithful prayers and the generous response of the Spirit of Jesus Christ, everything he wants to do in and through me will be done. I can hardly wait to continue on my course. I don't expect to be embarrassed in the least. On the contrary, everything

---

[7]   "Phil 1" refers to the New Testament book of Philippians, chapter one.

happening to me in this jail (hospital bed) only serves to make Christ more accurately known, regardless of whether I live or die. They didn't shut me up; they gave me a pulpit! Alive, I'm Christ's messenger; dead, I'm his bounty. Life versus even more life! I can't lose,' (Philippians 1:19-21, *The Message*).

"Your life is screaming right now!!"—brianb8888

Nate's life was indeed "screaming." People who had never met Nate were being touched by his story and by the groundswell of support that was developing. One member posted, "This is the first thread I read every day. Even though I've never met you, you've touched my life. Rest up . . . . You got a lot more waves to catch!"—datcat

A post from Ron Berwick (Seabass), another of Nate's friends, echoed that thought:

"Mornin' Kid. I am in the midst of last minute packing and planning for Costa tomorrow . . . . Anyway, I have a ton to do, and plenty to think about, but you are at the top of the list . . . . I know you don't drink, but there will be many an Imperial and Pilsen raised in your honor each sundown I witness down there in Centro America . . . . And a prayer every morning when I paddle out (Hey Nate, look at this friggin' AWESOME day God has given us. And while I'm on the subject, Lord, thank YOU for giving us Nate. Get my brother well . . . for the next swell).

"Keep on keepin' on brother o' mine, El Ride is with you!!!"—seabass

Ron "Seabass" Berwick's words were almost prophetic, because within the El Ride community, momentum had begun to build to do something for Nate and his family. For some time now, many of the surfers had been closing out their posts with the initials PFN, which stood for "Pray for Nate." Those three letters became a simple reminder to keep lifting Nate up in prayer.

A couple of the members took it a step further.

Surfncpa posted a photo of a sticker he'd designed: a surfboard with the letters PFN "riding" the board. That simple sticker touched off a movement that would soon become a juggernaut. The responses on the El Ride board were enthusiastic.

"MAW / CPA that sticker ROCKS!!!! Get them down here somehow!!"—g_scott

Later that morning, Seabass posted:

"MAW is doing a stealth delivery of PFN stickers to an undisclosed surfboard research laboratory in the U of H area . . . I plan on doing some 1ˢᵗ degree felonious sticker placement . . . down in the CR (Costa Rica). So stoked!!!! Thanks MAW!!!!!"—seabass

Like the proverbial snowball rolling downhill, the PFN movement took on a life of its own, progressing from a simple reminder to pray for Nate to a means for raising funds to help with his medical expenses.

Another El Ride member suggested that they expand on the sticker idea:

"How about a T-shirt? . . . . Content figure downloaded from one of the photos posted (I think by G) so permission would have to be given. Just a thought and other designs welcome. I couldn't commit to printing for a few weeks . . . but would be glad to work out something to help with the $$ drive."—datcat

Along with the post, datcat included a logo design that featured an image of Nate on a surfboard, riding a wave. Under the board were the letters PFN and a design of a dove in flight.

An online account had already been set up where people could donate. Now, with stickers and T-shirts, Nate's friends would have a tangible means of raising money for him. Throughout the day on Friday, June fifteenth and Saturday the sixteenth, the El Ride board was peppered with short messages, working out the details necessary to get PFN stickers and T-shirts into production as soon as possible.

Surfncpa: "I love that design Datcat. I'm trying to find FSB and see if he can make some screens. I'll buy the Ts." datcat: "It's 99% screen ready (just need to clean up some tiny flaws). Tried to keep it one color to keep the cost down so profits can stay high, but it would be easy to make it multi-colored as well. I'll be happy to supply the file. Anyone needing to discuss particulars can PM (private message) me for my cell #." wavehound: "That is one sweet design. When they're ready, let me know how to get stickers and t-shirts down here to Victoria. We could sell a buttload of them." seabass: "I'm on the horn to a screen printing buddy to see what he can do for us. I didn't know if FSB/Charlie have the equipment or they outsource, if someone would call and let me know . . . ."

Surfncpa: "We have all the equipment and probably already have enough blank shirts in stock. I just haven't heard from FSB to know if he's available to make the screens and do a print job." seabass: "Just got off the phone. My bro in Beaumont will print them for free. He suggested for t-shirts that we may wanna go down to Harwin and get some $1 shirts. If it is more than that he can get them for just a bit more. He will burn the screen and print them up. Somebody call me so I can pass them this guy's info, but please do it soon, my day is freakin' crazy right now." g_scott [whose photo of Nate surfing was used in the logo, added his support as well as his permission to use the picture]: "The design is AMAZING. So completely honored about the photo. Count me in for whatever is made from it." datcat: G . . . If you wanna supply Bones or any of the other artists on here the hi-res file of that pic, they could do a more realistic version of Nate's features and replace the figure in my design . . . . I don't have time to take on the chore myself due to prepping for the trip, but if the crowd would like to see something more lifelike I'll send them my file and they've got my permission to tweak the design." jsh: "That shirt is cool. I also have a connection in the shirt screening business. If things don't pan out with the current plan, let me know." hilldo: "Datcat . . . please send the file here before you go and we'll get it to FSB." wavehound: "I showed Nate's mom & dad the t-shirt design, and they loved it. First real big smiles I've seen in a while. A special request was made by some of the ladies in the waiting room for tank tops, so I'm passing that along."

JP1: "Thanks D for the update. I will take a bundle of those shirts. Nate another day with you on my mind. And the new PFN stickers on the Tacoma look sic."

MAW: "I will nag Ceep and FSB until they can't stand it. That is one AWESOME t-shirt. Cins, come on down and we can have a PFN shirt/ sticker party! Everyone welcome to come on over!!"

MAW: "Let's plan one . . . what day is good for anyone interested? I would love to have a house full of adults screaming through my house!" hurricane hopkins: "Nate, the Hopkins clan are praying for your quick recovery bro!!! Chuck, Dat Cat, I love the stickers and the t-shirt design. Let me know if you need any help." surfguru: "MAW . . . we need to get some stickers down to Dorados for a donation jar there also . . .

Bones, if you are down with designing [a] flyer, go for it. Lifting you up, brother . . . we love you Nate." hilldo: "The file is in the screen printer's hands!" jsh: "Will be down to Galveston tomorrow to get my stickers and can't wait for the shirts. Continued prayers brother."

Surfsesh: "Haven't been on in a few days but the prayers continue for you my brother. Count my family in on the T-shirts and stickers, they look great." mommasherrynpapat: "PFN'n still from the Cali side . . . . Hey, who can I talk to about sending an offering and a mailer for some t-shirts and stickers . . . ."

CHRIS SHANNON: "We could also have a batch on hand at our shop . . . t-shirts and stickers. We can put the sticker on the front door . . . and t-shirt in the display window and have both items available for folks to buy. We would just provide another place for those who want to support this cause. Hope I make sense here." datcat: "Good morning Nate! Got my T at the Mullet Gumbo showing last night. The slotted crew did a great job printing and honoring the art by adding your famous quote "Check out this freakin' awesome day God has made." nip: "I was at the surf movie tonight . . . and Surfncpa brought 40-50 t-shirts which pretty much sold out. Thanks to Ceep and MAW and the surfing community. We continue to PFN."

JP1: CPA some of us who could not make it last night would greatly appreciate the opportunity to catch a few of those tees. And tell MAW that the red PFN stickers were out at Surf Specs. If need be I will drive to your house to get the tees and the stickers . . . . my wife is threatening horrible things if I don't get her one. Love ya Nate, as always, PFN." poop: "Showed up a little late last night and all that were left were smalls so I gotta wait on my t-shirt. Did get some stickers for my car and new board."

Jammie Helzer: "Whoever came up with the T-shirt. ABSOLUTELY AWESOME. I will buy quite a few and I am sure that his buddies around here in Galveston would be proud to sport the shirt and let everyone know what it means and how much Nate "Dawg" means to us. Can someone out here hook me up with one or two of those stickers. I am not a surfer, but I am sure that my motorcycle and helmet can definitely sport them stickers with pride . . . . Help a biker honor his friend the best way I know how. I LOVE YOU MAN."

Tammy and Billy Lytle were deeply touched by the efforts of the surfing community in support of Nate. They had never met many of these people, but now they shared a strong bond in praying for Nate's full recovery. Even more than that, this was just one more sign that God was at work, even though they didn't know exactly what he was doing.

Friday evening, Tammy posted on the El Ride board:

"You guys are awesome! I love the stickers and the t-shirt! We want some here, too. I just can't believe how God is working in all this. Nate would tell me, 'No sweat Mom. God can do anything.' It's pretty strange when you've been raised in church, served in church (sang on praise teams for years, deacon's wife, taught Sunday School, etc.) and you come from a family of pastors, deacons and missionaries, that your 23-year-old son can have more faith than you do. It just goes to show that Nate truly has a call on his life and a relationship with God that is genuine and awesome."

Nate Lytle did indeed have a call on his life, but as he lay there in the ICU, the burning question was how that call would play out. Would Nate's impact no longer be by his words and his infectious personality? Would he forever be a silent witness? Or would he come back from the nether world in which he was now trapped to share God's love again?

Whatever happened, Tammy and Billy knew that there were scores of people ready and willing to help Nate—and them—in any way they could.

Chapter 12

Encouraging Signs

Friday, June 15th, 2007

Tammy was resolute. "I'm not opening another door until God closes this one."

She was convinced that Nate was supposed to do his rehab at TIRR Memorial Hermann in Houston. As she met with Myrna, Nate's social worker, to discuss places where he could do his rehab, she said, "I just know in my heart that this is where he's supposed to go. I've prayed and I've prayed, and I get a peace about TIRR. I don't get a peace about someplace else."

The problem was that Nate had no funding or insurance, and TIRR Memorial Hermann was one of the best rehab facilities in the country. Humanly speaking, it seemed as though Nate had about as much chance of getting in there as he had of walking on the moon.

In the meantime, now that it looked like Nate would survive, there were other issues that had to be addressed. Again, it seemed as if God was providing, even before Tammy and Billy knew what to ask for.

Nate was obviously going to need someone to take care of his bills and other payments, and Tammy had no idea where to start. She wondered about getting power of attorney or a legal guardianship of some kind, but knew that those things would have to be done in court. A few days earlier, she'd expressed her concerns to some friends in the

ICU waiting area. One of them was another friend named Connie. Tammy didn't realize that she worked in a law office.

"I can help you with that," Connie said.

True to her word, she showed up at the hospital Friday afternoon and got the paperwork started. It would be an involved and expensive process, but God provided every step of the way.

Another issue that had to be taken care of was Nate's wrist. He shattered his left wrist when he fell from the ladder, but up till now his condition had been so unstable that the doctors simply immobilized it by tying it down to his chest. That way, he couldn't injure it any further. But now that Nate's condition had stabilized somewhat, they needed to go in and try to repair the damage before Nate's left hand became permanently disabled.

Some questioned whether Nate was well enough to go through the procedure, but if he was to have any chance of using his hand again, the surgery had to be performed.

He went in for surgery at about four in the afternoon, and returned an hour and a half later with an external fixator attached to his left wrist.

The orthopedic surgeon, Dr. Charles Daniel, explained that Nate's wrist was so completely shattered that they felt that it would be better than trying to reassemble his wrist piece by piece. Tammy passed on the surgeon's explanation on a post to El Ride:

"Just wanted to let you all know Nate came through his wrist surgery okay. Yeah God! They put two pins in his hand, two in his lower arm and a bar connecting them together. They will turn the pins each day and give him therapy to try to help it heal correctly. His wrist was shattered pretty bad, so they thought this would work better than going in and trying to piece it back together. They said if all goes well, it should all be taken out in about six weeks."

Although the external fixator was a necessity, it also became a source of worry. Now that Nate's arm was no longer tied down, he was able to move it around. The problem was that now there was a danger that he might bring his hand up toward his head and accidentally hit the softball-sized hole in his skull that was now only protected by his scalp.

(He had always had a habit of sleeping with his left arm across the top of his head.)

Also that afternoon, Nate received a special visitor, whom Danny Vivian (wavehound) announced on El Ride: "Mike Forman, the sports writer for the Victoria Advocate, will be coming to the . . . ICU waiting room this afternoon at 3:00 to get info for a story to tell about Nate. I realize this is short notice, but anyone who can, and has a story to tell is encouraged to show up. I got Mike onto the El Ride forum so he could get some insight into what has happened over the past week and a half. This article will be a great opportunity for people to see what an impact the kid has had, as well as assist in getting the word out about assisting Nate financially."—wavehound

Mike Forman came to the hospital that afternoon, shortly before Nate went into surgery, and interviewed Tammy and Billy along with several of Nate's friends. Danny Vivian commented about the visit on El Ride:

"The newspaper reporter came with photographer in tow, and was there for over an hour, interviewing Nate's folks and friends. They got a lot of the surfing pictures of Nate and, hopefully, got a good idea of who Nate is and how remarkable he is. The article is supposed to come out tomorrow in the Victoria Advocate and should be available on their website. They also got all of the donation info. Let's hope they do the kid right."—wavehound

And although everyone hoped that the publicity about Nate would bring good things, no one could have imagined just how life-changing that article would be.

Saturday, June 16th, 2007

Saturday morning brought a report from the neurosurgeon. The results from Nate's EEG (Electroencephalograph) were in. Nate's EEG was not normal, but it didn't show any seizure activity, so they decided to take him off of his seizure medication. According to the neurosurgeon, Nate was no longer in a coma but rather in a very deep sleep.

Even though almost two weeks had passed since the accident, Nate still received a flood of visitors every day. Nevertheless, among all the visitors a few stood out.

Haley, a young girl who had been in Nate's sister Elissa's class at a daycare, had collected nearly $400 from friends and relatives and brought it in a jar.

Another young boy, Devon, came nearly every day and sat in the waiting room all day long.

"He just feels like he needs to be here, close to Nate," Devon's mother told Tammy.

Tammy wondered if it was good for Nate to have so many visitors but quickly put her fears aside. She could imagine what Nate would say.

"If it helps them, let them come."

However, even though they didn't restrict the number of visitors Nate had, they did lay down some ground rules. They asked people to keep the conversations upbeat and not to discuss Nate's condition while they were in the ICU with him—just in case he could hear them.

Nate seemed to be responding more and more but they still weren't sure if he was responding to commands: "He has been trying to reach the left side of his head with the right arm to scratch his head where the surgery was done," Tammy posted on El Ride. "He also scratches his neck. A few things happened today that we are praying were on command. After asking him twice if his arm was hurting, I asked him if he needed pain medication for it and he reached over with his right arm and gently put it on his left hand. The nurse said, 'I think he was letting us know it was hurting because he's pretty rough and quick with the right arm, but he very gently reached over with it and touched the left arm.'"

There were other indications that Nate was hearing them and responding to commands.

At the six o'clock visitation, Elissa asked Nate to open his eyes.

He opened them briefly.

"Nate, open your eyes," Billy said.

Nate opened his eyes for a second.

"Open your eyes, Nate," said one of Nate's friends.

Again, Nate opened his eyes for about a second, and then closed them.

Also that evening, Nate's physical therapist visited. She pulled his leg back and forth several times, and then said, "Okay, Nate. Now you do it."

Nate moved his leg two times.

As the day wrapped up, Tammy and Billy were encouraged. The timing of Nate's responses seemed too accurate to be coincidental. It appeared that he was hearing them and responding to instructions. Nevertheless, the doctors and nurses were still cautious in their assessment. They didn't want to raise false hope.

But the hope was already there, as far as Tammy and Billy were concerned.

"With all the things he has done today and the timing that he has done them, they are starting to think that maybe he is following commands. We know that he is, regardless of what they think."

One thing that amazed everybody was that Nate was moving his right arm and leg, even though the left side of his brain—which controls the right side of the body—was injured.

As the day wound down, Tammy wrote in her journal: *Father God, I ask you to continue healing Nate so that he can proclaim Your Word and love to the world. I know, Father, that with You, all things are possible!*

Sunday, June 17, 2007 (Fathers' Day)

Fathers' Day brought a change of venue for Nate. He was moved from the Surgical ICU to the Medical ICU, and the accommodations were much nicer. The SICU was one large room with curtains separating the beds. In the Medical ICU, Nate had his own room and even a window.

Tammy, Billy, and Danny Vivian arrived for the early visitation and found Nate with his eyes open. He didn't appear to be focusing on anything in particular.

"He did that several times during the night," the night nurse told them. "A few of those times, I think he was tracking me."

It was hard for Billy to spend Fathers' Day at a hospital watching his son as he lay unconscious, but almost as if on cue, El Ride posts trickled in, reminding him of just how special his son was.

Brian Brown posted about how Nate had helped a homeless man in Victoria about a year earlier:

"If you can imagine [Nate] struck up a conversation with him ... and shared God's love letter with him. Nate decided to take all the money he had and get the guy a room at La Quinta for a week on one condition: that the guy would go to church with him on Sunday. Here's where Nate got excited, the guy went and told another homeless guy about what Nate had done . . . he wanted to bless someone else, so he said he would share his newfound home with this guy. One beggar telling the other beggar where the bread is!"—brianb8888

Nate's friend Lawrence (nip on El Ride) added,

"Nate's life is a living testimony. He definitely walks the walk and talks the talk. I met him last year walking down the beach after a Gorda drift session and we have become good friends. I'm sort of a shy person and Nate was basically talking my ears off while we were walking together, but I could tell right away that he was special and had a heart of gold. I'm old enough to be his dad, but I look up to him as a Christian role model and he has motivated me to have a closer walk with the Lord and be thankful for the freakin' awesome day the Lord has made."—nip

Danny Vivian, who had visited Nate that morning and had seen his eyes open, commented almost prophetically about the challenges that Nate would be facing in the coming weeks and months:

"It dawned on me as I saw Nate's eyes open. Clear and bright, yet distant. It was the same look you see on a surfer's face when he is sitting in the lineup during a long lull between sets. Watching, searching, waiting. That's one thing about the sets. You can predict the size, the interval, and how they will roll in, but each set is different. Each wave is different. You don't really know until it arrives, your eyes widen, and you turn and paddle.

"That's the look I saw this morning.

"No one knows what the next set will be like that will roll in to Nate's path. It's over the horizon, beyond our vision. But the God who loves him does [know]. He knows the plans He has for Nate. Plans to prosper him, and not to harm him. Plans to give him hope and a future.

"Keep looking, Nathan. The next set's coming."—wavehound

That morning, the nurse told Tammy and Billy that it was okay to turn on a TV, particularly if there were any programs Nate liked to watch. It could help stimulate him. Billy told her that Nate didn't watch much TV, but he liked surfing movies. By mid-afternoon, Danny had brought a portable DVD player and put it at the foot of Nate's bed. The rest of Nate's day was a triple feature of surfing movies: *Step into Liquid*, *Siestas & Olahs*, and *ES 2*. Maybe Nate would hear them and wake up.

The evening brought more indications that Nate was indeed hearing and responding to commands.

At the 8:00 p.m. visitation, Tammy said, "I love you, Nate."

Nate raised his right arm and stuck it out as if reaching for her hand. When she took Nate's hand, he squeezed it for a second.

"Nate, do you want me to sing to you?" Elissa asked. "If you do, you have to open your eyes.

Nate opened his eyes for a second.

That was encouraging, but Nate put on a real "show" at the ten o'clock visitation.

As time was running out, Elissa again asked Nate if he wanted her to sing to him. "If you want me to sing, please open your eyes."

Nate opened and closed one eye, then the other.

"You cheated," Elissa said. "Do you want me to sing?"

Nate lifted his right arm, stuck out his right finger, and moved it as if he was directing music. Everybody in the room laughed, and then Elissa sang to her brother.

After Tammy got home that evening, she wrote in her journal:

Father God, I am amazed at all that is going on around me. I know that as hard as this is on me and our family, You know what You are doing and I know that Nate would have been willing to go through this to reach others for You. We know you have called Nate to ministry and that he has been ministering for a long time. Now he is ministering in an amazing way, without saying a word.

It was now almost two weeks exactly since Nate's accident. Given that he had not been expected to live, Nate had made great progress. However, he still had a long way to go. On top of that, a disturbing question nagged at Tammy and Billy. They had been told that frequently when people wake up from comas after a severe brain injury, their personalities have changed. In essence, they are not the same people they were before their accident.

When Nate woke up, would he be the same person they knew and loved?

Would he be the same guy who loved to call his mom and say, "Check out this freakin' awesome day God has made?"

Would he still have a passion for telling people about God?

Or would he be a stranger?

Chapter 13

Waves of Support

On Monday morning, June eighteenth, at the top of the Victoria Advocate's front page, a bold, half-inch headline—all in caps—proclaimed: **SURFER RIDES WAVE OF SUPPORT**. Just below the headline, taking up five columns of the six-column layout, was a large color picture of Nate riding a huge wave out at North Padre [Island] Beach.

Mike Forman's article came out a little later than everybody had originally expected, but it was a great tribute to Nate, not to mention his faith in God. The first half of the article was filled with stories from Nate's family and friends that highlighted his character as one who loved God and cared about people.

Forman recounted how Nate had bought a car for one of the teens in his youth group, "Recent Memorial High School graduate Garrett Geistman knows Nate's generosity first hand. Nate was Geistman's group leader at a Parkway Church camp and encouraged him to attend youth group after he returned. Geistman said Nate would often drive him from his home in the country to group sessions until one day, 'he said he was tired of driving me so he decided to get me a car and got some donations from his friends and used his money and bought me a 1999 Honda Civic.'"[8]

---

[8] Mike Forman. "Surfer Rides Wave of Support." *Victoria Advocate*. June 18, 2007, Pages A1, A2.

The article included another story about Nate's selfless lifestyle: "It was less than a month ago when Nate's . . . brother Will, who lives in Corpus Christi, totaled his car. Nate offered to give his pickup to Will, telling Tammy, 'I can ride my bike.'"

Forman's article continued on page two, framing a copy of the PFN logo that was now being printed into stickers and T-shirts by Nate's El Ride buddies.

Forman quoted Danny Vivian in the article, highlighting Nate's unique relationship with so many people who were older than he was, "'I started getting phone calls from Nate when he was in junior high,' said Danny Vivian, a frequent visitor who was one of Nate's surfing instructors at Parkway Church. 'I used to think it was funny but a lot of his friends are older. They are a very diverse group. One of the guys he surfed with is a pediatrician from Sugar Land who came down the other day, and another is a CPA. He's just a special young man who has a big heart for people.'"

Most important, the article featured a box on the Advocate's front page that listed the information necessary for people to give to the fund that had been set up to help cover Nate's medical expenses. Early Monday morning, Danny Vivian posted his reaction to the article for the others on El Ride:

"The article about Nate came out this morning in the Victoria Advocate . . . Front page, with a big photo of Nate making a bottom turn at Bob Hall Pier. Second page photo of the t-shirt design image. They did provide the link to the Nate Lytle Recover Fund site and the Wells Fargo account. Pray that God uses the article for Nate's good and His glory."—wavehound

On their first visit that morning, Tammy and Billy took a copy of the newspaper with them. Nate's eyes were open and he was staring at the window.

"Here's the newspaper article about you, Nate," Tammy said.

She held the newspaper in front of him and showed Nate the picture of him riding a wave. Tammy slowly moved the picture side to side and Nate tracked along with it. He stared hard at it, as if he was trying to focus on it or figure it out.

"What do you think about it?" asked Tammy.

Nate squeezed her hand.

Throughout the day, reactions to the newspaper article trickled in. Most of them were encouraging.

As Tammy was waiting to go in to see Nate, one of the Pink Lady volunteers came up to her and told her that she had seen the story in the Advocate that morning. She handed Tammy fifty dollars for Nate's benefit account. Tammy was reluctant to take the money, but the lady looked as if she might cry if Tammy refused the gift.

Besides, Tammy thought, Nate was going to need the help.

"Thank you for your kindness and generosity," Tammy said as she took the gift.

Before she could sit down, someone called her over to the waiting room pay phone. "Are you Nate's mother?" she asked.

"Yes," said Tammy.

"You have a call," the woman said, holding out the receiver.

Tammy walked over and took the phone. The caller had read the article and wanted Tammy to know that she had put Nate on her church's prayer chain and that she was sending Nate some money. Tammy thanked her and hung up, but before she could sit down, the phone rang again.

This time the call wasn't so uplifting.

It was another woman who had read the article about Nate.

"I'm not trying to be rude," the caller said, "I just want to prepare you. You need to know what you're in for. My mother fell and suffered a head injury years ago. As far as I'm concerned, my mother died that day. The person who lives with me today is not the same person. I love her, but her personality and attitude is much worse than it used to be."

Tammy didn't know what to think or say.

The woman continued, "You need to be prepared. Even if your son pulls through this, he will never, ever be the same person. You need to realize that you are dealing with the death of your son, whether he lives or not."

After she hung up, Tammy found it difficult to breathe. She knew the woman was trying to be helpful, but her words had a chilling effect on Tammy. She couldn't imagine God allowing Nate to live, but not allowing him to be the same person, to have the same heart.

To her, that seemed like a fate worse than death for this young man who loved God and constantly radiated His joy and life to others.

Tammy felt she would rather see Nate go home to be with the Lord. Later that day she wrote in her journal:

Nate, keep strong Son. I don't care what anyone says, I know you hear us when we talk to you. I am so proud of you for being such a fighter! I am still frightened of what the future holds. I am relieved that you are progressing, but scared that you might stop. Other people in similar situations have told me that they prayed that no matter what, if their child or loved one would live, they would do whatever they had to do to care for them, and that they prayed God would just let them live, no matter what. I have a hard time praying that way. I wonder if there is something wrong with me. As much as I love you and can't bear the thought of losing you, I continue to pray that if you must remain in this state the rest of your life, that God would take you home to be with Him. Part of me would die with you, but I know you and your heart and know that you would not want to live this way, so I try to put my pain of losing you aside and wait to see what God will do. This battle that you are fighting now is not only whether you will live or die, but what kind of life you will have if you live.

❈   ❈   ❈

The newspaper article in the Victoria Advocate was only the tip of the iceberg as far as support and encouragement for the Lytles was concerned. Some of Nate's surfing buddies, friends of the family, and people from the community had been talking about doing some kind of fund-raising benefit for Nate, but it seemed that after the publication of the article the benefit took on a momentum all its own.

Danny Vivian posted to El Ride:

"Big plans are in the works for a 'Nate's Birthday Bash' fundraiser in early August. Bands, raffles, silent auction, etc. The crew heading it up arrived at the hospital like they had just left a Red Bull party. There is a lot of enthusiasm about helping this wonderful family."—wavehound

The enthusiasm that Danny mentioned was certainly not lost on Tammy who had seen the benefit idea blossom. She wrote in her journal: "When Leisha (a wonderful friend from church whose family owns a renovated warehouse where it will be held) originally started working on it, she was talking about a BBQ and maybe a raffle. Now, they are talking about bands, silent auctions, and many other things too. They are having meetings every Monday night to pull it all together."

The stickers and T-shirts created by Nate's El Ride friends were also becoming a force. The shirts and stickers—along with donation jars—were now showing up in surf shops all over Galveston and Port Aransas. Soon, the shirts would be coming to Victoria as well.

Donation jars were also in restaurants around Victoria. One of Tammy's friends, Ruth, who owned a daycare, had already gotten orders for shirts for everyone who worked at her daycare.

And the online account that Nate's friend hilldo had set up was receiving donations.

Tammy and Billy were amazed at the generosity, not to mention the creativity.

One of Nate's surfing buddies named Dustin (surfguru on El Ride) was going to be married in about a month. He planned to put up a poster and donation jar for Nate at his wedding. He also asked Nate's sister Elissa to sing at the wedding, but instead of "wedding songs," he wanted her to sing the song she sang to Nate every night.

But probably the most incredible wave of support came in regard to TIRR MH.

Tammy learned that Myrna, Nate's social worker, had been talking to the people there and that she had sent them a copy of the newspaper article and requested paperwork for a charity bed there. Another surfing buddy from Houston was talking to people he knew at TIRR MH.

Humanly speaking, it was an impossible dream.

But Tammy was not willing to give up.

"I keep praying and not looking at any other rehabs," she wrote. "I am still determined that Nate will go there, until or unless God closes that door."

Chapter 14

Progress

June 19th, 2007

With the passing of each day it seemed, to Tammy and Billy at least, that Nate was slowly coming back to them. The day before, he had tracked along with the newspaper as Tammy moved it back and forth in front of him. Later, she held up some of his surfing pictures along with photos of his sister. Again, he seemed to be following the pictures with his eyes as Tammy moved them. Those small reactions were only the preamble to some stunning steps forward that Nate would take that week—steps that amazed his doctors.

Tuesday morning, Charlotte, Nate's speech therapist, came in to test Nate's ability to swallow. She tried to get him to lick a lemon lollipop. Nate wouldn't cooperate, so she stuck it in his mouth. He made an awful face—Nate hates lemon flavor—and licked his lips. As far as Charlotte was concerned, that was a good sign, so she followed up with a few spoonfuls of Jell-O.

Charlotte was about to leave when she said, "Nate, may I shake your hand?"

Nate kept his eyes closed, but raised his arm for her and she shook his hand.

There were also good reports from Nate's physical therapists. As they worked on his leg, Nate would do some reps on his own and occasionally pressed his foot against them as if he were playing with them.

Nate was not only making progress in his recovery; some of the medical issues he faced—specifically his pneumonia and infections—had finally cleared up. As Tammy talked with a representative from TIRR MH that day, she was told that with the medical issues out of the way, Nate could be cleared to go.

That was good news; however, it didn't mean that Nate had been accepted.

There were still significant financial hurdles to clear.

Even if Nate were to be awarded a charity bed at TIRR MH, should he have any medical emergencies and need to be sent to the hospital, Nate would have nowhere to go because he wasn't insured.

Tammy had scheduled appointments with Social Security and the Texas Rehab Commission, but the lady from TIRR MH was not hopeful.

"Even if those agencies were to give him benefits," she said, "it would take months to get them going. They'd never be in time to help your son get to TIRR."

Tammy was not daunted by the bleak picture the lady painted.

"They're doing a big benefit for him here in Victoria," Tammy said. "And if that's not enough I'll sell my house. I'll sell everything I have if you'll just take him."

"I read the article about Nate and everything he's done for others," the lady from TIRR MH replied. "I would like to accept him, but it's not up to me. I'll talk to the people here and the board will have to meet and discuss it," she said.

"Thank you for your help," Tammy replied. "There will be a lot of people praying about this."

And there were. Especially on El Ride.

On the previous night, Surfncpa posted: "Night time prayers for Nate. I'm hoping for some positive news from TIRR tomorrow."—Surfncpa

Tuesday morning, he added: "I just had a great call with Nate's mom. It is so incredible how Nate's ministry is touching so many people without him saying a word . . . . TIRR is now reviewing his case. Add an extra prayer for them to admit Nate into their care."—Surfncpa

Bronson Hilliard followed up almost immediately: "Dear Heavenly Father . . . We pray that you share the light of Nate's being into the hearts of the people at TIRR so that they may share in the joy of bringing his body back to full recovery. In Jesus's Name."—hilldo

Surfncpa responded: "I hear that the folks at TIRR have read the newspaper article and have even viewed the fundraising site hilldo created. I don't know how that factors in to their decisions but it certainly can't hurt."—Surfncpa

❊　❊　❊

As Tammy awaited news from TIRR MH, there were other pressing matters that needed to be taken care of. One of the most important of these was setting up a legal guardianship for Nate. In his semi-comatose state, he wasn't able to direct his own affairs, and Connie, a friend of Tammy's, had begun the legal paperwork to get her set up as Nate's guardian.

Before the guardianship could be finalized in court, however, Nate needed a *guardian ad litem* to represent him in court. For Tammy to be appointed as Nate's guardian, it would have to be evident that Nate needed one. That afternoon, an attorney named Rodney Durham came by the hospital to interview Nate.

Rodney talked to Nate and, although Nate opened his eyes, he stared straight ahead. The attorney explained to Nate what guardianship meant and asked if that was okay with him. Nate continued staring straight ahead, nonresponsive.

As Rodney left, he said to Tammy, "I have sons and I can't even imagine what it is like to go through this."

Later in the afternoon, Connie brought the guardianship paperwork for her to fill out. She also mentioned that someone would have to pay a large fee and agree to be responsible if Tammy should misuse Nate's money or belongings.

"I could never ask someone to do that," Tammy said.

"Don't worry about it," Connie replied. "It's already been taken care of."

❊　❊　❊

As the afternoon drifted into evening, Nate didn't show much change.

Tammy rarely took advantage of the small conference room, but she was exhausted, and the chatter and noise of the ICU waiting room had become overwhelming.

"I don't use it very often," Tammy wrote, "because I feel I need to be in the waiting area with the people that are there for us and to see Nate. I adore these people and appreciate them, but I also get so exhausted, I can't even talk or hear what they are saying sometimes."

She closed out her journal entry for the day with this prayer: "Father God, please forgive me, for I don't even have the strength to pray."

Wednesday, June 20ᵗʰ, 2007

In what had become a normal routine, Wednesday, June 20ᵗʰ on El Ride began with a flurry of prayer-posts for Nate.

"Morning prayers for Nate. Praying for some good news from TIRR today."—Surfncpa

"Amen, amen, and again amen. We're praying for you Nate."—jtownsurf

"Morning prayers for ya Nate."—RobHenson

"I am blown away ... by so many on here ... pray without ceasing ... Thank you God for Nate . . . and for the body of Christ."—CHRIS SHANNON

"Good Morning Nate!! Sending prayers your way my man!!! Thanks T-boys mom for keeping us up to date."—hurricane hopkins

Morning Nate! Just said a prayer for you. I'll just keep on prayin' for Nate!—ZigMund

Tell Nate we were thinkin' about him this morning. We paddled out before the sun came up, only two of us in the water . . . and the howler monkeys we could hear from the jungle. He woulda dug it ... especially when the tide started to move and the sets got a bit bigger."—seabass

Brian Brown's posts often set the spiritual tone for the day, and this day was no different:

"Thanks bro for the reminder to be like the moon today, and to position myself to reflect the Son—to be the mirror, not the light bulb, REFLECT! It's not about me, it's all about Him. When the creature fulfills the assignment of the Creator, the creature is as safe, as secure and finds more peace than you'll find anywhere else, doing anything else. Nate, you are safe, secure, & finding peace. Thanks for reflecting! Live by the one big rule: God gets all the glory! Embrace it!"—brianb8888

❈　❈　❈

It was to be a busy morning for Tammy, and quite a change from her routine of the past two and a half weeks. Ever since Nate's accident, she'd been spending nearly all of her waking hours at the hospital, either visiting Nate or waiting for the next visitation time, but this morning she had two crucial meetings to attend. The first was an emergency court hearing so that she could be appointed Nate's legal guardian. The second was a meeting at the Social Security Administration to find out if they would be able to provide any benefits for Nate.

The emergency court hearing was quick and easy and, after signing all the papers, Tammy was now able to take care of paying Nate's bills. The meeting at the Social Security administration was neither quick nor easy.

As she waited to be called in for her meeting, Tammy read through Nate's medical records. She had talked to the doctors, of course, and knew the severity of Nate's injuries. But seeing it all in print was so much more stressful. For the first time, Tammy saw in black and white what had happened to her son.

"Massive subdural hematoma extending into the frontal region, temporal region, parietal region, and occipital area."

"Several fragments of skull were identified that were depressed and were removed in piecemeal."

"After surgery the scalp was closed in layers."

"Before surgery his pupils were 5 millimeters and nonreactive and after surgery they were 3 millimeters and nonreactive."

She also read about the three hematomas removed from Nate's brain and how on June tenth—six days after surgery—Nate's Glasgow Coma Scale score was about a seven. Tammy had been reading about the Glasgow scale and knew that eight was the critical number. Statistically, fifty percent of the people who had a score of less than or equal to eight after six hours would die.

Another notation had a chilling effect on her. Written nine days after Nate's surgery—only about a week earlier—the doctor had written, "In the future, *provided that he survives this tremendous insult to the brain* [emphasis added], he will need to undergo a closed reduction of the left upper extremity by one of the orthopedic surgeons to have his left arm fracture stabilized."

Provided he survives this tremendous insult to the brain . . .

Tammy closed the folder. She couldn't stand to read any more.

Her meeting with the people from Social Security was stressful, as she had to relive and recount everything that had happened as well as update them on current developments. As the meeting ended, they told her that it would be at least a month, and maybe two, before she would know anything about benefits for Nate.

The problem was that Nate needed to get into TIRR MH—or wherever he was going—as soon as possible. If he was to have a chance to recover, to regain his ability to function, they couldn't delay his rehab.

Although the medical records painted a bleak picture, Nate seemed to be making significant strides every day. When Charlotte, the speech therapist, came for Nate's Wednesday session, she gave him a little toast and jelly, and he ate it. He also took some sips of orange juice through a straw. He also took a sponge tooth brush and pulled it back and forth across his teeth.

"Can you shake Charlotte's hand?" Nate's friend, Jaime, asked.

Nate raised his arm and offered his hand.

Charlotte showed Nate where his nose was, then said, "Can you touch your nose, Nate?"

He did.

"I've worked in a lot of rehab centers," Charlotte said, "and I'm amazed at what I'm seeing him do. I can honestly see Nate making a full recovery."

On another visit later that day, Charlotte gave Nate a spoon with some orange sherbet. He took the spoon and put it in his mouth, swallowing the sherbet without a hitch. It wasn't visiting hours, but the nurses brought Tammy and a few others in to watch this milestone. When Nate ate the sherbet, everyone in the room burst into applause.

As Danny Vivian described it on El Ride, Nate's accomplishment was bittersweet:

"The therapist came into Nate's room and stirred him, sat him up, and got him to eat some sherbet. Although he had some trouble, he was able to bring the spoon to his mouth and eat. It's difficult to watch a kid who is so strong have such a hard time with such a small task, but yet it's one of the most 'freakin' awesome' sights I have ever seen . . . . The nurse on duty this afternoon allowed a crowd in Nate's room, which literally erupted into applause when Nate ate on his own."—wavehound

Lawrence added his own comments:

"That is awesome. "Nate's mom said that he held the toast and ate it, also sipped juice from a straw, and raised his hand to say bye when the therapist was leaving."—nip

Lawrence's comment was followed up a few minutes later by a tongue-in-cheek suggestion from hilldo:

"Here's a good one for him . . . hand him a bar of [surfboard] wax and tell me when he starts making circular movements with it."—hilldo

As the day wore on, Nate had several coughing and choking spells. Later, his left arm seemed to be in pain so the nurses gave him morphine. Even so, when one of his friends left that evening, he raised his right hand and gave her the peace sign. And, in what had become a nightly routine, Elissa sang for Nate. As she was singing he glanced over at her.

It had been a full, amazing day, one of hope and progress.

Nate was making significant progress, yet as Tammy expressed in her journal that evening, their joy in Nate's progress was tempered by concern:

Father God, thank You for all the things that Nate is doing. Thank You that he is pressing forward. God, I pray that he will continue. The more I am learning about brain injury, the more scared I become. But Father, so many of the professionals at the hospital are amazed at Nate's progression. They are excited, but many of them warn not to hope for much more, because he is already doing what should medically be impossible to do. It is hard hearing what his prognosis is, but I know that You can change his prognosis and that it doesn't matter what the books say. You can do anything that You want to do.

Thursday, June 21ˢᵗ, 2007

Billy and Tammy Lytle's life had fallen into a routine that centered around the ICU visiting hours. They began their day at 6:00 a.m. with a joint visit to Nate. At 6:30, Billy left for work and Tammy retreated to the conference room and rested until 8:30. By 8:30, Tammy would go out to the waiting room, which was now filled with people who wanted to sit with Tammy and visit Nate. The rest of the visitations occurred at 9:00 a.m., Noon, 3:00 p.m., 6:00 p.m., 8:00 p.m. and 10:00 p.m. Billy would come from work for the Noon visitation. After he got off work at 5:30 in the evening, Billy would spend the rest of the day with Tammy and the others in the waiting room.

On Thursday morning, Nate was sound asleep through the first two visitations. That wasn't any big surprise because he had been so active the day before. He needed the rest.

Myrna, Nate's social worker, brought Tammy some good news that morning. She said that she'd spoken with someone at TIRR MH admitting, and all of the paperwork had been assembled and would be delivered to the CEO that day.

Shortly before the Noon visitation, the charge nurse called Tammy and Jaime to the ICU to see Nate. When they got back to his room, they were speechless.

They had Nate strapped into a chair, wearing a blue foam helmet.

Nate's eyes were closed, so Tammy bent down in front of him. "Can you open your eyes for me, Nate?"

He opened his eyes and looked like he was concentrating, trying hard to focus on her. Then he held out his hand.

Tammy took it.

"I love you, Nate. I miss your smile. Can you smile for me?"

He gave her a cute, crooked smile, then raised his arm and leaned forward as if he were trying to hug her. Tammy hugged him for a few minutes. It was the first time since the accident that she'd been able to hug her son.

A few minutes later, Billy arrived, on his lunch hour. When he came into the room, Nate reached out to his dad and they held hands. A few seconds later Nate tried to stand up, but Tammy and Billy had to tell him he couldn't. Not yet.

Nate seemed to be responding very well, so they tried a few other things.

They put a small cup of water in his hands and he drank from it. Then he used a tissue to wipe his mouth.

They gave him ice chips and—if they put the chips in his mouth—he chewed them. However, if they put the chips in Nate's hand, he would throw them. Because the part of his brain that was damaged also controlled sensation, Tammy wondered if the ice felt too cold for him.

It was then Tammy remembered hilldo's El Ride post from the day before: "Hand him a bar of wax and tell me when he starts making circular movements with it."

Nate's buddy Dustin had brought a bar of surfboard wax earlier, so Tammy picked it up and took it over to Nate.

"Nate, open your eyes," she said.

It took a little while, but finally he opened them.

She put the wax in front of his face.

Nate tried to focus on it.

"Do you want to hold it?" Tammy asked.

Nate reached up and grabbed the bar of wax.

"Do you remember what to do with it?"

Nate moved his hand around, making circular motions as if he were waxing a surfboard.

When the visit was over, Billy helped Nate stand up. Nate put his arm around his dad and hugged him, and then he leaned his head on Billy's chest. With Billy in front, holding him up, Nate scooted over and sat down on his bed.

Later, when Tammy posted about the visit on El Ride, she asked hilldo what he thought about Nate's antics with the surfboard wax. hilldo replied, "I think that is about the most kick arse thing I have heard in a very, very long time. He WILL surf again."

One thing that puzzled Tammy and Billy was Nate's blue helmet. Up to that time, he hadn't been given anything like that, and when they asked the nurses what it was for, they were told that "TIRR requires it and sent it."

But Nate hadn't been accepted yet.

Or had he?

They called to check and the mystery got even deeper. The people at TIRR MH said they didn't know anything about it.

In any case, Tammy and Billy knew it wouldn't be long before they had an answer. TIRR MH's finance board was scheduled to meet to discuss Nate's case that very afternoon. This was the last step in the process. That was what was foremost in her mind as she posted an update to El Ride that evening:

"Well, we didn't hear from TIRR today. Hopefully tomorrow because they are saying here that he needs to get out of here before he catches something. Also because he is soooo ready to try to do more and needs to be somewhere that they can do more rehab than here . . . . We have the ambulance on standby and sure hope it will be tomorrow so we don't have to wait until Monday. Please keep praying for TIRR to come through."—texasboy's mom

That evening, as Tammy read through the El Ride posts for the day, she came across one by Brian Brown that seemed to put the whole experience in perspective. She wrote in her journal: *I read Brian's post, 'Nate, God's been preparing you for this, even though it is so unexpected, you remember who you are, you are His child, be a warrior for Him to bring Him Glory!! From Him!! Through Him!! For Him!!' It reminds me of how often Nate talks about how surfing is not just a sport, but a spiritual thing for him. Then I think how ironic it is that he is pulling through this and beating death, partly because of his physical condition due to surfing. In Nate's life, God, surfing, and God using Nate, all fits together perfectly. It has given God the opportunity to use Nate all over the United States and possibly the world, to bring others to Himself.*

"Way to go Nate! Keep fighting! I love you so much!"

Chapter 15

Brianna

Brianna Hartman had just completed nursing school and started working at the hospital in the summer of 2007. When Nate had his accident, she was in Las Vegas, enjoying a brief vacation before jumping into her first nursing job. A few days after she got back to Victoria, her mother told her about a young man who had fallen at work and was now in a coma. Brianna had never met Nate, but they went to the same church, and they had some mutual friends.

Brianna's mother gave her a copy of the recently-published newspaper article about Nate. When she read the piece, Brianna was struck by the character of this young man. In a world where most people lived for themselves and their own interests, here was someone who would do anything for anybody, who lived his life to serve God, and who seemed so easygoing.

Nate Lytle was different from anybody she'd ever heard or read about. And for some reason, he got stuck in her head. She couldn't stop thinking and wondering about him.

How is he doing?

Why is he so special?

How could this happen to someone who seemed like such a great person?

These thoughts struck a deeper chord in Brianna's life, reaching all the way to her own relationship with God. Reading that newspaper article and seeing how someone lived out his life for God hit hard in a dark place for her.

She began to wonder what it would be like if she had been the one hurt? Or perhaps someone close to her?

She had been a believer in God all her life, and had always gone to church, but never knew what it meant to truly walk with Christ. And since starting college, Brianna knew that she wasn't living her life very well. She had intentionally made some bad decisions and wrong choices, essentially neglecting God in her daily life.

"Someday, Lord," she would say, "When I get over having all my fun, I'll try harder for you."

Over the last few months, the emptiness of her life had begun to catch up with her. She felt as though something was missing in her life. She also felt guilty and tired of doing the same old things. She had come to realize that a battle was being waged in her, a battle that had been going on since she was in high school.

She wanted to live her life for herself and, as a result, when faced with choices, she never chose God. But recently the tide had begun to turn in her life and Brianna decided to work on her relationship with God. And so, when she read the newspaper article about Nate, it resonated with her.

And God began to work in her heart.

When Brianna returned to work after her Las Vegas vacation, she felt strange knowing that this person she had read about was right down the hall, in the same hospital she was working at.

For some reason that she couldn't explain, she felt led to pray for Nate. She didn't know him, had never met him, but she started praying for him.

During the few weeks that Nate was in the ICU, Brianna prayed for him regularly. And a few times, she mustered up the courage to go by the ICU and see him. She always went at times other than visiting hours, and only the nursing staff knew about her visits.

A few of the nurses that she knew gave her updates on Nate's condition.

She went three times and stayed only a few minutes. As she stood there watching him, she was drawn to Nate. It was as if the light of Christ was radiating out from him.

She couldn't understand it. Here was a guy who was fighting for his life, and yet being around him—even when he was in a coma—was like a breath of fresh air.

Brianna resolved to pray for Nate. She felt that God had put him in her path for a purpose—maybe to lead her to a deeper relationship with God.

She didn't know.

But she planned to keep tabs on him. She couldn't wait to see what was going to happen.

Even though she had no tangible or logical reason for believing so, she felt that Nate was going to be okay.

Chapter 16

On the Move

Friday, June 22nd, 2007

When Tammy and Billy arrived for the 6:00 a.m. visitation on Friday, they learned that Nate would be moving out of ICU and into a room that day. Tammy received the news with mixed emotions. Moving out of ICU was definitely a step forward. On the other hand, Nate would no longer have a nurse with him constantly. She was particularly worried about the possibility of Nate lifting his left arm and accidentally hitting his head with the heavy external fixator that had been attached to his wrist. With the hole in his skull only being covered by Nate's scalp, one blow could kill him. Billy and Tammy decided that they would make sure that Nate was not left alone. One of them would be with him at all times.

Still, moving out of ICU was a plus because Nate would be allowed more visitors and they wouldn't have to follow the strict visitation schedule of the ICU.

At the mid-morning visitation, J. P. and Joey, two of Nate's surfing buddies from Galveston, showed up for a visit. They tried unsuccessfully to get some reactions from Nate, but he was apparently too exhausted from everything he'd done the day before. Nate simply lay there, resting. But J. P. and Joey were at least able to help Tammy move Nate's things to his new room on the third floor.

At about 10:30 a.m., an enigmatic post showed up on the El Ride board: "Tears of joy and overwhelm here. God is good. PFN."—Surfncpa

The post was accented by several smiley face icons.

Within a few minutes, Bronson Hilliard responded: "Letting a cat out of a bag?"—hilldo

"There are laws against that."—Surfncpa

When Tammy checked the site and saw the exchange, she began to wonder what was happening. Thankfully, she didn't have to wonder for long. Her cell phone rang, and she recognized TIRR MH's phone number.

"Hi Tammy," the lady on the other end said.

Tammy said, "Hi."

"Well, the board has made a decision. If you're sure that you will finance the medical end if he needs it, then we're going to accept Nathan."

"What?"

"We're going to give him a charity bed."

By now, Tammy was crying. "You're kidding me!" she said.

The lady from TIRR MH was nonplussed. "You sound surprised," she said.

"Well," Tammy said, "I am."

"But you were so sure it was going to happen."

"I was, but it's still amazing when it happens."

"I'm so glad he's coming here," the lady from TIRR MH said. "I can't wait to see how he does."

"When can he come?" Tammy asked.

"We're full at the moment, but just hang on. We hope to get him in here by the end of next week."

Tammy thanked her repeatedly. She could hardly believe it. Once again, God had done the impossible.

Nate was going to TIRR Memorial Hermann.

It didn't take long for the news to break on El Ride.

"Praise God! TIRR just called and accepted Nate. He's supposed to be transferred at the end of next week as they are waiting for a bed to open."—nip

"And they have NO idea what they are in for. Go get 'em Nate, run 'em ragged."—ratpak13

"Way to go Surfncpa and Lawrence, major props to all those involved in making this happen."—surfnsail

Later that afternoon, Tammy added her own thoughts in a post to El Ride: "Praise God TIRR accepted him. God is sooooo awesome. Now we just have to wait on His timing for Nate to go there. They said probably the end of next week. We can live with that, but we're praying for sooner. That would be a double blessing because Nate would get to go there and someone else would get to go home."—texasboy's mom

Brian Brown chimed in with a thought that put it all in perspective. "Sounds like lots of prayers being thrown skyward . . . dude, God responded in his timing. He's about to use you in a whole new arena! Chase that lion. Be a warrior!"—brianb8888

Again, even though Nate was semi-comatose, what was happening in his life was resonating with everyone around him. Like Tammy, Nate's friend Shad Estes had been keeping a journal since the day of Nate's accident. The journal was written as if it were a long letter to Nate, filling him in on all that had been happening since Nate fell. Many of the entries contained family news, particularly about Shad's children. But on this day, Shad reflected on what God was doing in Nate—and in him.

"God has really been working on me lately. I feel a peace about you, man. I know God has a plan that is going to blow our socks off. The thing that is the hardest is that we as humans are not patient enough to wait. God is teaching me patience and what really matters. I am anxious for you to be back with us in full capacity . . . . I had been specifically praying for you to open your eyes before and God allowed that to happen. Now I had been specifically praying for God to stir in a doctor's heart and for a rehab hospital to open up for you. I went on to El Campo Friday afternoon and I just made it there about 2:00 and your dad called me. He said, 'Are you driving? If you are, pull over to the side of the road.' Immediately, my stomach got sick because I thought something bad had happened to you. I told him to hold on a minute, I was fixing to pull up into my appointment at the bank. He proceeded to tell me that they had accepted you into TIRR hospital. They do not have a bed available until late next week, but you were accepted. I got chills all over my body and was so excited. Man, we have an awesome God."

❊   ❊   ❊

Tammy was thrilled that Nate was going to be admitted, but she was concerned about being so far away. Ever since Nate's accident, she, Billy, and the rest of the family had received so much support from their friends and members of their church. The support, prayers, and comfort from their friends had helped get them through this journey so far. Now Tammy and Nate would be two hours away.

Would the support continue?

She needn't have worried.

Before the evening was out, people were already asking if they could come to Houston to visit Nate. On top of that, many of the surfers on El Ride were from the Houston and Galveston areas. They began to post that they were planning to visit Nate.

One post in particular said it all: "It's going to get crowded. Might have to raffle off visiting time privileges."—surfnsail.

Saturday, June 23rd, 2007

It was a rough night, and Tammy got very little sleep.

Nate coughed frequently through the night and was becoming increasingly restless. He had also become very sensitive to sound. When machines beeped or alarms went off, he would pull his pillow over his head. He also wanted his iPod turned down or completely off.

Billy arrived early that morning and, since it was his day off, would spend the day with Tammy and Nate. Tammy was grateful to have him around as it had been a while since she had been able to spend much time with him. She was also thankful for the help, as Nate's coughing and choking had become almost a constant problem.

The nurses told them that Nate's trach was irritating his throat and that they would probably put a smaller one in soon. Although Nate was for all practical purposes breathing on his own, they didn't want to take out the trach until he got to Houston. In the meantime, the nurses taught Billy and Tammy how to suction Nate to help ease his choking spells.

Nate's change of rooms also brought a change in the nursing staff that cared for him. Now he had three nurses: Tina, Donna, and Brianna.

Part of the nurses' regular routine was cleaning the places on Nate's arm where the external fixator's metal posts were inserted. When the nurses cleaned Nate's arm, he opened his eyes, but Billy and Tammy noticed that Nate's reaction was different with one particular nurse. Whenever Brianna cleaned his arm, Nate would stare at her. Brianna was young and beautiful, with dark hair, big beautiful brown eyes and a dark complexion.

"He doesn't look at the other nurses like that," Tammy told Brianna.

Brianna looked up and gave Nate a big smile.

"She's cute," Tammy said after Brianna left. "You know, Nate's always liked girls with dark complexions. If this hadn't happened, she's someone he would have definitely been interested in."

Tammy knew that Nate would be a blessing to whomever he married, but privately she wondered if he would ever recover enough to have a wife. What Tammy didn't know at the time was that Nate had already made a deep impression on Brianna.

"Nate was transferred out of ICU to my floor after about two and a half weeks because he was medically stable enough and breathing on his own." Brianna wrote later. "I was assigned to care for him, along with another nurse because I was still on orientation. I felt excited that I would get to take care of him because it was almost like he was a celebrity. He had this following of people who were all spiritual and just different. You know, 'God' people.

"I got to see a different way of life through them and felt honored to be a part of it and to be able to care for him. He just seemed different than most people I'd ever known. It was a little odd taking care of someone my own age, let alone a male. I remember that several times when I was cleaning his arm and taking the staples out of his head, he opened his eyes and would just watch me for a minute.

"Those eyes touched my soul. I had never in my life felt such a sense of peace or purpose. I had never met someone that while being in a coma, made me feel such a desire to be the kind of person that he was. And I didn't even know him."

Later that evening, the connection became even more interesting when Nate's friend Dustin posted on El Ride: "Our good friend Brianna was the nurse on rounds there today."—surfguru

The next time Dustin came by to visit Nate, Tammy said, "So, you know Brianna?"

"Yeah," Dustin said. "She's a good friend of ours."

"Nathan doesn't respond to any nurses around here except her," said Tammy. "And he doesn't do anything except open his eyes and look at her."

"Did he ever tell you I was trying to fix him up with somebody?" Dustin asked.

"No," Tammy replied.

"He was telling me that he wasn't going to go out with anybody because he was going to Florida to start that church," said Dustin. "But Brianna is a good friend of mine and Jen's and we wanted them to meet. But he would not have anything to do with meeting her."

"Really?" Tammy asked.

Dustin nodded. "And this is who we were trying to fix him up with, Brianna."

"Well you were pretty much dead on," Tammy replied. "I really believe he thinks she's cute."

Nate had indeed taken notice. Even though he couldn't tell them at the time, later Nate said, "Bri was pulling the staples out of my head. When she pulled the staples out it kinda pinched and woke me up for a second. I remember seeing this angel with dark hair, bright eyes, pretty teeth and a warm spirit."

❖   ❖   ❖

Throughout the day Nate continued to improve in his ability to respond and communicate, even developing his own sign language. When he wanted a drink, he held his hand up like he was holding a glass. To signal that he wanted to brush his teeth, he put his finger in front of his mouth and moved his hand back and forth.

He also responded to instructions by opening his eyes, shaking his head yes and no, smiling, and waving when someone asked him to. When they would give him pictures to look at, Nate would take each picture and hold it up in front of his eyes, squinting as if he was trying to focus on it.

All of these improvements brought a mixed reaction from the doctors.

Tammy asked Dr. Norvill, the neurosurgeon, if he thought that Nate would continue to improve.

"I don't know," he said. "I didn't think he would get to this point, quite frankly."

Another doctor tried to temper Tammy's optimism, telling her not to expect Nate to be the same person.

A third was utterly amazed after seeing Nate. "After seeing his CAT scan," the doctor said, "I never thought Nate would progress, especially this quickly. We usually measure improvement in these cases by months. Not with him. With Nate, it's only been a few weeks."

Later, Tammy posted on El Ride: "It seems like it's been months, that's for sure. We do know that the only reason he has come this far is because of God, regardless of what the doctors say. He is the Great Physician and Healer! I am standing on His word and trusting that He is in this with us every step of the way. (Believe me, it's not always easy and I do have my moments, but He has brought us too far to start doubting him now.)"

Then she added some advice for all those who would read the posts. "Give everyone you love and hold dear big hugs and tell them you love them. You never know when it will be the last hug or how long it will be before you can have another one."

Sunday, June 24th, 2007

El Ride post from Brian Brown at 8:00 a.m.:

"Morning bro,

"'But David strengthened himself in the Lord his God.'

"Nate, you are His blessed, chosen, given, redeemed, forgiven, marked, been made alive, saved, raised up, seated with, created, brought near . . . that's who your Creator says you are. Find the strength from him today!

"Paddle hard, bro!

"Love you & praying for you."—brianb8888

❀　　❀　　❀

When Nate was injured, the conventional wisdom was that, if he survived, he would never walk, talk, or communicate again. Despite the skepticism of some of the doctors, it seemed that every day, Nate was proving that prediction to be incorrect. But if there were any remaining doubts that Nate would communicate again, they were erased on his last Sunday in Victoria. It had been a long day, with plenty of visitors, including a man who had suffered a brain injury himself. Nate smiled and waved to all the visitors, but when Shad Estes—one of Nate's best friends—arrived, Nate surprised everybody.

Nate took Shad's hand and turned it over; then he wrote the letter W with his finger on the back of Shad's hand. He followed it up with the letter A, but then ran out of room.

"Are you writing a W and an A, Nate?" Tammy asked.

Nate nodded.

They tried to guess what he was writing, but none of their guesses were correct, and Nate grew increasingly frustrated. They gave him a pen and paper to see if he could write down what he was trying to say, but Nate just became more frustrated.

"You can try again tomorrow," they told him.

It didn't take long for word about Nate's attempt to communicate to spread on El Ride:

"Hey gang at elride," posted Danny Vivian, "I just got a 'Danny, you're not gonna freakin' believe this' call from Tammy a few minutes ago . . . . tonight he was listening to our bud Shad Estes . . . talk to him about his kids praying for him, when he took Shad's hand and turned it over and began drawing letters with his finger on the back of Shad's hand. He apparently made a W and an A but ran out of room."—wavehound

Minutes later, Lawrence sent out his own post: "Nate hugged his friend and then wanted to write something in his friend's palm with his finger. He wrote out, "W ... A" and then ran out of room. He again wrote out, "W ... A", but didn't finish. Not sure what he was trying to say, but still another amazing step forward. He's gone from wondering if he could respond to commands a couple of weeks ago, to now trying to communicate."

El Ride members lost no time suggesting what Nate might have been trying to spell out.

"Tears just came to my eyes when I realized he *might* have been trying to write out WARRIOR! Be a WARRIOR!"—brianb8888

"I believe he was trying to say: 'waves'!"—Samb

"I think the WA was the start of 'WATUP'!" Great news, Nate.—fredmrtx

Whatever Nate was trying to say, there was no longer any doubt. This young man who was never supposed to communicate again had just made another leap forward.

That night, Tammy wrote in her journal: *Nate, once again you have amazed us. They told us you would not be able to communicate. After only 20 days you are already trying to communicate with us by spelling out letters in Shad's hand. Anything you do tires you out so quickly, but you continue to try. You are amazing!*

Chapter 17

Saying Goodbye

Monday, June 25th, 2007

"With each new day, Nate brings such inspiration to the lives of many people, and I'm by far no exception. He [God] and Nate both have given us all the purest gift of hope, love, miracles, and faith . . . just to name a few. To all the beautiful people that continually bound together through human crisis to help pass on these gifts, thank you for making this world a much better place! *Peace I leave with you, my peace I give unto you: Not as the world giveth, give I unto you. Let not your heart be troubled, neither let it be afraid. PFW PFN.*"—cinsdragonfly

❊   ❊   ❊

Only three weeks had passed since Nate's accident and he was already defying the doctors' predictions. He had not only survived, but was making rapid progress, even to the point of trying to spell out a word on his friend Shad's hand. But despite his amazing recovery to this point, Nate could stop moving forward at any time. It is not unusual for brain injury patients to get "stuck" at a certain level and then stay there for months or years—or even the rest of their lives. So, although Tammy and Billy rejoiced at Nate's improvement, their rejoicing was tempered by uncertainty. Would Nate continue to recover? Or would he spend the rest of his life trying to navigate through a fog?

When Charlotte, his speech therapist, came in for Nate's first session of the day, she asked him to pick out shapes and colors, which he did correctly. She also asked him to hold up one finger, then two, then three. Again Nate responded correctly. But as the session continued, Nate kept making writing motions with his hand, so Charlotte gave him a pencil and paper.

"Can you write your name, Nate?" she asked.

Nate began to write a name on the paper, but it looked something like Courtney.

Charlotte laughed. "Not *my* name; your name."

Nate started to write again.

His handwriting wasn't easy to read; it looked like it might if an able-bodied person were to try to write his name with the wrong hand. Nevertheless, there was no question that he had written "Nathan"—in cursive!

When word broke on El Ride about Nate's accomplishment, Lawrence (a physician) responded: "That is awesome. He wrote out his full name, Nathan, on a piece of paper. I betchya his handwriting is better than mine."—nip

A little later, Nate's sister Elissa dropped by to see him. She told Nate, "I sure do miss you giving me a pop on the side of my neck."

Nate raised his hand and she leaned over toward him.

He gave her a playful slap on the neck.

It was a small thing, but it was one more sign that the "old Nate" was still in there.

Later that afternoon, Tammy had to leave for a while, and so Danny, Ian Hampton [a friend of Nate's from Clear Lake, Texas] and Shad stayed with him. When Charlotte came in for the second session of the day, Nate wasn't in a cooperative mood. He lay in his bed with his eyes closed, as if he was trying to ignore her.

"Come on Nate," Charlotte said. "You've got to get up and stop sleeping all day or you won't be able to sleep at night."

Nate waved his hand at her, motioning that she should go away.

Charlotte didn't give up so easily. "Come on Nate. You've got to get up and eat."

Nate gave her "the finger," but he used his ring finger instead of the middle one.

Later, Shad wrote in his journal: "Danny and I were totally shocked. We said we couldn't believe you did that. Your mom told us that you do that when you are upset and don't want to shoot the real finger. You're a fart, you know that?"

Danny echoed Shad's comments in an El Ride post: "Quick update. Stayed the afternoon with Nate. He wrote his name on a piece of paper, ate a cinnamon roll, brushed his teeth by himself. Flipped off the therapist when she came back in and wanted him to do more work, but used his ring finger, so he wasn't serious. Slept without coughing for most of the afternoon. Overall a better day than yesterday, which was better than the day before, which was better than . . . well you get the picture."—wavehound

❧ ❧ ❧

While Nate and his family were anticipating a move to TIRR MH, his surfing buddies, friends from church, and people from the community were moving forward with fundraising. Leisha and a few others had obtained a copy of the PFN logo and had taken orders for T-shirts and stickers so they could have them in Victoria. Mark, a friend of Leisha's, agreed to make them. The shirts and stickers sold out quickly—even the nurses and hospital volunteers wanted them.

Not only were the PFN materials selling well, but plans for Nate's benefit were moving along. Dustin posted on El Ride: "Had a good meeting for the benefit this evening also . . . I need to know if anyone is gonna head down to help out . . . the date is Sunday, August 5th . . . Planning on serving about 2500 brisket plates so we definitely need some help with the plating process . . . and if anyone has things to donate for the raffle or silent auction hit me up and we will try to get things going asap.—surfguru

Tuesday, June 26th, 2007

Finally, the call everyone had been anticipating came through. Nate would leave on Thursday. Tammy was told he would be staying in a room with three other people, but she and Billy were delighted that he even got in. They weren't particularly worried about the accommodations.

Tammy's main concern was how Nate would react to strange surroundings, since he still wasn't fully aware and in a fog. She didn't want him to be afraid.

"Can I stay with him overnight?" she asked.

"If the other patients and family are okay with it, one person can stay with him at night. But keep in mind that you may feel uncomfortable. TIRR is a lockdown facility, and strange things can happen, because the patients who are there are not always in their right minds."

Billy and Tammy discussed it and decided that Tammy would stay with Nate during the day and most nights, but Billy would stay Wednesday, Friday, and Saturday nights to give her a break.

Now the only concern was whether or not the other patients and their families would be okay with it. As they had done with everything since Nate's accident, they committed the matter to prayer, asking God that the others in Nate's room would agree to someone staying with him.

In her journal, Tammy wrote her prayer, "Father God, thank You that we will be leaving for TIRR soon. Father, I am a little apprehensive about staying there, but I will not leave my son. Father I pray that you will go before us and prepare the way with the right roommates, nurses and doctors. Amen."

Wednesday, June 27, 2007

Wednesday morning, Tammy reluctantly left Nate to attend a meeting with the people at DARS, the Department of Assistive & Rehabilitative Services, a state-funded organization. They have a program for people who suffer brain injuries and offer help with vocational rehab through DRS—Division of Rehabilitation Services. Unfortunately, the news was not encouraging. Nate's caseworker, Megan Bennett, told Tammy that although Nate definitely qualified for funding, there were several things working against him.

First, DRS was currently out of funds and wouldn't get any more until September, still more than two months away. Even when the funds did come in, Nate was at the bottom of a long waiting list. According to Megan, there were a lot of people ahead of him who had been waiting for a long time.

Tammy was disappointed. Nate was guaranteed a charity bed for a short time, but what would happen when that time ran out? What if Nate still needed more rehab? She was tempted to worry, but then remembered how faithful God had been up to this point.

Tammy decided that the only thing to do was pray and leave the matter in God's hands.

It was very clear to both Tammy and Billy that prayer was—and continued to be—an integral part of Nate's recovery, and that Nate's friends on El Ride were a key part of that prayer effort. That same morning, Billy posted on El Ride:

"Hey Y'all . . . . I tend to ponder things deeply. As I look back on the last month and all that has happened, the Lord keeps taking me back to the Old Testament when the Hebrews were doing battle with the Amalekites. How, as long as Moses would hold his arms up, the battle would shift in favor of the Hebrews. As Moses grew tired, Aaron and Hur would come alongside him and hold his arms up til' the Amalekites were defeated.

"Well, Nate is doing battle, also. Fighting his way back to wholeness. I am so encouraged by all of you who are being the Aarons and Hurs for him! You 'hold him up' with your many prayers and outpouring of kindness. So eventually Nate will arise victorious! May God Richly Bless You!"—Billy

❄ ❄ ❄

Throughout the day, Nate continued to try to communicate, particularly through writing. Charlotte, his speech therapist, told Tammy, "I worked at a rehab facility for many years before coming here. It's a miracle that Nate is trying to write. I've seen many patients with far less severe injuries that have never gotten this far. And I've never seen anyone progress this quickly."

At one point during the day, Nate motioned for a pencil and paper. They gave it to him but weren't sure how well he'd be able to do. The day before, he'd tried to write something for about twenty minutes. But he couldn't manage to put the letters together, so he finally became frustrated and gave up.

This time, however, Nate managed to put together a message.

He wrote: "may sisye!! Sis csy sye sye"

Nate had a two-and-a-half year old nephew named Sye.

"Are you asking, 'May I see Sye?'" Tammy and the others said.

Nate breathed out what appeared to be a sigh of relief and nodded. Everybody in the room was excited. At that moment, Tammy turned away so Nate wouldn't see her tears of joy. It wasn't spelled or written correctly, but that didn't matter. Nate was trying to communicate!

It also seemed that Nate's little note turned on a switch. Throughout the rest of the day, as nurses and therapists came and went, Nate mouthed "please" and "thank you".

Nate had taken another step on his journey back.

❊   ❊   ❊

Word had spread that Nate was leaving for TIRR MH the next day, and so he had a lot of visitors that evening. His room was so filled with visitors that people were standing in the hall, waiting for a chance to wish Nate well before he left.

Mark, one of Nate's best friends, leaned over and spoke softly, "Hey Dude. I love you, and you're going to be fine when you go over there. Everything's going to be all right."

Nate's eyes grew big; he looked scared and began to cry.

It was the first time they had seen him express any emotion since the accident and, naturally, everyone thought Nate was afraid of going away.

Everyone in the room tried to reassure him. "It's going to be okay, Nate. Don't cry. Don't cry."

"What's wrong, Nate," Tammy asked. "Are you okay?"

He motioned for a pen and paper, but when he tried to write, only gibberish came out: "m9ld jouj no s fez on that you have that."

Nate tried to write several times, but finally threw the pen across the room.

Everyone tried to reassure him. "It's okay, Nate. It will come over time."

Next they gave Nate his cell phone. Before the accident he was a proficient "texter," so they thought maybe he'd be able to text whatever he was trying to say.

Nate tried, but that didn't work, either.

Then Tammy remembered that the speech therapist had given them a pointer and a board that had the alphabet on it. They hadn't tried it out yet.

"Nate, do you want to try to spell it out on the board?" she asked.

Nate nodded, and they brought the board over to him.

Using the pointer, Nate spelled: I M S O R R Y.

Everybody in the room looked at one another in disbelief.

"You're sorry?" Tammy asked. "What are you sorry for?"

Nate couldn't answer. He just kept crying.

One of Nate's friends laughed and said, "Typical Nate. He's worried about everybody else."

They all reassured Nate that everything would be okay.

It wasn't until several weeks later, after Nate awoke from his coma that they would find out what he'd been trying to tell them. Tammy asked him, "Do you remember when you were trying to write something and you got frustrated, then you spelled out 'I'm sorry?' What were you sorry for?

"I felt bad because I couldn't express myself verbally and I couldn't tell everybody I was going to be okay. I knew I was going to be okay. The whole time I was in a coma it was like my time with God. I had a peace about it, but I couldn't tell anybody."

For two full hours, visitor after visitor came to say goodbye to Nate.

Shad Estes brought his children by. A little later, as Nate had requested in his garbled handwriting, his nephew Sye came in and lay down on top of him for a few minutes. Nate tried hard to speak to Sye, but couldn't. Both visits brought a smile from Nate, who adores children.

As the stream of visitors continued, Nate hugged each one and mouthed "I love you".

Later, as the posts on El Ride reflected, Nate's friends and family realized they were witnessing a miracle in progress:

"As I was reading this morning, a verse hit me: 'I, Nebuchadnezzar, looked to heaven. I was given my mind back and I blessed the High God, thanking and glorifying God who lives forever.' Dude, if He would do this for a wicked king, he would certainly do it for you! '. . . hard pressed on every side, but we're not crushed; perplexed, but not in despair; persecuted, but not forsaken; struck down, but not destroyed.' Swim to the surface, follow your lifeline, He is your Deliverer. Thank you Lord for what you have already done!"—brianb8888

"Evening PFN. I am so stoked on Nate's progress. I hope the folks at TIRR can accelerate his recovery. I'm looking forward to surfing with him in a few months."—Surfncpa

"Spoke with Billy earlier this evening. They haven't heard exactly when he will be transferred, but it will probably be tomorrow morning. He is doing much better with the smaller sized trach as his cough is much better. Last night, he whispered to his dad, 'Go to bathroom' which Billy said was clearly audible. His recovery has been and continues to be remarkable."—nip

"What a diff a couple of days make. Got back from College Station this evening and went by the hospital. There were probably a dozen or more visitors there, taking turns talking to Nate. He would smile, reach out, and hug each one, and would periodically start to cry. He is very frustrated at not being able to move and communicate like he feels he should . . . . We told him how proud we are of him, that his recovery was a miracle that had brought together people along the entire Texas coast and far beyond. Each person there told Nate what an impact his life had had, and was still having, on those he came in contact with. We told him how God was using him and this experience to do freakin' wondrous things.

"It is amazing to see how far Nate has progressed in such a short amount of time. It seems like just a few days ago that it was hard to tell whether he really recognized people or whether he was hearing and understanding when you spoke to him. Now he is communicating by hand signals, facial expression, and writing. His sense of humor is still there, and the love for his friends and family clearly shows on his face and in his embraces. His appetite is there, too—I watched him devour half a PBJ in 3 bites.

"We also made sure he knows that he has a bunch of folks in Houston/Galveston waiting to see him when he gets there. (Along with a steady stream of Victoria folks.) It may be a lengthy and frustrating recovery for Nate. He will get impatient, I'm sure. But he will recover, and he will have a fascinating and inspiring story to tell.

"Treat him well, TIRR. Your newest patient is a true miracle. Treat him well."—wavehound

As Billy witnessed Nate's incredible progress and the love that was evident as people came to say goodbye, he reflected on how God was at work both in Nate and in those around him: "How do you measure the depths of God's love? Can it be measured by human standards? Can you catch a reflection of it in the life of a man?

"To witness the seemingly endless parade of people for two hours that came to bid Nate farewell as he heads for TIRR tomorrow was the beginning. To watch Nate's face well up in tears as he had to hug each one . . . . To watch him whisper the words 'I love you' over and over to each person and finally get to the point that he was compelled to try and write something. After several attempts the frustration set in; he motioned for the spelling board.

"Then he spelled the words . . . 'I'm sorry' and his tears flowed again . . . . God's love demonstrated. WOW!

"Even in the midst of his own suffering he was worried about everyone else.

"God's love transcends this shell we inhabit called the human body into the very depths of our spirit. For certain ones like Nate, we get to witness how deep God's love really is.

"PFN for he PFY."—Billy

Chapter 18

First Days at TIRR Memorial Hermann

Thursday, June 28ᵗʰ, 2007

"Morning bro! Praying for you and the next steps in your journey with our Father! 'From the days of John the Baptist until now, the kingdom of heaven has been forcefully advancing, and forceful men lay hold of it.'

"Be a warrior for our King!! Be strong and courageous!

"God speed, paddle hard!"—brianb8888

❈   ❈   ❈

On June 28ᵗʰ, Tammy and Billy began the day with mixed emotions.

On the one hand, this was a huge step forward for Nate. He would soon be on his way to TIRR MH, one of the best rehab centers in the world for people with traumatic brain injuries. Hopefully, his recovery would not only continue but accelerate. However, the two-hour relocation from Victoria to Houston also meant that they all would have to leave the support that they had grown accustomed to at the local hospital. Going to TIRR MH not only meant leaving behind the medical staff that had taken such good care of Nate but also the friends who had faithfully come to the hospital and provided everything from prayers and encouragement to meals. Since the day of Nate's accident, Billy and Tammy hadn't had to worry about a single meal. Friends had even brought cake, vegetables, and cookies to the hospital for the nurses and doctors that were caring for Nate.

Life at TIRR MH would undoubtedly be different. The question was, how different?

There were other nagging concerns. Even though Nate had been coughing less with the smaller trach, he was having more difficulty keeping it in. Lawrence (nip) posted on El Ride: "[Nate] tried to get out of bed 3 times last night and once was able to walk with assistance to the bathroom. On one attempt, his trach came out and his oxygen level (pulse ox) was still very good, so they left the trach out and he seems to be fine without it. They decided to transfer him without it."

In her journal, Tammy admitted that she and Billy were concerned about Nate traveling without the trach: "Nate has had less coughing with the smaller trach, but has been having trouble keeping the smaller one in. It is coming out again this morning, so his pulmonary doctor decided to take it out and leave it out. We are concerned because they wanted it left in for the trip to TIRR. The doctor assures us that Nate has been breathing so well on his own that he thinks it will be fine."

Early on Thursday morning Tammy, Billy, Elissa, and a few of Nate's friends assembled to see him off. Tammy left briefly to buy some of the things Nate was required to have—among other things, shirts and shorts that would serve as workout clothes for his physical therapy sessions. She also had to write a check to the ambulance service as a deposit for the transport fee, which was paid out of donations that had been coming in.

Again, God had provided in advance for Nate's needs.

When Tammy arrived back at the hospital, Brianna, one of the young nurses who had taken care of Nate over the past few days, was taking the staples out of the incision on Nate's head. Nate reacted to the pain as Brianna removed the staples, looking at her for a long time as though he was trying to focus on her.

Tammy recalled that this beautiful young woman was the one who Nate's friends, Dustin and Jen had been trying to fix Nate up with. She couldn't help wondering whether they would have made a good couple if things had been different.

By 11:30 a.m. everything was ready and it was time to leave for Houston.

Nate was put on a gurney for the ambulance ride, and Tammy noticed that he looked frightened. As they wheeled him down the hall toward the elevator and the waiting ambulance, Tammy and the others tried to reassure Nate and explain what was happening. They couldn't tell whether or not he understood, but Nate's friend Shad was confident that Nate was in good hands.

Shad wrote in his journal: "They came to pick you up about 11:30. Your parents, Elissa, Connie, Laura, Michelle, Danny and I were all there when you left. You looked at me a couple of times and winked and I knew God was going to take care of you."

It was a difficult goodbye for those who were being left behind. Danny Vivian posted on El Ride: "It was happy and hard to see Nate head out for TIRR. Happy because he will get the help he needs to recover, hard because the look on his face was one of fear and uncertainty . . . . Our prayers and thoughts will continue for you, Nate. Stay strong, stay hungry, stay positive. When frustrations come, you have a merciful God, a loving family, and good friends to hold you up and encourage you. 'For God has not given you a spirit of fear, but of power and of love and of a sound mind.' Paddle hard, brother."—wavehound

The ambulance ride was rough. It is also among the few things that Nate can remember from the six weeks he was in a coma. Throughout the bumpy, two-hour trip Nate kept waking up enough to see the EMT who was sitting beside him—a young man with glasses. He also felt nauseated and thought he might throw up. True to Nate's character, he was more worried about the EMT's welfare. "I'm going to feel so bad if I throw up on this guy," Nate thought.

Nate didn't throw up, and by 1:45 p.m., the ambulance had arrived at TIRR Memorial Hermann. Even though he hadn't become sick during the trip, the rough ride had taken a toll on Nate's left arm. He looked pale and kept motioning to it with his other hand. Tammy, who rode in the ambulance with Nate, took care of his admission forms and paperwork while Billy and Elissa went with him to help get him settled into his room. They were delighted to discover that Nate had been put in a semi-private room rather than in a room with three other patients.

As Tammy filled out Nate's paperwork the people in the admitting office told her that Nate's charity bed was for four weeks. That came as a welcome surprise because she knew that a bed paid for by Medicaid was only for two weeks. She didn't know what would happen if Nate needed to stay longer than four weeks, but she just added that to the list of things she was praying about. God had provided abundantly so far. She was confident that He would provide something else by the time the four weeks was up.

❖   ❖   ❖

Even though he was exhausted from the trip, Nate's first day was full of activity. Therapists came in and checked on him, helped him stand and turn his back to a wheelchair and sit down in it. They even got him to move the wheelchair with his feet.

Dr. Sunil Kothari, the doctor who would be overseeing Nate's rehab, also stopped in to see him. At first, Tammy was disappointed because she had been doing some reading and was hoping for a doctor there that she had read about. But several of the nurses and therapists reassured her and told her that Nate had gotten the best doctor there. Tammy wrote in her journal: "[The nurses and therapists] said he spent more time with the patients and always answered any questions family members or patients had. I realized that once again God was in control."

Dr. Kothari put Nate on medications that would help his brain to wake up, sleep aids so that he would get enough rest for the therapies he would be going to in the daytime, and one particularly nasty shot in his belly each day to prevent blood clotting. After reviewing Nate's chart and comparing his injuries and progress, Dr. Kothari told Tammy and Billy, "I am encouraged and plan to have him walking and talking in thirty days."

Tammy and Billy knew Nate was right where he was supposed to be.

By the end of the day—most of which was spent in evaluations—Nate was exhausted. Billy and Elissa returned to Victoria, and Tammy stayed with Nate. Unfortunately, nighttime at TIRR MH was nowhere near as quiet as it had been at the hospital in Victoria. "Things are a little noisy here," Tammy posted on El Ride. "Nate is right by the nurses' station and his roommate likes to stay up very late watching TV."

That night, in strange—and at times frightening—new surroundings, Tammy prayed: "Father God, I am a little scared here. I am a little nervous about my new surroundings. God I pray for protection and for some rest tonight. I still don't rest well, as I worry about Nate hitting his head with the metal on his arm. Father, please keep him safe and me also while we are here. Please give him a good night's sleep. Amen."

Friday, June 29th, 2007

It was not a quiet night.

Nate appeared to be uncomfortable, perhaps from lingering pain in his arm after the long ambulance ride. The man in the other bed didn't help matters. Throughout the night he kept getting out of his bed to yell at the nurses. But despite a less than restful night, Nate and Tammy had a full day ahead of them.

The nurses came in at 9:00 a.m. to get him started on his day. As they did, Nate pointed down and tried to get out of bed.

"You have a catheter, Nathan," they tried to tell him. But Nate kept trying to get up and go to the restroom. "All right," they finally said. "We'll take the catheter out and put britches on him."

"What are britches?" Tammy asked.

"Adult diapers," was the reply. "It usually takes a while to retrain the bladder after someone has had a catheter. It could be a few days before he can fully control his bladder again," the nurses said.

Tammy knew Nate wouldn't like the idea of britches at all.

They put him in the wheelchair and took him into the bathroom. To everyone's surprise, Nate had no problems using the toilet, even after having had a catheter for over three weeks.

Once again, Nate proved that things don't always go the way the medical books say.

❧ ❧ ❧

Nate's day was filled with activity.

Physical therapists worked with him in the morning, helping him to relearn to walk and later encouraging him to use his feet to move his wheelchair. At noon, they took him for stomach and chest X-rays, then had him sit up in his wheelchair for a while, to help him regain upper body strength. A breathing treatment followed at 1:00 p.m. and another therapist came in to work with him at 1:25.

Later, after having Nate do some tongue exercises, his speech therapist, Laura, said, "Nathan, today is Friday, June 29th."

She went on to other things for a few minutes, then showed Nate three dates on a piece of paper. "What day is it, Nathan?" she asked.

Nate pointed to "Friday, June 29."

Then she showed him a picture of a bus, a car, and an ambulance.

"How did you get here?"

Nate pointed to a picture of an ambulance.

Next Laura held up a paper full of numbers. "Can you point to your age, Nathan?"

Nate pointed to the number 23.

"Very good," she said. "Who is your mom? Can you point to her?"

Nate pointed at Tammy.

Finally, Laura showed Nate a piece of paper with the city names: Victoria, Corpus Christi, and Houston. "Can you show me where you live?" she asked.

Nate stared at the paper but wasn't able to point to his hometown.

By the time his last therapy session was complete, Nate was exhausted, and he slept most of the afternoon. That evening, a nurse, Ms. Mele, came in to clean around his central line, feeding tube, and the external fixator on his wrist.

Tammy could tell that it was painful for Nate.

"Hold on to my hand and squeeze it as tight as you need to," she told him.

Nate squeezed Tammy's hand, but when Ms. Mele began to clean around the feeding tube in Nate's stomach, the pain was too much.

"STOP!" Nate shouted.

Tammy was overjoyed. "Nate, you did it! You spoke," she said.

This was the first time since the accident that he had spoken above a whisper. His voice was still not as strong as it was before, but he definitely spoke out.

"Can you say it again?" Tammy asked several times, but each time Nate just faintly whispered, "I can't."

After Ms. Mele finished cleaning the area around Nate's feeding tube, he motioned toward the bathroom, but as the nurse was trying to help him get out of bed and go to the bathroom, a wire attached to his feeding tube got caught on the bed frame and pulled the feeding tube out.

Instantly, Ms. Mele was in a panic.

"I need help here, stat!" she called out.

Some other nurses came in, and all at once a flurry of activity began.

"What's wrong?" Tammy asked.

"If we don't get another tube in there fast, the hole will close over and he'll have to have surgery to get a new feeding tube put in," one of the nurses replied.

They worked quickly, trying to insert a smaller catheter line in place of the feeding tube.

As Tammy watched the nurses and aides furiously working on Nate, she could tell that her son was in pain. The hole where the feeding tube had been was so raw and sore that Nate had shouted "Stop!" when Ms. Mele was merely cleaning it. Now they were forcing another tube in that hole as Nate lay there.

He didn't call out this time, but Tammy could see the pain etched across his face.

When they finally finished, one of the nurses said, "He'll have to have an X-ray in the morning to make sure the catheter is properly placed." Until then, they couldn't give Nate anything through the feeding tube, so he would only be able to receive his fluids by IV that night. Nothing through the stomach.

Even after all the commotion—and exhausted as he was from his long day—Nate kept motioning that he wanted to go to the bathroom, so Tammy and Ms. Mele wheeled him in. Again, Nate had no problems making it to the toilet.

Even though he'd been wearing "britches" all day, Nate hadn't soiled or wet himself once. So from then on, he was allowed to wear his own underwear.

Both Nate and Tammy were exhausted by the end of the day.

Before she retired for the night, Tammy wrote in her journal: *Father, thank You for today and the amazing hope it has given me. I pray they will get the feeding tube thing worked out in the morning. Please help Nate with his pain. Thank you, Father. Amen.*

I continue to pray for and with Nate every morning, several times throughout the day and every evening. We are kept so busy with therapies and me helping Nate when the nurses can't and trying to journal everything about this journey for Nate, that I don't keep a prayer log while at TIRR.

Saturday, June 30ᵗʰ, 2007

The weekend brought a lighter routine for Nate and a total change of pace for Tammy. Billy, who had spent the night in Sugar Land with Nate's friend Lawrence (nip) and his wife, came up to spend the day with Nate while Tammy and Elissa (who had stayed overnight at a friend's house) went back to Victoria to attend Dustin and Jen's wedding.

Up to this point, the moral, emotional, and financial support of family and friends had been no less than overwhelming. Several donation accounts had been set up. In Victoria, people had brought food to the hospital and been there to pray and encourage. But nothing could have prepared Tammy and Elissa for what they saw when they arrived at the wedding

When they came through the door, there was a huge poster of Nate with a donation jar in front of it. If that weren't enough, in the middle of the ceremony, Dustin and Jen took time out to tell everyone Nate's story and asked them to pray for him and help with donations if they could. To cap it off, they asked Elissa to sing the song that she sang to Nate every night at the hospital. She sang, and there wasn't a dry eye in the house.

Looking around at everyone at the wedding, with all the emotions going on, Tammy wondered, *Will Nate ever get to find his true love and get married?*

Tammy wrote later:

I was overwhelmed that this wonderful couple would take time out in their wedding to think about and ask for help for their friend. Any money that they got at the wedding, they gave to Nate's benefit fund.

After the wedding, Tammy thanked Dustin and Jen and told them that she couldn't believe they had done this for Nate.

"Nate is always doing for others," they replied. "It was an honor to be able to do it for him."

Another surprise at the wedding came in the form of Brianna, the young nurse who had removed Nate's staples just before he left for TIRR MH. She came up to Tammy, hugged her, and asked how Nate was doing.

It was an amazing day, as once more Tammy saw how many lives her son had touched, just how many people loved and cared about him, and how God had put wonderful people in their lives.

❖   ❖   ❖

At TIRR, Nate had a fairly light routine in comparison with the previous two days. Mid-morning, they took him down to X-ray to make sure that his feeding tube had been properly placed. Although the tube looked good, the area around it was inflamed, so they would have to watch for infection.

Now that Nate was in Houston, his surfing buddies from Galveston and the surrounding areas began to take up the roles of visitors and encouragers. Lawrence, his first visitor, posted on El Ride: "I visited Nate last night and this morning. He was pretty tired last night and he just got back from therapy this AM, but he is awake and occasionally says a few words. They are trying to encourage him to talk as opposed to doing hand gestures . . . . I mentioned there may be some visitors this weekend and his eyes lit up. He then signaled for paper and wrote, 'JP', 'Mike R', and 'James'. He is scheduled for OT (Occupational Therapy) sometime today, but the weekend schedule is sort of open. He also has a nice PFN sticker on the front of his helmet."—nip

Nate was asleep when J. P. showed up later in the day, but J. P. said he wouldn't leave until Nate woke up. About twenty minutes later, Nate opened his eyes and indicated that he needed to use the restroom.

J. P. commented on the incident later on El Ride:

"Nate has the profound ability to call me when I am on the can. At least 70% of the time he calls, I am in the Kimchi Squat. My GI issues

149

are a constant harassment to my brother Nate. We would talk for like 10 minutes and then he would hear me flush and he would be like, 'Were you dumpin' the whole time? You are sick. Just gross.'"

"Well, after visiting for a while he started pointing to his stomach and stated, 'OOOWWW.' After a while, we figured he had to utilize the porcelain. Well, in typical Nate payback fashion he unloaded. I think he saved it for me for a few days. I thought they were going to have to evacuate the whole wing of the hospital, but to me it was the sweet smell of brotherly retribution."

On a more serious note, J. P. added, "He is trying hard, and his frustration serves as a good sign as he wants to do more than he actually is able to do at this point. He must have been worn out after I left because he exerted a lot of energy while I was there. It's like he was trying to tell me that he is going to be OK, and that I just need to have faith and be patient for his return.

"Nate, I love ya brother and I will wait and try to be by your side as much as possible in the coming months . . . . I really feel, I mean in the depths of my inner core feel that it is going to be his family and friends that are going to be the greatest encouragers of his rehabilitation. As always, liftin' 'em skyward. PFN."—JP1

Almost as if in answer to J. P.'s call, other posts floated into El Ride over the next day:

"Good day Nate . . . ya boy guru got married yesterday . . . your Mom and sister came to the ceremony . . . your sis sang us a song and it was beautiful . . . so glad they were able to make it . . . we also put out a pic of you and a li'l story behind what's been going on . . . We had a donation point set up . . . and you got some more money to help out with the medical expenses . . . we love ya brother, you have touched the hearts of many people and will continue to forever."—Dustin~

"Hey Nate, Praise God for your continued progress. As I am typing this my 5 year old daughter . . . came up and gave me a big ol hug. Oh how precious and delicate life is. We watch our children grow from an infant to adulthood and everything in between. Man I can't even imagine how proud your parents must be of you. The last few weeks has to have been so hard on your parents watching their little boy (even though you're now 6'3", 200 lbs.) go through this whole thing. But I know they have hope. The one thing that Jesus offers us is hope. The hope that if we have faith in him, all things are possible and can't believe that God would take you this far in life just to stop now. There is no doubt in my mind that you will be fully restored. I get on this thread 2 to 3 times a day and find myself smiling and shedding tears all at the same time when I read that you continue to make progress every day. You are a living miracle. What an inspiration you and your parents have been for the last few weeks for all of us that know you and even those who don't."—jsh

"Nathan: Keep working, keep pushing. It will come in time. You've already come so far so quickly. You've also brought a lot of people closer to each other and closer to God. We're praying for you daily."—wavehound

"Thank you all again and again for sharing all the updates. It's one of the only few pieces of news I look forward to reading several times a day. Please let Nate know that he has been a HUGE inspiration and testimony to so many of us!"—cinsdragonfly

"This is the BEST thread ever. Reports like this are a DAILY record of a true miracle in action. Inspired and renewed daily, through Nate. If that is not a ministry, I don't know what is. Bless all who are helping him heal, all who have visited, and all who continue to Pray for Nate."—g_scott

"Thanks for the wonderful reminder that God can lead us through even the most painful tragedies if we ask Him for His wisdom and allow Him to help us make sense of our lives."—brianb8888

❖   ❖   ❖

Billy spent Saturday night with Nate so that Tammy could spend a night in her own bed. Throughout the night Nate got up every three hours or so to use the restroom, but Billy didn't mind at all.

"I never thought I'd be so happy to see my son use the restroom," he wrote later. "It's awesome."

As Billy looked at his son, asleep in the hospital bed, one prayer flashed through his mind.

"Nate, I pray for your healing every waking moment."

Chapter 19

Baby Steps

Sunday, July 1ˢᵗ, 2007

By Sunday morning, Nate was becoming more accustomed to getting around in his wheelchair. After Tammy arrived, she and Billy helped him into his wheelchair, and after that he used his feet to pull himself down the hallway outside his room. As Billy, Tammy, and the nurses all cheered, Nate went faster and faster. Then he gave them a "thumbs up" sign. A little later, when Lawrence was visiting, Nate showed off his wheelchair skills by doing a full lap, all the way down the hall and back, and then wheeling back into his room—on his own. Given that his friend was there, it's possible that Nate was "ramping up" his performance a bit.

"Nate really seems to try harder when he thinks someone is coming or after someone has visited him," Tammy posted on El Ride. "He usually has so much strength and stamina, but with his head injury and his arm hurting all the time (also been having problems with the feeding tube coming out several times) he does get discouraged more than usual. When I tell him someone is coming, he works a lot harder to keep trying."

Lawrence recounted the story in an El Ride post: "Nate looked really good today. He had a shower earlier and enjoyed that and looked a lot more alert. He is able to walk sitting on his wheelchair pretty fast down the hall and is able to turn it around. When he came back he cruised right into his room (built in GPS)."—nip

But as well as Nate was able to navigate in his wheelchair, it was not his favorite place to be. As part of Nate's rehab, to help him regain upper body strength, the therapists wanted him to sit in his wheelchair for three hours at a time. Nate still tired easily, and he much preferred being in his bed. Unfortunately for Nate, he was belted and buckled into the chair.

Nate kept working at the buckle, trying to free himself, but without much success.

Finally, he became frustrated and said, "Gosh, dang it!"

Up to this point, Nate had been mostly saying one word at a time, and even then it was little more than a breathy whisper. This time, he spoke out clearly, and it was more than one word.

Once Nate was finally allowed back in his bed, Tammy decided to turn on the TV to give him something to focus on. However, although Nate enjoyed watching movies, he was never much of a TV watcher.

He found the remote control and pressed buttons until he hit the power button.

Tammy turned the TV back on.

Nate turned it off.

"You're a stinker." Tammy said.

Nate just gave her a weary look and sighed.

❋   ❋   ❋

One ongoing source of encouragement for Nate were the posts on El Ride, which Tammy read to him regularly. Among others that morning, she read Brian Brown's most recent post. The post ended with a characteristic word of encouragement: "It would have been easy for some to lose their faith in God through this situation, yet through your sacrifice you have been a source of inspiration, love, and hope for many! Love you."—brianb8888

Nate motioned for a pen and paper, and then wrote down Brian's name.

"Would you like me to call Brian so you can talk to him?" Tammy asked.

Nate nodded.

Tammy was excited that Nate wanted to talk to Brian. Laura, his speech therapist was emphasizing the need to get him talking more, so this seemed like a prime opportunity. She called Brian and put Nate on the phone. Of course, most of the conversation was from Brian's end, but at the end, after Brian told Nate that he loved him, Nate responded.

"I love you, bro."

It wasn't much more than a whisper, but it was loud enough for Brian to hear it.

Brian lost no time passing the news on to the surfers on El Ride.

"FREAKIN' AWESOME!! Tammy asked [Nate] if there was anybody he wanted to talk to and he wrote my name. She called and I talked to him for a few minutes and then he said . . . 'I love you!' That's the most excited I will ever be to hear those words come out of a guy's mouth!!! Nate is truly a miracle happening before our eyes! Give God some glory and thank Him for allowing us to watch Him work!!! Paddle hard my brother!!"—brianb8888

Nate had a few more visitors that day, but he had difficulty staying awake because of his pain medication. Earlier, the nurses asked him to rate how bad the pain in his wrist was on a scale of one to ten. Nate told them it was a seven. They gave him a Lortab pill—a combination of acetaminophen and hydrocodone. Nate rarely took any medications at all—not even Tylenol—so his system wasn't used to such a powerful drug. Nevertheless, when his friends Fred and, later, Mike dropped by, he at least tried to open his eyes while they were there.

Monday, July 2ⁿᵈ, 2007

"Morning bro! Thinking about you this morning as I was reading this passage:

'Satan's angel did his best to get me down; what he in fact did was push me to my knees. No danger then of walking around high and mighty! At first I didn't think of it as a gift, and begged God to remove it. Three times I did that, and then he told me, "My grace is enough; it's all you need. My strength comes into its own in your weakness." Once I heard that, I was glad to let it happen. I quit focusing on the handicap and began appreciating the gift. It was a case of Christ's strength moving in on my weakness. Now I take limitations in stride, and with good cheer, these limitations that cut me down to size—abuse, accidents, opposition, bad breaks. I just let Christ take over! And so the weaker I get, the stronger I become,' (2 Corinthians 12:8-10, *The Message*).

"Rely on His strength today, and the friends who God has placed in your life for encouragement. Love you! PFN—brianb8888

❊   ❊   ❊

Even though Nate was progressing much faster than the doctors and nurses expected, it was still difficult for those who knew him before the accident to watch him trying to get through little things that had been easy for him before. On Monday, Shad Estes came up to visit and stayed with Nate through his physical therapy session so that Tammy could run some errands.

Shad was glad to be able to help, but it was hard to watch his friend, especially when he looked like he was struggling just to keep going.

"I came Monday to see you at TIRR," Shad wrote in his journal. "I thought you might be more excited to see me but you looked down. You were very frustrated looking. I stayed with you during your rehab time while your mom had some time to go take a shower and stuff. I helped your therapist walk you and do some different exercises. You just didn't seem up to it. I would try to talk to you some but I could tell you just wanted to go back to the room. We took you back and you wanted to lie down but you couldn't. You tried to write some but got frustrated because it didn't come out. You said . . . 'Gad doggit this is dumb.' I don't know if you realize I am there or not. I could tell you were getting frustrated so I asked if you wanted me to pray with you and you said yes. I prayed. Nate, I know it's tough but you have to fight and get through this. I miss talking to you buddy. I wish we were able to have some Coke® float time. I have to be patient and let God heal you. It's just I want it to be now and I am impatient."

But even though Shad found it hard to watch his friend struggle, Nate was making significant steps forward every day. He could now ride a stationary bike for about a minute, and completed a swallow test so he could begin to eat again. (Nate had eaten a few bites of food at the hospital in Victoria, but the doctors at TIRR Memorial Hermann wanted to do a swallow test with dye before they would allow him to have solid food.)

One of Nate's most notable accomplishments was that he figured out how to unbuckle his seatbelt and would now try to "escape" from his wheelchair instead of sitting in it for hours at a time. His newly-achieved liberty was short lived, though, because while some of Nate's friends were visiting, his occupational therapist, Ms. Irene, came in and put a different latch on his seatbelt. This one required that a "key" of sorts be pushed through a hole to unlock it. The key was attached to the back of the chair with Velcro®, where Nate couldn't reach it.

After his friends left, he was allowed to go to the restroom, but had to get right back into his wheelchair. Nate was getting frustrated because he couldn't figure out how to get his seatbelt unlocked. He began to hit on the arm of his wheelchair.

Tammy had been talking with Nate's case worker, but when she came over to him, Nate stuttered, "Mom, I'm sore and I been sittin' here a long time. P-p-p-lease, b-bed."[9]

Tammy cried when she heard those words, partly because she felt so bad for Nate, but also because he had put so many words together. He still spoke barely above a whisper. And he stuttered. But he was talking.

Tammy undid the buckle and helped him back into bed. He looked exhausted.

"Thanks," Nate said.

Then he drifted off to sleep.

❋   ❋   ❋

Speech therapy was another part of Nate's grueling daily routine. He had to answer questions, point to the correct objects when asked, and count to ten, among other things. He struggled with saying the days of

---

[9] Author's note: When Nate began to speak after his accident, he stuttered badly, and it took many months of speech therapy for him to overcome it. However, to make Nate's dialogue easier to read in this book, his stuttering has been minimized.

the week, but overall he did well, at least until he got tired. His writing was improving as well, although it was still very messy and contained misspellings.

"He has aphasia and apraxia," Laura, the speech therapist, told Billy and Tammy. "With aphasia, people have a hard time producing or comprehending spoken or written language. With apraxia of speech, people have a hard time saying what they want to say correctly and consistently. They know in their head what they want to say, but getting it out of their mouth is hard. With these conditions, people can also have a hard time writing. Thinking thoughts, then getting them from their head to their hand can be very difficult."

"Nate is very blessed then," Tammy replied. "Before he could say one word, he was able to do a little writing."

"That's the first time I've ever seen a patient do that," Laura said. "Most of my patients begin speaking before they can write."

Amazingly, in spite of all he was able to do, Nate was still in a sleep stage and hadn't fully awakened from his coma.

But that would begin to change very soon.

Tuesday, July 3ʳᵈ, 2007

Aside from an encouraging visit from Seabass, Tuesday was a long, difficult day for Nate.

Not only did he have a hard time with his therapy sessions, he was in a lot of pain. His feeding tube had come out three times now, and the area around it had become very red and infected. If he could only start eating three full meals a day they could remove the tube and be done with it. However, Nate wasn't eating much, and when he tried, he became nauseated.

Nate had also started saying, "Stop!" or "That's enough!" when the nurses or therapists were doing something that he didn't like. Even then, his concern for others would shine through because he'd immediately say, "I'm sorry."

"Why do I have to be here?" he began to ask. "Why can't we go home?"

The therapists told Billy and Tammy that Nate was progressing to the next stage of awakening from a coma. The patient realizes that something is going on and becomes confused and irritated. Sometimes they become angry.

Tammy and Billy pray that Nate will pass through this stage quickly, as he has with the other ones.

Because the next day was the Fourth of July, Billy came up from Victoria to spend the night with Nate. Tammy planned to spend the night with Fran, a friend who lived in Houston. As Tammy got ready to leave, Nate became agitated.

"What's wrong?" she asked.

Nate spoke quietly. "I j-just w-want y-y-you here."

"I'll be back early in the morning. I promise," she said.

"I-I-I'll b-be here." Nate replied.

As Tammy drove to Fran's apartment, she thought about Nate all the way.

"Father, it is so hard to see my wonderful, smart, caring, can-do-anything, motivated, self-sufficient son struggling to walk, talk, and now afraid to be alone. Please let him progress and get past this stage."

Chapter 20

Changes

"Happy 4th of July!

"I know this day has such significance for you, you loved serving our country and following in the shoes of the men and women who fought for our freedom! But more importantly it has a greater significance for us because our freedom was bought and paid for on the cross . . . . Our Freedom came with an expensive price tag. Let's not waste it.

"I know how proud you were every time you put on the Coast Guard uniform, but I know it meant more to you to wear the uniform of 'one of the washed!' Live FREE today. Live in those open skies. Live to tell the story of the miracle you are. Live to tell how your freedom was bought and paid for by a blood-stained cross!

"One of the washed!"—brianb8888

❖   ❖   ❖

Independence Day brought Nate a temporary reprieve from his therapy regimen, and it was well timed. An infection had developed around his feeding tube, and he was running a low-grade temperature. To make matters worse, the infection around the tube was painful, which made it difficult for him to focus on his therapy. The holiday meant that Nate would be able to rest for the day.

Tammy kept careful track of how much food Nate was eating, and also of his trips to the bathroom. The ideal solution to the problems with his feeding tube would be to remove it entirely, but the doctors were reluctant to do that until Nate was eating more consistently. In the meantime, he would just have to live with the pain.

There were some positive changes for Nate on that July fourth holiday. His roommate moved out, and so they were able to move him to the other side of the room, closer to the windows. An added plus was that, at least for the present, Nate had the room to himself, so it was much quieter.

Tammy turned on the TV and gave Nate the remote.

Unlike a few days ago, Nate didn't turn the TV off this time. He took the remote in his left hand and began flipping through the channels. This was the first time he'd used that hand on his own.

Nate kept toggling through the channels and finally stopped on a *King of the Hill* marathon. Even though the sound was turned completely down, Nate began to laugh out loud. Tammy began to laugh even though she couldn't see the TV; she was laughing from the joy of finally seeing her son happy again, if even for a short time.

Nate's friend Lawrence stopped by for a visit, and later commented on El Ride: "Nate was watching *King of the Hill* and it was neat to see that he kept laughing off and on. Since the TV is on his left side, he has been using his left hand to operate it (fractured side).

"Nate's receptive language is there and his expressive language is coming around. He definitely is talking more, but sometimes he's 'said' something in his mind and thinks he's actually said it. The speech therapist has been working to reestablish that neuropathway.

"He's been able to walk to the bathroom with assistance. He seems less frustrated today. Another day and some more improvement. It's nice to see a miracle unfolding before our eyes. Praise God and keep battling buddy."—nip

Nate's improving speech abilities were clearly on display the next day when he talked on the phone to some of his friends. Danny Vivian told him that he was going to bring his family up to visit soon, and Nate said, "Come fast!" However, even though his voice was getting stronger, he stuttered and tended to get words mixed up, sometimes using one word when he meant something else.

And the feeding tube was still giving Nate trouble.

"Nate really needs our prayers about his feeding tube," one El Ride poster wrote. "It is infected and causing him a lot of pain. He wasn't able to do much physical therapy today because of the pain around the tube. The doctors came in and looked at it. They are going to start him on antibiotics and will discuss removing it or not tomorrow. Nate has been eating and drinking really well. If the doctors feel he can manage without it they will just take it out. That would be the best case scenario."—Barney

Even though Nate was still in a semi-conscious "sleep" state, his battle for recovery, chronicled through the posts on El Ride, was a daily source of encouragement for many.

"It's difficult sometimes to understand the walk we are all made to endure. Each one of us are made to stand for an example to others . . . whether it's an immediate crisis, life-threatening or just simply heartbreak, we are setting examples to ourselves and to others.

"Nate's walk has made such an impact in so many ways to me alone. Above all else, it's been his truest convictions and faith through this maze of the unknown. Whether he is struggling, having a bad moment, or conquering big or small tasks, it's his faith that reminds me to be patient and count the smallest of blessings.

"I log on each day several times to what I call my 'moment of inspiration', for he/He has been my guiding light through my darkest hours."—cinsdragonfly

As the day wound down, one more change came into Nate's world and this change would present a whole new challenge.

He got a new roommate.

Friday July 6th, 2007

Nate's new roommate was another young man with a severe head injury, only this young man was not as far along in his recovery as Nate. He couldn't get out of bed, and he stayed awake all night, moaning and making loud "owwww" sounds almost constantly.

Nate got very little sleep that night and it showed the next day.

For his morning physical therapy session, Christina, his therapist and Billy took Nate on a short field trip. Nate was now walking well with assistance and a little on his own, so they helped him walk downstairs and outside the building. They even made it across the street and back. Nate cooperated that far, but when they tried to get him to sit in the passenger seat of a car, he wouldn't do it. Instead, he told them that he needed to go to the bathroom.

They took him upstairs, but instead of going into the bathroom, he reached across to his bed, climbed into it and wouldn't get back out.

Laura, his speech therapist, didn't have any better luck.

She worked with him for about twenty minutes, trying to get him to say "I'm hungry."

Instead, Nate said, "Want something to eat."

Throughout the day, Nate repeatedly kept telling his therapists "thank you" and "bye," apparently hoping that they would take the hint and leave.

After Laura left, Nate asked Billy, "Why can't I remember anything?"

"You fell and hit your head," Billy reminded him. "You're here to get better."

❖   ❖   ❖

A huge step in "getting better" would be getting Nate's feeding tube and central line taken out. And although Nate chowed down on two of his favorites, Cinnamon Toast Crunch® cereal for breakfast and "PB and J" (peanut butter and jelly) for lunch, he was a long way from taking in enough nourishment to justify removal of the tube. Since his accident, Nate—lean to begin with—had lost about forty pounds. The doctors told Tammy and Billy that they couldn't risk removing the tube until they were sure he was eating enough to keep up his strength.

It didn't take long for word to spread among Nate's friends and surfing buddies that he needed to eat more. Later that day, Lindsey and her mom, some friends from Victoria, came up and brought a huge basket full of candy, crackers, fruit, and other kinds of snacks. They also brought along a pizza, and Nate managed to eat a few bites.

At supper, however, it was a different story. The menu included chopped steak, which Nate refused to eat. Not to be so easily defeated, Billy went down to the cafeteria and bought a hamburger. Nate devoured the whole thing, along with three Reese's Peanut Butter Cups® and a root beer.

When the doctor stopped by to see how Nate was eating, he told Tammy and Billy that if Nate ate half of his food and drank Ensure® over the weekend, they would take the feeding tube out on Monday.

Brian Brown added some encouragement along with a humorous perspective in an El Ride post:

"Pondering the whole feeding tube thing . . . how do they get that Circle K hotdog through that? NAAAAAW! Give me that crooked smile! Seriously, my little brother, here's a little encouragement for you today . . . He's coming back!!!! Live deeply in Christ. Then we'll be ready for him when he appears, ready to receive him with open arms. Walk bold and confident towards our King today! Love you!"—brianb8888

Saturday July 7ᵗʰ, 2007

Nate's new roommate was heavily medicated and sleeping, so Billy was hoping that Nate would have a good night's sleep. Unfortunately, that was not to be. At about 2:30 in the morning, the fire alarms went off. It was just a malfunction, but it startled Nate and he wet the bed. Surprisingly, it was the first accident Nate had had since his catheter had been removed. Nevertheless, Nate had to wait until the sheets were changed and the fire alarms repaired before he had a chance to go back to sleep.

He got a good start on eating that morning, finishing his breakfast. But he steadfastly refused to drink the Ensure®.

"It's bad," Nate said.

He didn't eat quite as much at lunch, although he still did manage to get about half of his food down. And again, he wouldn't drink the Ensure®.

That afternoon, two of his friends, Mark and Anecia, came up from Victoria and cheered Nate up with their visit. Mark had lived with him in Michigan briefly when Nate was stationed up there the second time.

Nate laughed when Mark reminded him how cold it was in Michigan and how much they hated it up there. But Mark got the biggest laugh when he tried to get Nate to rub his big belly.

"You ain't right," Nate said, laughing. "You ain't right in the head."

But when Mark said that it was time to leave Nate's emotions swung in the opposite direction. He began to cry.

"I'll visit you again and bring you some chocolate ice cream," said Mark.

"C-c-call me when you get h-h-ome," Nate stuttered.

❖   ❖   ❖

Throughout the day, more and more signs of agitation presented themselves in Nate—another indication he was moving through the next stage of coming out of his coma.

At one thirty that afternoon, something triggered the fire alarms again. It was then that Billy and Tammy realized that something in the accident had caused Nate's hearing to become very acute. The loud noise of the fire alarms—which continued for almost five minutes—was overwhelming to him. Loud noises even tended to nauseate him.

Later that afternoon his good friends Dustin and Jen dropped by and even though Nate did his best it was hard for him to visit. Lack of sleep, stress from the fire alarms, and the continued pain from his feeding tube were making it difficult for him to cope.

Nate often appeared to be frightened and would repeatedly ask questions like, "Why am I here?" and "Why can't I remember things?" He couldn't seem to understand why he was weak and unable to do things, and he always kept his eyes wide open, with a faraway look in them.

In the midst of Nate's confusion, Tammy, Billy, and everyone around him worked to reassure him that God was doing something great in and through him, and that things would get better.

Privately, Tammy prayed that Nate really would continue to get better. The nagging fear that she and Billy faced every day was that Nate could get "stuck" and not progress any more for a long time—or ever.

That evening, she posted on El Ride: "We continue to have ups and downs, but more ups than downs. Nate had an emotional day today.

He is really starting to realize that something is wrong . . . . He misses everyone and will start to cry when he asks about family and friends . . . . I know this has been going on for a while now and you all have busy lives. I really appreciate all of you for continuing to keep in contact all this time. Please continue your prayers for Nate."—texasboy's mom

One thing that was absolutely certain: Nate was having a huge impact on others, many of whom had never met him.

"I wish I knew Nate personally. He has been such an inspiration to me, and I don't know how to thank him. Get well, Nate! I'm praying for you homie."—ZigMund

"I'll be real honest right here. I am undoubtedly very rough around the edges and have a semblance of hypocrisy from how I talk/type and what I really believe, but Nate's witness has me re-examining my understanding of the Bible and has me seeking an understanding deeper within myself of what it means to be faithful. Thanks, Nate."—hilldo

"Last night I went back and read all 25 pages of posts. Nate has certainly made a day-to-day improvement, but looking back week-to-week, his progress has been rather remarkable. Like wondering if he would open his eyes to now speaking some sentences. Like wondering if he could move his arms and legs and now being able to walk down the hall with assistance. Like wanting to step out in faith and start a ministry and how the Lord has used him to minister to many people and to be thankful for the simple things we take for granted, and reexamine what's really important in life.

"Little steps each day in an unfolding miracle."—nip

"As things seem to drag on, it is encouraging to step back and put things into perspective. It was not that long ago that it was a day-to-day thing as to whether Nate would even still be with us. His progress has been amazing. The impact that Nate's life and his recovery have had on so many people has been even more amazing. But Nate serves an amazing God.

"Surfed Port A[10] yesterday with my son. As I was walking across mounds of washed up seaweed, and wading through soon-to-be washed

---

[10] Port Aransas, Texas

up seaweed, and waiting for the occasional semi-clean knee-high swell, I just kept thinking, 'Check out this freakin' awesome day the Lord has made.' Before Nate's accident, I would probably have been griping about the conditions."—wavehound

"Surfed a place called Cape San Blas yesterday. The whole Florida Gulf Coast was basically flat, but this place sits way out in the gulf, so it catches anything out there. Yeah, it was ankle slappers, with an occasional surprise, but loggable.

"Drew was having a blast on my log, chest high waves for him at times. He had been surfing for awhile and, frustrated about paddling, he said, 'Dad, I'm tired of paddling back out.' Thinking of you, I said, 'Paddle for Nate, push for Nate!' He surfed the rest of the afternoon. Man, my boys would do anything for you! Thanks for making a difference in their lives . . . .

"Bro, on those days when you get frustrated and don't think you can go, remember there is a 9-year-old boy in Tallahassee pulling for you and thinks you can!

"PFN—Pray for Nate

"PFN—Paddle for Nate

"PFN—Push for Nate

"Love you!"—brianb8888

Sunday, July 8th 2007

Sunday brought more visitors, including Danny Vivian (wavehound), along with his wife Connie and their son Travis. Even though Sunday was a "rest" day—no scheduled therapy sessions—Danny and Travis helped Nate out of bed and he walked the long hallway outside his room four times. The best part was that Danny and Travis only had to steady Nate if he started to lose his balance. In just a little over a month, Nate had progressed from not being expected to ever walk or talk again, to walking nearly on his own down a long hallway.

But such excursions quickly tired Nate out and when they got back to his room, Tammy asked him if he wanted a root beer to drink.

Nate shook his head and began to get agitated.

Tammy and the others could tell that he wanted something but couldn't figure out how to say it.

As Nate became more frustrated, Tammy knelt down beside his bed and tried to help. "Calm down, Nate. Start with one word or letter at a time.

"HW," Nate said.

She held up the can of A&W® root beer.

Nate sighed and shook his head.

Then he stuttered, "U-used to d-d-drink on t-trips."

Tammy couldn't figure out what Nate was asking for and fought back her own tears of frustration.

The room grew uncomfortably silent as everyone watched Nate struggling to communicate.

Tammy kept running Nate's words over in her mind: *HW, HW, trips.*

And then she had it.

"A&W Cream Soda®? Is that what you want?"

Nate breathed a sigh and brightened immediately. "Yes, yes, yes!"

When Nate was younger, A&W Cream Soda® was a regular part of any of his family's trips to the beach or vacations.

Danny and Connie rushed downstairs and checked all the soda machines, but there were no A&W Cream Sodas® to be found. But they were undaunted. "We'll be back," Danny said. "We are going all over Houston until we find some A&W Cream Soda®!"

It wasn't long before they were back with plenty of A&W Cream Soda®.

Nate was ecstatic.

Later, as Danny and his family were about to leave, Danny asked, "Can I take a picture of you to show to everyone who has been praying for you?"

"Sure," said Nate.

Danny took a picture of Nate in his "net" bed—a special bed with a thick netting around it that can be zipped up from the outside to contain a patient who has become violent or unruly or who tries to get out of bed without assistance. Up to that point, Nate hadn't had to be zipped up inside his bed.

In a few days, that would change.

Chapter 21

Trying to Remember

"I know people have said this before, but it is so true how blessed we are and yet we still take it for granted sometimes. I find myself needing to come here to check on Nate's progress but also as a reminder to how lucky I am to be in the position I am in. Thanks, Nate, for keeping me grounded. You truly are a role model and a hero!"—RobH

Monday, July 9th — Wednesday July 11th, 2007

Nate was gradually becoming more aware, even though his brain was technically still in a "sleep" state. Although Nate's increasing awareness of his surroundings and circumstances was another step in the right direction, this particular "progress" created a new set of problems.

For one thing, Nate got around much more quickly now, and he preferred to walk wherever he went. This was at least partially due to the fact that he couldn't unbuckle himself from his wheelchair. In Nate's words, he didn't want to use "that chair." But even though he could walk on his own, Nate still occasionally would lose his balance and stumble toward his left. That meant that Tammy needed to keep pace with him. Even though Nate walked fairly slowly, he was still over six feet tall. At 5 feet, 4 ½ inches, Tammy practically had to run to keep up with him. She didn't complain, though. She was glad her son was walking.

Nate also appeared to be struggling with what was real and what wasn't. He remembered falling but also said he needed to go home to see where he used to live and remember it. It was as though Nate was trying to figure out if his present life was a dream or if the memories of his past life were dreams.

Short-term memory loss was also a problem. All over his wall there were pictures of Nate, of his family and friends, home and room. Although he could now look at the pictures and describe what was going on when they were taken, Nate had difficulty remembering things that had happened recently, and it frustrated him.

Tammy shared about Nate's frustration on El Ride:

"He is still asking why he can't remember things. It's hard for him to understand that he really is progressing every day. Two days ago he was asking me about things in the pictures in his room and having a hard time remembering them. Today he was telling me who was in the pictures and saying that he remembers the events. So he is questioning why he can remember those things, but not new things. He still has a hard time telling me what it is he wants. He can say, 'Mom, can you,' but can't think of the word or can't get it to come out right. He is so patient with me when I can't figure it out."—texasboy's mom

Earlier that day, when Nate had been particularly frustrated, he asked Tammy, "Pray with me."

Tammy reminded him, "Remember Noah and the ark. Noah had to wait forty days and forty nights going through a tough storm. We have to pray and wait on God's timing and trust him like Noah did."

"I know, Mama," Nate replied. "But it's just so hard."

"God doesn't give us more than we can handle, even though sometimes it seems like He does," said Tammy. "When we're weak, He is strong. The doctors said you wouldn't walk again, but you're walking. Nate, you are a miracle. God must have something very special for you to do for Him to work this miracle in you."

Tammy prayed with Nate and then called Brian to pray with him, too.

Nate also had finally begun to realize that he was in a hospital.

"I'm sorry for all this trouble. Who's going to pay for all this? It's going to cost so much."

"You just need to concentrate on getting better," Tammy said. "God is making many provisions, and you have wonderful friends and family who are all helping us in so many ways."

"I know, Mom," Nate said.

As they went to bed that night, Tammy hoped that they'd be able to get some sleep.

Unfortunately, that was not going to happen.

❀   ❀   ❀

Once again, Nate's new roommate was awake and spent much of the night moaning and calling out, "Ooowwwwww!"

The loud noise began to wear on Nate, and he finally yelled out, "Please shut up!"

His roommate could only say a few words, but he was able to respond in no uncertain terms: "Yoooouu shut up!"

"Shut up!" Nate repeated.

"Yooouuu shut up!" came the young man's reply.

This exchange went on several times until Nate finally appealed to Tammy for help.

"Mom, please make him stop. It's hurting my head."

Tammy was torn. She was frustrated for Nate, but she also felt sorry for the boy in the other bed. He evidently was in a lot of pain and had no one there to comfort him. She went over to his bed.

"Are you okay?" she asked.

"Owwwwww!" was his only response.

Tammy talked with the boy a while, then she sang to him and prayed with him. Finally he fell asleep. She and Nate were able to sleep for a little while, but it wasn't long before it started all over again. That night, they only got about three hours sleep. The next day Nate stayed in bed, running a low grade fever.

The next afternoon, Nate's roommate gave them another scare.

Several techs came into the room and were unable to wake the young man. He just lay in his bed, staring straight ahead.

"We need help in here, stat!" one of the techs called out.

For several minutes, the room was filled with chaotic activity. Techs, nurses, and doctors—about eight people in all—ran in and frantically tried to wake the boy. Finally they decided to take him to the hospital.

Nate was so exhausted from the night before, he slept through the whole thing.

Tammy learned later that Nate's roommate had had a seizure and that he would be returning later.

It wasn't until around six in the evening that Nate finally woke up and started to feel better. Tammy gave Nate his iPod and he listened to his favorite music and tried to sing along. It wasn't pretty, but to Tammy it was the most beautiful music she'd ever heard.

When bedtime came, noise of a different kind was coming from Nate's roommate's side of the room. He had several visitors and they were laughing and talking. They had had a terrible scare earlier in the day, and they were relieved and happy that he was okay.

But Nate was so much more sensitive to noise than he had been before the accident. He began to get frustrated because the noise from the other side of the room was too loud. Tammy talked to Nate and tried to keep him calm until they left.

But although they hoped for a quieter night, it was not to be.

❖　　❖　　❖

Nate's roommate was up most of the night moaning in pain.

Nurses and techs came in and out most of the night trying to get him to calm down and go to sleep. They had been trying to get him transferred to a different room so that Nate could get some rest, but all the rooms were full. Tammy had mixed emotions about it all.

She definitely wanted Nate to be able to get the rest he needed. Otherwise, he wouldn't be able to do his therapies and his progress would be slowed down. On the other hand, she had begun to develop a relationship with Nate's roommate, and she saw a young man whose parents couldn't be with him most of the time, because they had to work. She felt sorry for the boy, but that afternoon he would make an indelible mark on her and remind her of just how blessed she and Nate were.

Tammy was feeling particularly down that afternoon when Nate told her that he needed to use the restroom. Helping Nate walk to the bathroom was something she did routinely now. But she hated to see him go through this. Nevertheless, it was something that had to be done.

So Nate put on his helmet, got out of bed and walked over to the restroom, with Tammy by his side and holding his arm. She helped him sit on the toilet and then closed the door part way, to give him a little privacy.

"Let me know when you're done, Nate."

She felt so bad that a twenty-three-year-old man needed to have his mom help him when he was done using the toilet. She knew that if he were fully awake, he'd be deeply embarrassed at needing to have someone help him use the toilet. As she sat there waiting for Nate, a wave of self-pity washed over her.

But then she looked across the room and saw Nate's roommate's father.

Tears were streaming down his face.

"Are you all right?" Tammy asked.

"You are so blessed," he said. "Your son can stand and walk and use the toilet. I'm praying for the day my son can do some of those things."

Tammy knew that this young man had his accident six months before Nate. Yet he wasn't remotely close to where Nate was in his recovery.

"I've been praying for your son, too," Tammy told him.

Privately, quietly, Tammy apologized to God and thanked Him for how far he'd brought Nate.

❁   ❁   ❁

Later that day, they moved Nate to a new room. His new roommate, an older man named Mr. Willie, was a rancher. He had been out among his cows when he fell and hit his head. Amazingly, the cows gathered around him and protected him from the hot July sun until someone found him. Mr. Willie said that the cows were his angels.

In addition to a new room, Nate received a status upgrade of sorts. Among other things, the color of a patient's wristband identified that patient's "security level." Nate's red wristband was switched for a yellow one, which meant that Tammy could now take Nate downstairs without having to have someone accompany them. It meant a lot more freedom of movement.

Nate's progress was also evident at speech therapy that day. He was able to write the numbers one through ten without someone telling him which one came next. He was also able to make associations, correctly writing answers like "pepper" after the phrase "salt and." When Laura, his therapist would show him objects on flash cards, Nate could name them correctly. However, in spite of a good session at speech therapy, the lack of sleep definitely took its toll on Nate. After lunch, Nate tired quickly, only staying for part of his group therapy. He refused to do afternoon speech and occupational therapy, and went back to his room.

That evening Nate brought up his now-daily question about why he couldn't remember things. Clearly he was becoming increasingly frustrated and confused as he tried to process what was happening to him.

A highlight of the day was a visit from Shad, Nate's good friend from Victoria. Shad brought one of Nate's favorite treats: a Subway® sandwich. Seeing his friend struggling like this was tearing Shad up. A few days before the visit, he wrote in his journal: "Hey man, I talked to your mom tonight and she said you were having a hard time trying to figure out everything. You kept saying you want to go home so you can remember everything. Dude, my heart really hurts for you, man. I wanted to cry tonight when I talked to your mom because I can't even image in my mind what you are going through. I can only hurt and wish God wouldn't have allowed all this. But then I remember that it's His plan and we are not allowed to ask why. Dude, I wanted to talk to you tonight and tell you that I need you back, man. I want you to be back here, just like the night of the 3rd of June when everything was okay. The world changed June 4th and you were set back. In my mind, I try to figure out what it will be like in a month, in a year, in two years. I wonder if you will be back the same again or different. I really miss you man and I want you to know that I am always here for you whatever . . . . I miss the talks we have. I miss the deep conversations we had. I miss being challenged spiritually. I just pray that you will all be back to normal soon. I love you man and I will see you tomorrow. Don't forget, I will always have your back."

Like Tammy, Billy and everyone else, Shad wondered if Nate would come back all the way, and if he would be the same person as he was before the accident. And, like the others, Shad prayed that Nate would be back to normal soon.

What Shad didn't know at that time was that God was indeed going to bring Nate back, and in only a few days.

But things were going to get worse before they got better.

Chapter 22

This Is Not Real!

Thursday, July 12th, 2007

On Thursday, Nate's behavior took a turn for the worse. After breakfast he refused to do his therapy. When they went down with Ashley his therapist for PT, Nate just kept sitting down.

"I'm tired," he stuttered.

Tammy noticed that Nate was becoming more and more irritable and he wasn't acting like himself. He kept insisting that they go back upstairs to his room, so finally Tammy and the therapist agree to take him back up, on one condition.

"You have to walk the hall for therapy if we go back up there, Nathan," Ashley said. "Will you do that?"

Nate agreed, and up they went.

But when they got up to the floor, he headed straight for his room.

"Lay down," Nate said repeatedly, but Ashley and Tammy were insistent.

"You promised to walk the hall," they said as they led him down the hallway.

A new bed was being put in a room several doors down from Nate's room and the old bed was out in the hallway. As soon as Nate spotted it, he walked over, climbed into it, and refused to get back up.

After a few minutes of unsuccessful cajoling, Ashley said, "Okay, Nate. If you get up and walk to your room, you can go back to bed."

Nate went back to his bed, but his attitude progressed from uncooperative to shocking.

Later that morning, when a female therapist leaned over his bed to talk to Nate, he reached up and tried to touch her breast.

She grabbed his hand and said, "That is inappropriate."

Tammy was mortified. This was completely out of character for Nate. He always treated women with great respect. She apologized on Nate's behalf, but the therapist wasn't bothered and reassured Tammy that Nate's behavior was not unusual after this type of injury.

"This happens at a certain time when the brain is healing," she said. "Patients often don't realize that something may not be appropriate. When they see something that they like, or that feels good, their instincts take over and tell them to do it."

As the day wore on, even Nate seemed to realize that something was not right.

As he was about to leave the bathroom one time, he saw himself in the mirror and walked over for a closer look. Since the accident, Nate, once a lean, strong, muscular young man, had lost about forty pounds. His frame was now thin and frail looking. Nate looked at his reflection.

"I-I-I'm l-l-l-ittle," he said.

He turned his head and looked at the place where his skull was missing.

"I have a dent."

Tammy reminded him about the accident. "The doctor is going to fix the dent when you get better."

After staring at himself in the mirror for almost five minutes, Nate looked down and walked out of the bathroom. His mood was subdued, and he looked depressed.

"Mom, I'm not doing too good," Nate stuttered.

Tammy could tell that Nate was scared. She prayed with him and tried to encourage him. Even though her own heart was breaking, she kept her emotions hidden. He was trying so hard and she didn't want to discourage or frighten him.

"Will you please try to eat some lunch?" she asked after she finished praying.

After Nate finished his lunch, Tammy turned on his iPod. He tried to sing along, and with each new song that came on, Nate said, "My favorite."

That afternoon, Nate did better in his therapy sessions and after he was back in his room he stuttered, "M-m-mom, I think I'm doing b-b-better now."

❀   ❀   ❀

During their stay at TIRR Memorial Hermann, as she and Nate were out at therapy sessions, they had the opportunity to meet and interact with other patients. During those times God opened many doors for Tammy to minister.

On this day, a lady came up to Tammy and asked, "How can you smile and be so strong?"

"My heart is hurting, too," Tammy replied. "I'm not as strong as I seem. But I do know God and I am trusting Him to take care of Nate."

"I don't know God," the woman said. Then she asked, "Are my husband and I so bad that God wanted this to happen to us?"

"No," Tammy answered.

"What have I done so wrong that God would want this to happen to my husband?"

Tammy listened as the woman poured out her grief and frustration. When the woman finished, Tammy asked, "Can I pray for you?"

She smiled, "Please."

From that day forward, Tammy prayed with her every day and they became friends.

❀   ❀   ❀

In addition to Nate's new "uncooperative streak," his moods began to swing, sometimes quickly and suddenly.

Later that day, two of Nate's friends, Allan and J. P., stopped by for a visit. Allan had come to cut Nate's hair for him, because Nate didn't like his hair being long. But after Allan arrived, Nate decided that he didn't want a haircut and refused to sit up in the bed. Allan stayed and visited with Nate, but the next day he posted on El Ride about how suddenly Nate's actions and attitudes could change:

"Yesterday Billy (Nate's dad) said Nate wasn't eating too good and wasn't wanting to talk much. All of the sudden, just like a light switch, he insisted on getting out of bed, walked over to the tray. I lifted up the cover to reveal roast beef and potatoes. He sat down and began to devour it, not even giving his dad time to cut it up. It was gone in just a few minutes. He then wiped his mouth and climbed back in bed and resumed the position.

"His dad, with a big grin says, 'That was good.'

"Later JP shows up and the same thing happens. Just like a light switch [Nate] just turned on and started gabbing away.

"God is healing him at an alarming rate.

"Pray for his family to have rest and strength. They are taking turns staying with Nate every night and then driving back to Victoria. It's a five-hour round trip. They both looked very tired when I saw them."—Barney

After Allen [Barney] and J. P. left, Nate slept for a while, and Billy returned to Victoria so he could be at work the next day. After Nate woke up he told Tammy that he wanted to go for a walk down the hall. By that time, it was 9:30 p.m. and many of the patients were trying to go to sleep.

"Okay," Tammy said. "But we'll have to be quiet."

When they got down near the elevators, Nate went over and pushed the "down" button.

Nothing happened.

The third floor at TIRR MH is a locked-down floor, and the elevators require a pass key to work, but Nate didn't understand that, and he interpreted the lack of functionality very differently.

"If this place was real, the elevator would work when you push the button."

They were standing near a Plexiglas partition. Nate turned suddenly, walked over to it and punched it. Nate thought it was glass and it should break when he hit it. All he succeeded in doing was hurting his good hand. But the failure of the glass to break added to his confusion and agitation.

Nate felt as if he was trapped in a dream world, and he couldn't figure out a way to get out of it.

But he intended to try.

Back in the room he said, "I want to go home."

"We can't leave yet," Tammy told him.

"I have to go to the bathroom," Nate said.

Before Tammy could react, Nate jumped out of his bed and headed toward the bathroom. But he passed by the bathroom door and headed for the hallway.

Tammy caught up with him. "You can't go out of the room without your shoes and helmet."

There was a counter near the door where his roommate's things were kept.

Nate reached over and swept Mr. Willies things off the counter.

"Nathan, stop!" Tammy grabbed Nate's arm but he shoved her backward and she fell to the floor. She got up and tried to go after him. By this time the nurses and techs had become aware of the disturbance and they came running.

They tried to convince Nate to go back to his room willingly.

"It's dangerous for you to be walking quickly down the hallway without your shoes and helmet, Mr. Lytle!"

It finally took four aids to get Nate back to his bed and, for the first time, they had to zip him inside the net bed.

"This sucks!" Nate kept shouting. "Let me out! Let me out!"

This was more than Tammy could take. She was crying when she called Billy in Victoria.

"I can't handle Nate right now. He's too strong for me."

Billy had just gotten home and into bed, but he dressed and made the two-and-a-half-hour drive back to Houston. After he got there, Tammy went to her friend Fran's apartment, hoping to get some rest, but she couldn't sleep because of worry for Nate. For the first time since Nate had begun to come back, he was acting like a totally different person. This wasn't the loving, kind son she knew.

Deep down inside, the fear surged. Was this just another part of Nate's recovery or, as some had predicted, was his personality changing? Was he transforming into an unkind, violent young man before her eyes?

"Please get him past this, Father," she prayed.

She went to sleep reminding herself that Nate would have to get worse to get better.

And he would indeed get worse.

Friday, July 13th and Saturday, July 14th, 2007

Friday morning, Nate began his day as if nothing had happened the night before. In fact, he went through what might be described as an "almost normal" routine. He got dressed—mostly by himself—and then he walked down to the elevators and back. Next, Nate removed his shoes, then went into the bathroom and peed—standing up. It was the first time he'd stood up to use the bathroom since his accident. After he returned from the bathroom he sat down on his bed briefly and then walked over to a chair by his breakfast tray. He then sat down and ate a breakfast of pancakes and milk.

After breakfast, Nate took a tablet, looked at a piece of paper taped to the wall, and then writes the day's date: Friday, July 13, 2007 on a new piece of paper and tapes it on the wall in place of the other one. This is part of his regular morning routine, and he always gets the date right.

Based on the calm start, it looked like Nate might have a good day.

But it was simply the calm before a series of major storms.

❊   ❊   ❊

Billy had spent the night with Nate and planned to stay with him all that day as well.

"I'm going to go downstairs and get some coffee," he told Nate. "I'll be right back."

By the time Billy got back to the room, Nate had put on his shoes and wanted to go for a walk.

"You've got to put your helmet on," Billy told him.

Nate was reluctant, but finally agreed.

"Where do you want to go?" Billy asked.

Nate didn't answer. Instead, he tried to push past Billy.

"You have to stay with me, Nate," Billy told him.

They went down to the first floor and Nate decided that he wanted to go outside. When they were outside, at one point Billy told Nate he had to sit down.

Nate got angry and cursed at Billy; then he took off his helmet and threw it.

It was the first time Billy had ever heard his son curse or use foul language, but Billy maintained control.

"We're going to have to go back inside if you won't listen to me," Billy told him.

Nate responded by taking off his shoes.

Having to step back into the role of a father disciplining a young child, Billy made Nate go back upstairs to his room.

Nate cursed Billy again—but he went along.

❈   ❈   ❈

Friday wore on with Nate going through a cycle of resting, walking the halls, resting, and walking again. Staying with him was becoming more stressful for both Billy and Tammy because Nate's combative moods were continuing.

They went to bed Friday night, but Billy had difficulty sleeping. Nate did not wear a helmet when he was in his bed and still had a heavy fixator attached to his left arm. He had a tendency to raise his arm up toward his head when he began to fall asleep, and Billy needed to watch him to make sure he didn't accidentally hit the place on his head where the skull was still missing. Such an accident would be disastrous, if not fatal.

At 2:45 a.m., Nate got up and told Billy that he had to go to the bathroom.

"You've got to wear your helmet," Billy said. "And when you're done, you've got to go right back to bed."

Nate agreed, but when he came back from the restroom, he took a slight detour over to where some soda bottles were kept. He started picking up bottles and trying to open them. He couldn't get the Sprite® to open, but finally opened a cream soda and drank it down.

"Get in bed now, Nate," said Billy.

181

Nate walked over to some pictures that had been set up. He picked up a framed picture of him surfing and raised it over his head as if he were going to throw it. Billy grabbed Nate's arms and stopped him, but after he put the picture down, Nate picked it up and tried to throw it again.

Billy spoke more forcefully this time. "Get in the bed, Nate."

When Nate complied, Billy thanked him.

Nate cursed at Billy again. "This place sucks!"

Billy tried repeatedly to calm Nate down.

"Shut up! This is NOT real!" Nate stuttered again and again.

Nate continued his rant until about 3:45 a.m. and finally began to run out of energy. He was asleep by four.

Later that morning, one of the doctors came in to check on Nate. After Billy told her about how agitated he had been earlier that morning, the doctor suggested they give Nate a "day off" and let him stay in bed if he was willing.

And, for most of that day, he was willing.

Throughout the morning and afternoon it seemed almost as though Nate was trying to determine the reality—or non-reality—of his world through his sense of smell. A surfing buddy brought by a bar of Mrs. Palmer's® surfboard wax. Nate kept it close and smelled it repeatedly. Later he asked for his shampoo and smelled it.

By mid-afternoon, after a visit to the restroom, Nate wanted to walk the hallway. He put on his helmet, but when Billy told him he had to put on his shoes, he wouldn't cooperate. He walked over to his bed, but would not sit down, so Billy had to put the shoes on while Nate was standing.

On his way out of the room, Nate walked by a fan and knocked it over. Next he walked down the hallway and tried to go into the hospital staff office. Billy intervened and brought Nate back out of the office.

Billy led Nate down the hall and back, but when they got back to the end of the hallway, Nate detoured over to the wall and hit the fire alarm cover with his fist. Then he walked to the nurses' station and with a sweep of his hand sent a stack of file baskets flying off the desk and clattering to the floor.

Nate glared defiantly at the nurse and stuttered, "W-w-what do y-you think a-about that?"

Billy tried to help. "Nate, you have to go back to your room," he said, but Nate remained defiant.

Another nurse, Bernadine, asked a security officer to intervene.

The officer walked over to Nate. "You need to go back to your room, Mr. Lytle."

Nate took one look at the uniformed officer and returned to his room, but when he got there he began to hit himself in the head—he was still wearing his helmet—with his right hand.

Billy gently asked him to stop. "I'm proud of you for remembering your songs and other things today."

For whatever reason, that seemed to trigger a shift in moods. Nate ceased being combative and began trying to explore, to decipher, the strange world in which he found himself.

"Can I see my pictures?" he asked.

Billy brought him all of the pictures in his room and, one by one, Nate examined each one. He held every picture up close to his eyes and studied it. But he seemed to focus on two pictures especially: one of his sister Elissa and one of his nephew Sye.

Tammy and Elissa arrived at about 6:30 Saturday evening.

Nate was especially happy to see his sister, as she hadn't been able to visit for a while.

Tammy also brought a special "gift" for Nate: his cell phone.

Nate was delighted. He barely had it in his hands before he started calling people. And for the next two and a half hours, Nate talked to his friends.

He was still in a fog, still trying to figure everything out, still stuttering. But it was as if a little light turned on when he held that phone in his hands. And as delighted as Nate was to be able to call some people he knew, his friends were even more delighted.

"I got a call a little while ago and it was Nate! He was talking clearly in sentences and was saying how he felt so weird, like he was in a fog. I told him he's doing very well and has come a long way and he said, 'Thanks man.' We only talked a few minutes, but I was so stoked that he called. I couldn't believe when my caller ID had Nate's name."—nip

"SO FREAKIN AWESOME!! Nate just called me on his cell phone!!!! What a freakin miracle he is! Someone tell me that prayer doesn't work, go ahead! Thanks God!"—brianb8888

"So stoked to get a call, unfortunately I missed it. I was surprised to see a missed call from Nate and he even left a message. He kept saying that he was sorry and that he would be praying for me. Just speechless."—JP1

After Nate's cell phone marathon he took a shower and by 9:45 was ready to go to bed. Unfortunately, his new roommate, Mr. Willie, was already asleep—and snoring.

Irritated, Nate yelled, "Turn it off!"

As if on cue, Mr. Willie let out one final, loud snore and then stopped. The rest of the night was quiet.

That was a good thing, because Nate would get no sleep at all the next night.

Sunday, July 15th, 2007

All around, Sunday was a much better day.

That morning, Nate went through what had become a regular routine: get up, go to the bathroom, brush teeth, put on deodorant, get dressed, eat breakfast, and write down the day and date.

Because it was a Sunday, there was a long parade of visitors, and Nate interacted well with everyone. Nate had a few visitors everyday, but the weekends were busy with visitors from Victoria, Corpus, Houston, Galveston, etc. Although he was in a much better mood, Nate still seemed to be analyzing and processing everything around him. He took time to examine his Bible, backpack, pictures, clothes, and everything else he had.

In the afternoon, Billy, Tammy, and Elissa took Nate downstairs for a walk. Nate spotted Billy's truck in the parking lot and recognized it.

"Can I sit in it?" he asked.

Then he saw Tammy's car. "Mom, that's yours!" he said, and he wanted to go sit in her car, too.

As they were sitting in the car, Nate and Elissa turned on the radio and started to listen to the songs. Nate began to sing along, and then started switching stations to find more songs that he recognized.

As afternoon transitioned into evening, it was time for Billy to head back to Victoria so he could go to work in the morning. But even though Billy was leaving, they had a surprise for Nate. Elissa planned to spend the night along with Nate and Tammy.

Back in the room, Nate, Elissa, and Tammy sat and talked for a long time. Finally, Elissa decided to go down the hall to take a shower and get ready for bed.

A while after Elissa left, Nate stuttered, "M-mom, c-c-come h-here p-p-lease."

He was in his net bed, so Tammy leaned in to him.

Nate looked at her and whispered, "You know this is not real."

"What do you mean?" Tammy asked.

"W-we're all g-going to wake up and see that this is not real," Nate said. "It's like one of those movies where you think it's real but you wake up and it's a dream."

Tammy tried to reassure him. "This is all real, Nate. I know it's hard, but it's getting better."

Nate shook his head. "W-watch this." Then he screamed as loud as he could, "Hey! Come here!"

"Nate, stop," Tammy said. "Mr. Willie is sleeping."

Nate laughed, "If this was real, people would come tell me to be quiet."

Tammy started laughing along with Nate, and soon they were both laughing so hard they couldn't stop.

"Hey! Come here!" Nate yelled again. "See?" he said, still laughing. "No one comes."

"They're too far down the hall to hear you." Tammy said.

"Look at that chair over there," Nate said. "Elissa was sitting there and she said she was staying the night, but now she isn't there."

"She went to take a shower and change clothes," Tammy said.

Unconvinced, Nate said, "That radio keeps playing the same songs over and over."

Tammy laughed again. "That's your iPod and somehow when you were playing with it you set it to repeat the same four songs, and I can't fix it back."

As they were talking, Elissa came back into the room.

"Hey, Nate," she said. "I'm back."

Elissa leaned over Nate and he smelled her shampooed hair. He always liked that smell.

Nate looked at Elissa, then at Tammy.

He paused, looked stunned, then stuttered, "M-mom, this is real, i-isn't it?"

"Yes, Son, it is. You had an accident at work in Dad's shop. You were in the hospital in Victoria and now you're at TIRR."

It was almost as if a light went on over Nate's head.

"Mom," he said, "I remember. I fell off the ladder and hit my head and broke my hand. It was hanging down. And then I started talking weird. And then I tried to text and call my friends to pray for me on the way to the hospital because I knew something real bad had happened."

Then a concerned look came over Nate's face. "Mom, I think I was very mean to some of the nurses and people here. I didn't mean to be and I feel so bad."

That surprised Tammy because the staff had assured her and Billy that patients don't remember what they do when they go through the agitated state and very rarely remember details of such a tragic accident and severe brain injury. Nate remembered it all.

Nate looked up at Tammy and smiled. "Well," he stuttered, "i-i-if this is r-real and we gotta be here, we're gonna make it fun, Momma!"

"Yes, Nate," Tammy replied. "We will make it fun."

Nate was full of questions, and the three of them stayed up talking until Tammy couldn't stay awake anymore. Since Elissa was there to stay with Nate, Tammy said, "I'm going to go down and try to sleep in the car for a while."

The nurses and security guards told her as she was going down that it might not be safe to do that, but Tammy was so tired, she decided she had to risk it. She climbed into the back seat of her car with a blanket and went to sleep.

Nate's nephew, Sye with his new bike September 2007

Nate with his sister, Elissa spring 2007

Friends from Parkway Church fall 2006 Caleb, Chase,
Mark, Courtney, Garrett, Nate, Michelle, and Heather

Nate with his family at TIRR Memorial Hermann nephew, Sye,
Nate's mom, Tammy, Grammy, and brother, Will July 16 2007

Nate wide awake from his coma with Lawrence, Danny,
and JP (nip, wavehound, JP1 on El Ride) July 18 2007

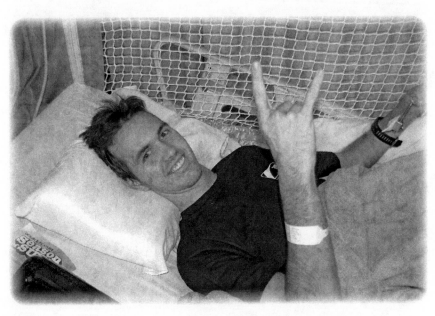

Nate awake and smiling in the net bed at TIRR
Memorial Hermann July 18 2007

Mr. Willie and wife, Mrs. Mary, at TIRR Memorial Hermann

Nate's speech therapist, Laura (right). at Tirr Memorial Hermann.

Nate with his nurses, Ms. Mele (left), at TIRR Memorial Hermann

Part Three

More God

Chapter 23

He's Baaaaaacck!

Monday, July 16th, 2007

When Tammy came back to the room at about six in the morning, Nate and Elissa were still talking. They hadn't slept all night. On Nate's part, that was partially from excitement and partially from fear. Nate was afraid that if he went back to sleep he wouldn't wake up again.

They continued talking until it was time for breakfast, and Nate was laughing at everything.

When one of his nurses came in, Nate said, "Ms. Mele, I think I was mean and yelled at you one day when you were giving me a shot in my stomach."

Ms. Mele replied, "Yes, Nathan, but it is okay."

Nate shook his head and stuttered his reply. "No, it's not. I am so sorry. Can I please give you a hug?"

It took a while for him to get that sentence out, but it was one of the most beautiful things Tammy had ever heard him say. She knew that, even though he stuttered, her wonderful, kind son was back. With that one sentence, Nate swept away her fears that his personality might change.

Ever since his accident, people had tried to prepare her for the possibility that Nate might be a different person when he woke up. She had even been told about pastors whose entire personalities changed after accidents far less severe than Nate's. These men had become violent,

195

would curse and, most frightening of all, many of them remained that way. For weeks, Tammy had lived with the fear that something similar might happen to Nate and, given his combativeness over the past few days, that had seemed like a possibility.

If any doubt remained that the old Nate was back, it disappeared as Tammy spent the next day with him. Throughout the day, Nate went around with a big smile on his face, greeting everyone he saw. "Hey, what's up?" or "How are you?" he would ask. The hospital staff members were all amazed at the change. Nate had been polite before, but now he virtually glowed.

"Do they have pur-r-r-r-ple wal-l-l-ls here?" Nate asked Tammy before they went downstairs that morning. "I remember that. I remember thinking this place can't be real because no one would paint walls purple in a hospital. Can we go see them?"

As they walked toward the elevators, Nate noticed the Plexiglas wall near the nurses station.

"Mom, did I hit that glass wall with my fist?"

"Yes, you did," replied Tammy. "And you hurt your good hand pretty bad."

"I just kept thinking, if this place is real then when I hit this glass it will break." When it didn't, it made me think this was all a dream."

Tammy explained that it was Plexiglas, and that's why it wouldn't break.

"Why don't the elevators open?"

"This floor is locked down. You need a staff member to work the elevators."

"That's another reason I thought it was a dream, because elevators don't usually lock."

They took the elevator down to the first floor and walked down the main hallway—with its purple walls.

"I knew it," said Nate. "I knew they were down here."

When they got back upstairs and Nate was settled in his room again, Tammy told him about his time at the hospital in Victoria and all the visitors he had.

"Who was the girl with the teeth and the eyes?" Nate asked.

"I don't know," replied Tammy.

Tammy had kept a log of all Nate's visitors, so she got it out and read through all the names. Even though she read through several hundred names, none of them rang a bell with Nate.

"I didn't know her. Never seen her before," he said.

"I've got no clue who you're talking about," Tammy said.

Finally, Nate said, "Mom, I think she was an a-a-a-a-angel. My a-a-a-angel."

Throughout the day, Nate continued to astound everyone around him. He told the doctors and nurses that he had fallen off a ladder and he remembered his hand dangling and that he was "talking weird." The medical staff had a difficult time believing that Nate remembered the accident so well because with this type of injury, people usually remember nothing.

"Did you tell him about it?" they asked Tammy.

"No. I only told him that he had an accident and was in the hospital for a month."

"It's just God," Nate said.

Nate also spent a lot of time that day apologizing to various staff members. "I'm sorry if I was mean to you or said mean words. I was just scared and trying to wake up. I thought it all was a dream."

Now that Nate was fully awake, he was eating just about everything in sight. As a result, the doctors decided that his feeding tube could be removed. Needless to say, Nate was ecstatic. For the first time since the accident, he had no tubes attached to him at all.

When he went to PT that day, they put him on a stationary bicycle. Previously, he rode it very slowly and didn't stay on long. This time he rode for ten minutes straight, and when Ashley, his therapist, told him that his time was up, Nate said, "Is that all?"

Then they had him walk on a balance beam and then try to bend down and pick objects up off the floor while on the beam. Nate performed almost flawlessly.

"It must be all those surfing skills," Ashley said.

Later that day, Nate asked Tammy, "Who's paying for all this?"

She explained about the charity bed and also how they were waiting to hear from DARS about more funding, and that there was going to be a big benefit for him in Victoria in just a few weeks. "Nate, you will not believe this, but everything at TIRR will all be paid for."

Nate smiled. "Mom, did you really think God wasn't going to take care of things? It's just more God."

From that time forward, every time something good happened, Nate would just grin and say, "More God."

❅   ❅   ❅

It didn't take long for the news to go viral on El Ride.

Nate was back.

"OMG! He's baaaaack . . . . Well, it happened last night; the fog was lifted. Nate said first he had a memory of when his brother and him were together as little kids. He remembers the accident and hitting his head on the pipe. 'I almost died, dude.' His memory has pretty much come back. I just talked to him for about 30 minutes on the phone and he is overwhelmed with all the prayerful and financial support from everyone. God is awesome and does indeed answer prayer."—nip

"Got a call earlier while driving to my in-laws. It was Nate on the caller Id. I was like whoa. Nate's mom said, 'I have someone that wants to talk to you.' . . . . Nate gets on and just starts talking up a storm about how much he misses everyone and how bad he was hurt . . . then how about it felt like a dream all this time and something just came back to him . . . . he even remembered about his board smacking him in the head at Gorda a few weeks before the accident."—surfguru

"In FREAKING TEARS HERE!!!! That is the BEST post I have ever read, Lawrence and surfguru. Thank you seems meaningless, but it carries with it all of my heart and beyond . . . THANK YOU!! SPEECHLESS. Keep on, Nate."—g_scott

"Wowser, got a great call from Nate earlier. As mentioned above he is definitely coming back. Or as he stated, 'I'm back, Bro. It's just soo weird.'"—JP1

Brian Brown, whose El Ride posts for the past month and a half had put Nate's injury and God's working in perspective, summarized it well: "God is so awesome, the great physician, the great healer!!! My prayer through all of this was 'God your will be done, but my desire for you is to show off' . . . GOD, THANKS FOR ANSWERING OUR PRAYERS!!!!"—brianb8888

❖   ❖   ❖

Back in Victoria, someone else was rejoicing in the news about Nate's amazing recovery. Brianna Hartman, the young nurse who had cared for Nate briefly before he left Victoria, had been praying for him and following his progress through their mutual friends, Jen and Dustin.

"I was so excited when Jen told me that he had woken up. My first thought was that I had to meet him; I had to be able to tell him how he had touched my life. Mind you, this was all so strange to me, knowing that here is this kid that's my age, fighting for his life, facing probably the hardest thing he will ever have to go through, and on top of that I was his nurse for a short while, and he has brought up all these emotions in me and motivated me to want to really find Jesus."

Brianna didn't know it then, but she would have the opportunity to meet Nate in only a few weeks—when she volunteered to help at Nate's benefit.

Chapter 24

Friends

Monday, July 16th — Friday, July 20th, 2007

Nate had awakened from his coma, but he knew he had a long way to go to make a full recovery. However, now that he was awake and aware of the challenge that lay before him, he was ready to meet it head-on. He knew that he had a story to tell, and he would do whatever he needed to do to be able to tell it.

"Mom," Nate said, "We need to write a book about this so everyone can see how good God is."

"I know, Son," Tammy replied. "God told me a long time ago that you would want to do that, so Dad and I have been keeping a log of the events that happen every day so others can see your journey unfold."

"I think the title should be *More God*," Nate told her.

Another sign that "the old Nate" was back became evident as he noticed all the other patients. Now that he was aware of their condition and their needs, Nate felt bad for them. So bad, in fact, that he began to feel guilty that he was doing so much better than many of them.

"It hurts my heart when I see them. I want to pray for them."

Tammy assured him that she would help him learn every one of their names and that they would pray for them every day. Indeed, Tammy had already learned most of their names and had been praying for them and their families.

Back in his room, Nate called more of his friends, laughing and talking well into the evening. It was after 9:00 p.m. and Tammy was concerned that he might be bothering his roommate, Mr. Willie, and his wife. She apologized to them and said she'd try to get Nate to quiet down.

"No," they both said.

Mr. Willie, tears in his eyes, said, "He's a good boy. It's so nice to hear him laugh. Let him go as long as he wants."

By 9:30, Nate was exhausted. He had been awake for more than thirty-seven hours. But even though he was desperately tired, he was still afraid of going back to sleep. Tammy promised him that she would personally wake him up in the morning and, as she prayed for him, Nate closed his eyes and went to sleep.

But over the next few days he would reconnect with his friends in ways that were nothing less than stunning.

Seabass

By Tuesday morning Nate was eager to get back to therapy and work toward his recovery. Normally this didn't pose a problem, but on this particular day it gave his friend Ron (Seabass) Berwick quite a scare.

Ron had visited Nate several times before, but every time he'd visited Nate had been asleep. So, even though he'd heard that Nate had awakened from his coma, he had no idea how completely he had come back. Ron knew the way to Nate's room, but when he got there the room was completely clean and the bed was made. What was worse, all of Nate's belongings were gone.

Later, Ron described the experience: "When you've been going to the hospital for that long with somebody in that bad a condition, and you walk in and everything's gone, it's like on a movie. 'Oh no! What happened?'"

In a panic, Ron asked a nurse, "Hey where's my buddy?"

She took one look at his face and said, "Oh, you're the guy that's in here all the time. No, no, no. He's okay. We're just cleaning his room and rearranging some things. They took some of his stuff home to get it out of here and get it uncluttered. Nate's down at physical therapy. He walked down there a while ago."

Ron looked at the nurse as if she'd just told him that Nate landed on Mars.

"What do you mean, 'He walked down there?'"

She just smiled and shook her head.

Ron knew exactly what that smile and head-shake meant.

"He just got up and decided he was walking down there today," she said.

Disbelief was still written across Ron's face.

"I'm dead serious," the nurse said. "He didn't even have a nurse. He just walked down there. Wouldn't let us help him."

Ron could hardly believe what he was hearing. A couple of days before, Nate had been in a coma. Now he's walking down to rehab? By himself?

Ron took the elevator downstairs and went to the rehab area, a large gymnasium-like room. Because he'd had a friend that was a paraplegic when he was growing up, he was used to seeing someone doing physical therapy, whose whole task for the day was simply to squeeze a ball. So when he went through the double doors into the gym, he knew what to expect.

At least he thought he did.

When Ron stepped inside the gym, he saw Nate clear across the room. Nate was pale and frightfully thin, and he almost looked comical standing there with his blue helmet on. But that wasn't what amazed Ron.

Nate was standing there, challenging his therapist to race him up some stairs.

Ron stood back and watched to see what would happen.

The therapist wouldn't race Nate up the stairs, but she did agree to a contest of their leg strength. The challenge was for both of them to put their backs to the wall and see which one of them could squat the longest.

Nate won.

Ron laughed and started walking across the gym and Nate finally spotted him.

"Seabass!" Nate called out, and began to make his way over to Ron.

"He comes walking across this room—and it's a big room," Ron said later. He's limping, gimping, metal stuck in his arm, hole in his head, hair sticking out of the side of his helmet, he's pale, he's skinny. So he's coming across and I'm looking at him. He looked in bad shape when he was in bed, but once he was standing up I realized, wow, this is how far he was going to have to go with this. And he opens his arms up wide and says, 'Look how awesome God is.'"

"Hey man, I almost died!" Nate went on. "Then yesterday—or the day before—or yesterday, I started remembering all my friends and wanted to call everybody."

"Now the guy is talking a million miles an hour," Ron posted on El Ride later that day. "Thanking all of us, thanking God, wanting to go surfing and just . . . well it's just amazing. I'm freaking out right now, too stoked and too happy to put it in the right words. All I can say is that Nate is one strong man, God is a strong God, and we are all blessed to see this happen."

As he watched Nate talking about how good God is, Ron thought, "You know, this dude right here is something else. He's like nobody else I know. Not even close."

Later as Ron walked down the hall on his way back to his car, the one thought running through his mind was, "Who am I to complain? Where are all these problems I think I have?"

Almost as if on cue, a teenager came rolling down the hallway in a wheelchair. He had a punk rock band shirt on and skateboarding stickers plastered all over the wheelchair. As the boy came closer, Ron thought, "Okay, this kid's probably about seventeen-eighteen years old, action sports guy, and here he is in a wheelchair. Man, that's gotta suck."

As they passed each other, Ron said, "Hey man, how's it goin'?"

"Pretty good, bro," the boy said. "I've still got wheels under me. I'm rollin'."

The boy cruised on by, and Ron stopped in his tracks and looked behind him. By now, the hallway was empty, and Ron was looking at the doors to the rehab room.

I have no reason to complain about anything, thought Ron. *None at all.*

Hilldo

Throughout that day, Nate was visited by an almost constant flow of visitors. Surfing buddies from Galveston, friends from Victoria, his grandmother, brother, and even his two-year-old nephew Sye came up to see him. At one point, there were too many visitors for the room, so they all gathered in the common area on Nate's floor. As they were all visiting, Bronson Hilliard (hilldo), who launched the online donation site for Nate, dropped in.

That meeting made a profound impression on hilldo, as he posted later on El Ride:

"I stopped in to see Nate yesterday and though Seabass called to tell me how floored he was to see Nate up doing stairs with the therapist, I really didn't know what to expect. I hoped I would not show up and find him sleeping, but as I looked for his room I noticed a group of younger girls and guys sitting at a table talking.

"It was Nate and his friends, sitting at a table having a conversation!

"I walked up and said 'Hi' and Nate got up and hugged me and started telling me how much he was blown away by everyone's support on El Ride. Keep in mind that Nate and I have only spoken in person a couple of times . . . at the last TGSA in CC and at the Grom Roundup in Galveston almost two years ago.

"He [Nate] is VERY stoked and praising God. He told me about what happened and seemed to be a little mad at that stupid pipe that got in the way of his fall. He has a little trouble with some words and gets frustrated a bit and apologizes for his difficulty in communicating, but there's no reason to apologize. I was frankly astonished to be sitting there carrying on a conversation with a man who up until a few days ago was not communicating too much at all.

"I looked at his broken arm and said, 'Ouch . . . that looks like it hurts . . . ' He shrugged it off . . . 'Yeah, it gets a little sore at times . . . but DUDE . . . I almost DIED . . . . I'm just glad to be here!' Amazing . . . he never complained once.

"He explained being in a haze and feeling like he was in a dream for so long and all the sudden HE'S BACK! He said they said that he might he might not walk again and now he's walking around and doing all these things! He is soooo stoked!

"I told him about when I was praying for him a few weeks ago, when I felt a feeling of peace come over me letting me know he was going to be OK. I got a little misty-eyed and he could see it coming so he broke it up and said, 'Dude . . . DON'T START CRYIN!'

"Nate's gonna be all right, folks. Keep praying and witness God's healing grace!"

Joey

Another of Nate's friends, Joey (Jsh on El Ride), posted about his visit with Nate: "I went to visit Nate around noon today [July 18th] and was blown away when I walked through the door. Like Seabass and Hilldo said yesterday . . . he was sitting on the side of his bed eating lunch and when I came in he got that big ol' grin on his face, said 'Hey, Dude,' stood up and gave me a hand shake and a big hug. He must of shook my hand 5 or 6 times while I was there. He was talking 90 to nothing. Said it's like he's been in fog for a while, trying to get out, talking to God, and then all of a sudden he just snapped out of it. Absolutely amazing! He seems to be blown away and very appreciative with all the support from everyone.

"I couldn't stop smiling when I saw him. He was so alert and talkative. He said he remembers surfing the Pro Am in Galveston the day before the accident (and drawing Morgan Faulkner in the first heat), falling from the ladder and all sorts of stuff. I'm still smiling while I'm typing this post. When I left he gave me a hug and told me that he loved me. The stoke I had when I left the hospital felt like I just dropped in the best wave of the day."

Wavehound

Nate's friend Danny Vivian (Wavehound) added his thoughts to the mix on El Ride:

"Got a call from Nate today [July 18]. He's called several times this week when I wasn't able to take his call, and . . . I called him back on the phone. What a difference since Sunday. Like all of you that have posted have said, HE'S BACK!! He was talking so fast, he would have to stop and apologize, then start talking again. He was [overwhelmed with][11] all the flood of memories and reality coming back to him. He kept saying, 'It's just so much, man . . . .' He even talked about things that had happened when he was in the hospital in Victoria when I [didn't know if he] was comprehending what was happening around him. He also kept saying how awesome everyone [has been and how] much he loves his friends and family. Just the excitement in his voice was overwhelming.

"Thanks, God. You raised my friend from the dead and are making him whole again. You are the Great Healer.

"Keep paddling, Nate. The next set's coming . . ."

Jammie Helzer

On Friday, July 20th, Jammie Helzer, Nate's former supervisor from the Coast Guard, made an emotional post:

"Man, I had the best night of my life last night. Let me set the tone for you all. I was sitting there on my couch with my two step-children when my phone starts ringing. I asked my son, Jacob, to get my phone out of the kitchen, so off he goes. He yells into the living room, 'Jammie, who is NATE DAWG?'

"Man, my heart just about jumped out of my chest. I ran in there to answer the phone, and there he was. The first words out of his mouth were, 'What's up, Dude?'

"I will never forget this. Time just seemed to stop . . . . He sounded so good. I could have talked to him for hours. It was a little funny because before I could ask him how he was doing, he was asking me how I was. Nate, the man that is always worried about everyone else and never takes the time to worry about himself . . . .

"Anyways, he was talking so fast. He has a lot to say and not enough time to get it all out. He is so appreciative of all of our prayers, and he

---

[11] Author's note: The printed text in this post was clipped at certain points. The words in brackets were supplied by the author and represent a "best guess" at what was originally written.

kept thanking me for keeping him in my prayers, but I was thinking last night when I was laying there in bed that I should be thanking him. He has made a 31-year-old man grow more through this whole thing . . . .

"Nate, much LOVE for you man. The Seawall is calling your name. I am going down to Ohana Surf and Skate after work to spread the news. I am soooooo excited for the Nate Dawg. Hurry up and get better. We have some catching up to do."

Indeed, Nate had a lot of catching up to do, and not just with his friends. Even though he had snapped out of his coma—a mere forty-two days after surviving what Dr. McNeill called "a non-survivable event"—a long stretch of rehab lay ahead of him. Nate was going to have to relearn the basics: reading, walking better, speaking, things that he used to do without even thinking about them. Unfortunately, TIRR MH was not the place where he could do all of that.

TIRR Memorial Hermann was an "acute" facility. The staff there specialized in working with those who couldn't walk or talk. Now that Nate was up and around, he needed to go to a "post acute" facility. The question was, where would he go?

And who would pay for it?

Chapter 25

Moving On

July 18th-July 31st, 2007

In just a few short days, Nate morphed into a cheerful, upbeat, and encouraging patient. Although still a patient himself, Nate quickly assumed the role of cheerleader—for everybody. Part of his daily routine was walking all over his floor, greeting and hugging staff and patients alike. "How are you doing?" he'd ask the other patients. "You're looking great! Keep fighting and pressing on."

One day as he was playing checkers with a female patient he asked her, "What do you think about God? Don't you think He's awesome?"

She looked at him, nodded and smiled.

When anybody asked Nate why he wasn't angry about what had happened to him, he would tell them, "If one person comes to know Christ or is touched by this, then it's all worth it."

In addition to being an encourager, Nate was now a model patient, eating like a horse and throwing himself fully into his rehab. He even began asking if they could give him homework to do in his room. His reason was simple.

"I want to get well so I can go home."

Nate's positive attitude notwithstanding, he knew he was facing an uphill battle.

"I was awake and I knew what was going on, but my brain wasn't working right," he said later. "I knew I was really messed up, but I didn't comprehend it."

Most of his struggles related to speaking and processing language. While most of the other patients spoke in slow motion, Nate stuttered. And he had difficulty finding the words he needed to communicate. As he went through his different therapies every day, this became increasingly clear.

At one small group session focusing on creativity, the therapist encouraged the patients to write a song. She asked each one to give a word to go in the song. One person suggested the word "car." When Nate's turn came up, he knew that he should choose a word that rhymed with car, but he couldn't quite come up with one. Finally, he said, "It was not dark."

In another session, the therapist gave Nate five traffic cones, each a different color. His task was to line the cones up and then walk down the line, weaving in and out through the cones. As he passed each cone, he was supposed to name the color.

He walked by the first cone, a green one.

He knew what it was, but he couldn't find the word "green".

"It starts with a 'g,' Nathan," said the therapist.

Nate stared at the cone, trying to say the word, but it just wasn't there.

The therapist tried to help. "It's like a "gr" sound."

Still no good.

Finally, the therapist said, "I'll help you out on this one. It's green."

The next cone was purple.

Nate stared at the cone again, willing the word to come out. But it wasn't there. Finally he managed to say, "Urkl."

Why is this so hard? Nate thought. *I really do have some problems.*

Speech therapy also highlighted to Nate just how far he had to go. The exercises they worked on were barely at a first-grade reading level. The worksheets didn't have sentences; they had single words. Nate would see a picture of an egg and a car, and he would be asked to identify the egg, or vice-versa. Again, when he was asked to name things, he knew the word was in the back of his head, but had difficulty finding the word and speaking it.

One day, as he was down in the gym, another patient rolled over to him in a wheelchair and said, "Hey man, I really want to tell you, you're an inspiration, dude."

Nate was taken aback.

"What? I can't even talk, man. Look at you. Your speech is perfect."

The man smiled and said, "Yeah, but my goal is to walk."

"I just want to be able to talk," Nate replied.

Privately, he wondered if he would ever regain enough ability to speak so that he could tell people about God and minister to others the way he used to.

❉   ❉   ❉

As Nate was struggling with his ongoing speech problems, Tammy was facing other uncertainties. She was concerned about how she would break the news that Nate might not be able to go home right away. He was so looking forward to getting back home to the places and people he was familiar with. She began praying about how she would explain to him that he would need to go to another rehab facility, possibly before he went home. She had already been investigating the possibilities and found a couple of options nearby.

TIRR MH had its own post acute program called Challenge. The problem with Challenge was that it was an outpatient program. Nate would be there for about eight hours during the day and then go home in the evening. That would necessitate Billy and Tammy finding somewhere to live in Houston for the duration of Nate's rehab. Another possibility was the Transitional Learning Center (TLC) in Galveston. TLC was an inpatient program, but that had its own downside: Nate would have to stay there by himself. He would only be allowed visitors on weekends. Problem was, Nate still had a "dent" in his head where his skull hadn't been replaced. Tammy was concerned that if he should forget to put on his helmet and then fall and hit his head, he could be seriously injured. A third possibility was a rehab facility near Austin, but that was so far away.

The other consideration was money.

At TIRR MH, Nate had a charity bed, but that arrangement would not continue at TLC. Tammy and Billy had been hoping to hear something from DARS but as of yet there had been no word. Other families who had applied for DARS funding told her not to expect anything very soon because their money had taken six months to a year to come in.

That was why Tammy was floored when Nate's social worker came in and asked, "Did you hear anything from DARS?"

"No," said Tammy. "They said it would be September before we heard anything. What's going on?"

"I was out and when I got back one of the people in the office said there was a message on my machine about funding for Nathan, but when I tried to listen to it, it was garbled and I couldn't understand it," the social worker replied.

"No," Tammy said. "I haven't heard anything from Megan [Nate's DARS caseworker in Victoria]."

"Maybe you should call her and see what's going on," the social worker said.

Tammy quickly called Nate's DARS counselor in Victoria. "Megan, what's going on?"

"What do you mean?" Megan asked.

"Nate's social worker up here is asking about his funding. Have you heard anything? Is he going to get it in September?"

"Tammy, he's already got funding."

Tammy couldn't believe what she was hearing. "How does he have funding? You don't get more money until September."

"We had this big lump sum that came in that was unexpected," Megan said.

"But there were so many people ahead of Nate," Tammy said.

"Well, the last funding didn't come through on time, so a lot of the people on the list got funding at other places or no longer needed it. And his name soared right to the top of the list."

"Are you kidding me? It's only been a couple of weeks," said Tammy.

"Tammy, I don't know. But I'm telling you, just like we've all been talking about from the day this kid fell it's been one thing after another.

It's just another one of those things. Who knows? It's crazy. I haven't seen it happen like this before."

"Well, when will it start picking up Nate's bills," Tammy asked.

"We've been picking up Nate's bills at TIRR since last week on the thirteenth."

"How long will it last?"

"He can stay at TIRR till September."

Tammy explained that Nate would have to leave TIRR MH by the end of July and asked Megan to check into whether DARS would pay for him to go to TLC in Galveston. She called back a little while later and told Tammy that they would cover his expenses at TLC for up to six months—in full.

Some quick decisions now had to be made. As she had since the day of Nate's accident, Tammy asked others to pray. That evening (July 18th) she posted on El Ride:

"Wow, God continues to bless Nate. We found out today that his DARS funding . . . came through . . . . We thought he was leaving TIRR July 28 because of funding and would be home at least a month, then would hopefully have funding for something in Sept. Now that this funding has come through, we have to make some quick and tough decisions. They are telling us they moved his discharge date to July 31. They don't feel at this time that he needs to stay here any longer than that because he is walking, talking, and doing things for himself.

"They said he needs to focus on cognitive rehab and logistics (like looking for cars when crossing the street, etc.). I was told that is not the strongest point here and that a post acute center would be better . . . . The good thing about the post acute residential is that TLC in Galveston is one that DARS pays for. That would mean he could at least be somewhere that he knows the city and has friends around some in the evening, and that could visit on the weekends.

"Please pray that God will show us clearly what needs to be done and that Nate will be accepting of it.

"Sorry for continuing to ask you guys for prayer, but it's just working so well and we know that through all this, God has been our only hope. What a marvelous hope He has been. Love you guys!"—texasboy's mom

Two days later (Friday, July 20th), Tammy decided it was time to talk to Nate about TLC. She'd been praying about it and felt that the sooner they discussed it, the better. She hated to break the news to him that he wouldn't be going home as soon as he'd hoped, but she needn't have worried.

"Mom," Nate said, "whatever we gotta do to get on with this, I can do it."

Despite his positive outlook, Nate wasn't particularly thrilled with the idea of having to live at TLC by himself, but when he found out that TLC was in Galveston, he was delighted.

"We'll come every weekend to visit, and your surfing buddies down there have promised to check on you and try to visit during the week."

Nate looked up at her and said, "We can do this, Mom."

Day Pass

Billy stayed with Nate on Friday night (July 20th) and Tammy stayed at a friend's house. Everyone hoped for a restful night because that Saturday they had a day pass. Nate would get to spend the entire day away from the hospital. The question was, where would they go?

Tammy had noticed some of Nate's friends posting on El Ride about the possibility of visiting him on Saturday, so before she went to bed she got online to tell them about their plans for tomorrow and hopefully to set up a surprise for Nate.

"Hey guys. Noticed that some of you wanted to visit Nate tomorrow. We got him a one day pass, but he has to be back by 6:00 p.m. We'll probably try to get out of there by 8:00 a.m. We don't have time to go all the way home and it is supposed to rain tomorrow, so I have no idea what we will do. If you want to see him at TIRR, it would have to be after 6:00 p.m. Butttttt, if a couple of you want to meet up somewhere and surprise him, I know he would love it . . . . Give me a call in the morning and let me know if it works out or not. He would absolutely die if you guys showed up at some restaurant or somewhere that we would be."—texasboy's mom

By the time Tammy arrived on Saturday morning (July 21st), Nate had already eaten and was ready to go. Before they left, Tammy logged on to El Ride to see if anyone had responded to her post.

At 5:14 a.m. on Saturday, Allan one of Nate's friends (Barney on El Ride) had posted an invitation: "Christian Surfers gathering at the beach. You guys could come by and have some worship with us in front of God's ocean. We start at 10 a.m. but something tells me we could be flexible if we knew you and Nate were going to stop by. We usually sing some songs, have a message, and just hang out and teach some folks to surf. It will be across from the Academy, where the dolphins are. We will have a canopy set up."—Allan

Tammy now knew exactly where they were going, but they'd have to hustle to get there on time.

"Let's go," Tammy and Billy said to Nate.

"Where are we going?" Nate asked.

"Why don't we go down to Galveston and look at the water?"

Nate was ecstatic, but he had no idea that a bigger surprise than the Gulf waited for him.

When they arrived at the beach, Nate exclaimed, "Mmmom, the gggguys are oooover thhhhere!"

Nate got out of the car as quickly as he could and began to run clumsily toward the tent. It was all Billy and Tammy could do to keep up with him. A few of the Christian Surfers group saw Nate coming and ran over to help. Some of the others pulled out cameras and started taking pictures. Many of them were as surprised and amazed as Nate was. Here was their friend, whom they'd been praying for and reading about, back from the edge of the grave and walking toward them.

After the reunion, Nate looked out over the Gulf of Mexico.

Nate said, "Ahhhhh, look at the water. I want to go in it."

Tammy was reluctant to agree. It was a steep walk down there and there were a lot of rocks. But four of the surfers stepped in and said, "We'll help him."

With his buddies around him, supporting him, Nate took off his shoes and they walked him down to the water. They walked out until the water was coming up around his calves. Nate was in heaven. "I want to drink it!" he shouted.

After Nate had a chance to get his feet wet, his friends escorted him back up the beach to the tent that the Christian Surfers group had set up. They all sang praise and worship songs together, which was the first time Billy, Tammy, and Nate had been able to be at a worship service since Nate's accident. When the service was over, Nate joined his friends, handing out surf wax to people on the beach and talking about God when the opportunity presented itself.

The rest of the day was filled with activity.

They had lunch at La Madeleine in Clearlake with some friends who'd come up to Houston, hoping to see Nate. One was Emily, a pre-med student who had read Scripture to Nate and prayed with him when he was in the ICU in Victoria. After that, Nate wanted to go to Bed, Bath, and Beyond to buy a belated wedding present for his friends Dustin and Jennifer.

When they left Bed, Bath, and Beyond Tammy asked Nate where else he would like to go, Nate said, "The Galleria."

"You really want to go to The Galleria?" Tammy and Billy asked him.

"Yeah! There's lots of people there. I want to see people living their lives."

After being in a coma for six weeks, Nate just wanted to walk around and people watch. See the ice skaters. Listen to snatches of conversation. Savor the sounds of life.

While they were at the Galleria, Tammy got a call from Bernie at TIRR MH.

"We need to move Nate to a new room again. We need the room close to the nurses' station for a new patient who is more acute than Nate, so they can keep an eye on her."

"That's fine," said Tammy, "But Mr. Willie will have to go, too."

Now that Nate was fully awake, he and Mr. Willie talked a lot between their respective therapy sessions and they had become fast friends. Mr. Willie told his wife that God sent Nate and Tammy to be his guardian angels, and when she couldn't be there, Nate and Tammy took care of him.

When they got back to the hospital at about 6:30 p.m., they found Nate's new room at the end of the hall. And to Nate's great joy, they had moved Mr. Willie, too. They would still be roommates.

There was one more benefit to Nate's new location. It was right across the hall from the freezer where they kept the ice cream. Nate was allowed to get it any time he wanted it.

And he did.

Going Full Circle

Over the next few weeks, Nate continued to pour himself into his therapy. An art-tech class was added to his regimen, giving him a full schedule of rehab every day: Physical Therapy, Phoenix, Art Tech, Lunch, Communication, Occupational Therapy, and Speech.

He even asked the speech therapist for some "homework" to do in his room.

He still struggled with his speech, particularly with finding the right words to say. In occupational therapy, Nate practiced activities such as doing laundry and even making cookies—although he was afraid to eat his own cookies. Again, it came down to language and communication. He tried hard to read the recipe and follow it, but when he would try to read, he would lose letters. Some of the writing would look like gibberish. As a result, he wasn't sure if he got the cookies right. He told the nurses, techs, and therapists that they could eat them if they wanted.

"Go ahead," he said, "but I'd be afraid to try."

Although Nate was fully cooperating with his therapists now, at times he grew frustrated, feeling as if they were treating him like a child. Everything was baby steps and the therapists were constantly hovering over him, watching his every move. Nate didn't complain, but it grated on him. He knew what he was going to do. Everything inside was working. He just couldn't express himself, so it made it look like he was going to hurt himself.

More good news came from TLC. Nate and Tammy met with a representative from the Transitional Learning Center and she said that Nate was a perfect candidate for them. Now the prayer was that a bed would become available so that Nate could start in August. There was some concern that Nate might lose his DARS funding if he had to go home first. Generally, insurance companies wouldn't pay unless the patient went directly from one facility to the next. But since TIRR MH was discharging Nate so they could free up an extra bed, and since TLC didn't have a bed ready for him, DARS agreed to allow Nate to go home until a bed opened up. That would give Nate the opportunity to make a brief appearance at the benefit that was going to be held in Victoria on Sunday, August 5th.

❊   ❊   ❊

On Wednesday, July 25th, less than a week before Nate's scheduled discharge, Tammy became concerned about Nate's left arm. Nate's hand had become swollen and an infection appeared to be developing at one of the points where the external fixator's pins entered his wrist. She showed it to the doctors and they decided that Nate should get it checked out by Dr. Daniel, the orthopedic surgeon who inserted it. That meant going back to Victoria.

They made it to the surgeon's office by 3:00 p.m.

The doctor inspected the site and confirmed that an infection was developing. It had been five and a half weeks since the fixator had been attached, so he thought it would be safe to remove it.

"It didn't heal as straight as I would have liked," the doctor said. "I think you'll regain most of the use of your arm and hand, although it may look a little strange. When you get done at TLC, if you haven't regained all the use of it or if it looks too strange, I'll consider doing another surgery to try and straighten it more."

As they left the surgeon's office, Tammy pointed across the street. "There's the hospital you lived in for a month."

"Can we go over there?" Nate asked.

"I guess we can," replied Tammy.

They went over to the ER and asked if they could go back so Nate could see the people who saved his life.

At first, when they walked back toward the ER treatment area, nobody recognized Nate. Who was this tall, skinny kid with the blue helmet?

Then they saw Tammy and Billy. They looked back and forth between them.

Tammy said, "Nate, did you have something you wanted to say?"

Nate struggled to get the words out, "H-h-h-how do I say thanks to someone who saved my life?"

Almost as one, the nurses and other staff said, "Nathan?" They couldn't believe what they were seeing. Only six weeks earlier, this young man had lain on a treatment table, not expected to live. Now he was walking and talking and hugging them all.

217

Nate looked across the room and saw Dr. McNeill. The doctor's eyes were filled with tears.

Nate walked over to him and gave him a hug. Tears now streaming down his face, Nate said, "I-I guess it was you. W-w-what do I s-say to the guy who saved my life?"

Dr. McNeill smiled and replied, "You don't have to say anything. Just seeing you walk in here is enough."

As Tammy and Nate drove out of town on their way back to Houston, they spotted a marquis in front of the Weinerschnitzel restaurant.

On it were the letters that had become so familiar on El Ride.

PFN

❊   ❊   ❊

Nate was formally discharged from TIRR Memorial Hermann on Tuesday, July 31st. Although he was sad to leave, he knew that it was time to move on.

"I knew that I needed to go forward, get more extensive rehab, but I was also a little wary [of going to TLC] because the people at TIRR were so helpful. But at the same time I knew that I needed more rehab and I was ready to go. I knew that I was ready to go to the next phase of my rehab. I wanted to get back to a halfway normal life."

When Nate arrived back in his home in Victoria, as soon as he was inside the house he stopped and inhaled deeply.

"Home," he said. "It smells good."

Chapter 26

The Benefit

Not long after Nate's injury, it became clear that no matter what happened, his medical bills were going to be astronomical. Yet in the weeks following his accident, God had provided in ways that were nothing less than amazing. Bronson Hilliard (hilldo) set up a donation account. Other surfing friends made and sold stickers and T-shirts with the PFN logo. Donation jars were set up in surf shops and other businesses in Galveston, Victoria, and other places along the Texas Gulf Coast. And friends back in Victoria were busy making plans to hold a benefit for Nate.

And what a benefit it was going to be.

Leisha came up with the idea and began to coordinate the event. Her family owned Power Avenue Warehouse, a venue where people could hold meetings, events, and receptions. She offered to host a benefit at their place and people all over town began to get on board. Before long, the benefit committee was meeting every Monday evening and had ballooned to almost fifty members.

The idea of having a benefit wasn't all that unusual to the folks in Victoria, a close-knit city of about 65,000. When one of their own was in need, they were quick to reach out by having a barbecue, a raffle, or some similar event. But the benefit that was being planned for Nate Lytle was unlike anything they had ever done. It may have started small, but it quickly grew into a juggernaut, an event that—at least for Victoria—would be "the mother of all benefits."

Danny Vivian posted on El Ride about the event on June 18th, only two weeks after Nate's injury: "Big plans are in the works for a 'Nate's Birthday Bash' fundraiser in early August. Bands, raffles, silent auction, etc. The crew heading it up arrived at the hospital buzzin' like they just left a Red Bull party. There is a lot of enthusiasm about helping this wonderful family."—wavehound

About a week later, Danny followed up with some more details: "Had a good meeting for the benefit this evening . . . . I need to know if anyone is gonna head down to help out. The date is Sunday, August 5th. Planning on serving about 2500 brisket plates, so we definitely need some help with the plating process. And if anyone has things to donate for the raffle or silent auction, hit me up and we will try to get things going asap."—wavehound

It didn't take long before donations for the raffle and silent auction began to roll in. Some items were modest and inexpensive; others were almost unbelievable.

A few days before Nate woke up from his coma, Tammy posted an inventory of the items that were going to be raffled. Among other things, the items included a seven-foot handcrafted pine plank table valued at $2700, a guided fishing trip for three people (a $1000 value), a migratory waterfowl cloisonné stamp collection (1933–1999) valued at $3000, a custom made surfboard, four tickets to the Houston Astros vs. Chicago Cubs, a custom made rod and reel, and a stainless steel tabletop grill.

In addition to the items donated for the raffle, about fifty things were donated for a silent auction, including one very special surfboard.

Nate's Surfboard

John Olvey, a surfer and artist from Corpus Christi, had only met Nate in person one time, and then only in passing. They had been trying to find a time to surf together for quite a while, but it never seemed to work out. Nate messaged John one day to let him know that he was in the water, but by the time John got there, Nate was already toweling off and getting ready to head back to Victoria. So John's knowledge of Nate was primarily through their interaction on the El Ride board.

As John watched Nate's story unfold through the PFN thread on El Ride, he had an idea, a way to communicate a simple message: "We're pulling for Nate. God's got it. It's under control." He wanted to take an old surfboard and paint a picture that would symbolize Nate's testimony, the prayers of his brother surfers, and God's work in the whole process. So John put out a call, asking if someone had an old board they could donate. It wasn't long before John received a call from another of Nate's friends, Chris Shannon.

"I've got a board for you," Chris said.

"Cool."

"No," Chris replied. "I've got *the* board for you. I've got *Nate's* board."

"What? How do you have Nate's board?"

Chris explained that a while back he had asked if anybody had any used surfboards that he could use for benches in front of his surf shop. Nate had been one of the first ones to respond. He drove down to Corpus and gave Chris a short board, his first surfboard.

"So how come this board doesn't have holes in it with concrete?" Olvey asked.

"God only knows," said Chris. "It's still in my garage."

So John picked up Nate's old board and painted a tribute picture for Nate. When requests went out for items to sell in the benefit's silent auction, John Olvey donated the board and posted its story on El Ride:

"Chris had wanted to make a sitting bench in front of his surf shop made of old boards. Nate drove down and gave this board to Chris and told him this was his first surfboard, use it as he saw fit. He hoped it would help Chris.

"God is a weaver of men and events. I believe that God planned that this board never be made into a bench. From Nate's act of kindness to the terrible accident that happened and the pure miracle of his recovery, I can witness how God's hand has taken control of Nate, his family and his friends and the fate of this board.

"This board was never made into the bench. It was for God's purpose that it be recycled into a gift to help Nate. This board shows what the power of faith can do. This board gives glory to God while providing help for Nate.

"There is a picture of Nate surfing that has been used on the Internet. It says simply: Pray for Nate below the image of Nate.

"As an artist, I do not often paint pictures that tell a story. This board does.

"The painting is of the fellowship of Nate's surfing brothers, standing at water's edge with their heads bowed as they pray for Nate. The SON has risen and transforms the surfboards into the sign of their faith on the sand. The wave has partially collapsed and the final outcome of this ride is uncertain. Yet Nate through his faith has pushed his hand out of the shadow of the wave and placed it directly in the light of the SON. It is a beautiful, true story.

"Please remember that the proceeds of this board will glorify GOD and provide for Nate. Perhaps this board will return to Nate. The board has come full circle. First from Nate; now for Nate.

"God recycles lives by giving you his SON, Jesus.

"John Olvey, Artist and fellow surfer."

The board, which started as a random act of kindness from Nate to Chris Shannon, had now been transformed into a work of art that would both tell Nate's story and help pay his medical bills.

The Benefit

As the date of the benefit drew near, and now that Nate had fully awakened from his coma, his friends wondered if he would be able to attend. Tammy and Billy were cautiously optimistic, but were also quick to let everyone know that Nate's appearance at the benefit would be very brief.

On July 19th, just a few days after Nate woke up, Tammy posted on El Ride: "Some of you have been asking about whether or not Nate can be at the party on the 5th. We are trying to work that out. He won't be able to stay and hang out long, but we are working on trying to have him there for 30 minutes or so. He would like to get up on the stage and thank everyone for everything. They still don't want him to get over stimulated, nervous, or anxious. He is already so overwhelmed by everyone and everything. We should hopefully know by late next week if he can be there or not. We are praying it will work out. I know it would mean so much to him. If it is doable, we will let you all know and let you know what time he would be arriving."

By July 27th, the plans for Nate's attendance at the benefit had solidified. Tammy wrote, "We are kinda thinking that we could have Nate (if he goes) to the benefit around 1:00 or 2:00 . . . . We will probably get him on stage to try to thank everyone, then get him back to the car."

Those were the plans. But when Billy and Tammy brought Nate to the Power Avenue Warehouse on the day of the benefit, all plans went out the window. When they pulled into the parking lot, there were cars as far as Nate could see. "It looks like a concert venue," he said.

"We're only going to stay an hour," Tammy reminded him. "The doctor says you don't need to get over stimulated."

"Okay, sure, Mom," replied Nate.

"If you get overwhelmed, you tell me and we'll leave earlier."

They went in the front doors and down a short hallway. There were people all around, and Nate hugged every one of them. When he rounded the corner and entered the main room, Nate was indeed overwhelmed, but in a very good way.

The room was filled with hundreds of people, all there for him. And there were tables full of things for the silent auction and the raffle: paintings, a brand new surfboard, a photo shoot, and so much more. Bar-B-Q plates and PFN caps, shirts, and stickers were also being sold.

"I've never felt so loved in my whole life," he said. "Mom, you see all these people? I've got to thank every one of them."

And with that, Nate plunged into the crowd.

Seabass posted later on El Ride: "Nate was in full force, working the room faster than a vinyl siding salesman at a hurricane shelter after a storm. He was sooo freakin' pumped up and excited, making sure he said hey to everyone. He is super thankful to all the people that have done everything from just post a comment of support or helped arrange hospital accommodations, donations, no matter how big or small the effort, he made sure each and every one knew how much he appreciated it.

"It was quite an experience seeing all this transform in just 60 days, from coma to cruisin' his own benefit bbq. Nate is an amazing young man whose faith in God seems to be VERY much a reciprocal relationship, utterly amazing. I'm not one to be too preachy about my relationship with God, but I recognize his work when I see it. And I have seen it in the last 60 days. I'll leave it at that."—seabass

Nate stayed for the duration of the benefit, talking and visiting with everyone, and making a point to thank each person. An official head count wasn't taken, but they had planned to sell 2500 barbecue plates and they ran out.

As the event wound down, Nate took to the stage, thanked everyone and led them in prayer. And then it was time for a final surprise for Nate.

As the benefit had been in progress, a quiet bidding war had been underway in the silent auction. The prize was Nate's surfboard, now a breathtaking work of art by John Olvey. Several of Nate's buddies, John Olvey and Chris Shannon among them, wanted to make sure that one of them "won" Nate's surfboard. Their plan was to give the board back to Nate as a surprise at the close of the benefit. However, there was one small glitch in the plan. Someone else desperately wanted to win it.

A photo of the board had been posted on El Ride, and even before the benefit MAW (Surfncpa's wife) expressed a desire to win it: "I want that board!!! I know that the right thing to do would be for it to end up with Nate, but I might have to work out some kind of rotation schedule with him if I win it. It can live with Nate for 3 months then live at my house for 9 months! That is a great piece of art and I hope to win it. CPA, get your checkbook out and win that for me for our anniversary gift that you didn't get me yet!!"

As the silent auction progressed throughout the afternoon, so did the bidding war for the surfboard. At first Chris Shannon—who had given the board to John Olvey—bid against the others, not knowing that they had formed a small coalition of Nate's buddies who were so determined to win the board for Nate that they agreed to pool their money if necessary.

"I was driving there to the event in a frantic . . . hoping the bidding would not be over, as I had full intentions of buying the board and giving it to Nate. I was very stressed all the way there, not knowing Mike R. and others had a plan. I outbid them while they gathered for a picture.

Just after the picture we talked and I was relieved to know we all had the same goal. The board belongs to Nate. Always has been his."—CHRIS SHANNON.

Eventually, the Christian Surfers won the day, and the board. And even though MAW didn't get to take the surfboard home, there were no hard feelings. Later, she posted on El Ride: "When Tammy brought Nate over to sit with the Christian Surfer group, I just sat there and stared at that miracle boy in total awe! Nate is a walking/talking miracle and I just hope that his story will help others realize that God does do miracles! I know that Nate has brought my family closer to God, and we will be forever thankful for Nate. We had a great time.

"I want to thank Mike R. for snapping me to my senses and telling me straight out, with a very stern look on his face, 'Don't even try to outbid me MAW, I have backers for that board.' The board did end up in the absolute right spot, with Nate."—MAW

MAW might have been disappointed in not winning the board, but that disappointment was short-lived. A large, 8'x2' banner-sized replica of the board had been printed as one of the wall decorations for the benefit, and Tammy made sure that the banner went home with her. MAW was delighted: "Thanks to Tammy I have an 8'x2' print of the board going up in my house very soon. This whole experience has been amazing and I can't wait to see what God has in store for us next!! PFN."

MAW's husband posted on El Ride a little later: "I never figured we'd win the board, but I bid to make sure it wasn't sold too cheap. I think the threat to hang it up at my house made the CS [Christian Surfers] bidders even more determined to save it from me"—Surfncpa.

MAW wasn't the only one who had reserved a spot for the board in her house. Another of Nate's buddies posted, "When I first got there I had the same intentions as you [MAW]. I have a spot in my study that would be perfect for the board. However, I think it was Dustin that mentioned the board needs to be in Nate's hands. From then on, it was not going anywhere else as long as we could help it."—fredmrtx

At the end of the afternoon, while Nate was still on stage, his buddies brought the painted surfboard up to the stage and presented it to him. On one side of the board (the bottom) was John Olvey's painting; on the other side, all of his fellow surfers, friends, and supporters had signed it.

Later, Tammy posted on El Ride: "Okay, now for the big THANK YOU. With tears streaming as I type this, I just want you to know how thankful we are to everyone who helped out with the board making its way back to Nate. We wanted it so bad and hoped Nate could somehow have it. We even talked about possibly borrowing some money to get it, but knew that wasn't possible right now. We just prayed that God's will would be done. I couldn't let any emotions go at the benefit because I knew I wouldn't stop. When I got home, I went in the restroom and couldn't stop crying. You will never know how much you mean to us."—texasboy's mom

When all was said and done, the benefit pulled in over $45,000 for Nate. Combined with the online account and other fund-raising efforts, Nate's friends, family, and community raised over $60,000 to help cover his medical expenses. But the event was far more than a fund-raiser. Lawrence (nip) summed it up quite well in an El Ride post: "Awesome event. It was amazing seeing how the Lord through Nate brought a small town community and the surfing community together and that Nate's stoke and miraculous recovery seemed to permeate the whole atmosphere. Lots of love and generosity and a sense of true fellowship."

And, although the benefit was a huge blessing for Nate, the greatest blessing he would receive that day was not financial.

Nate's Angel

Brianna Hartman was shy and the idea of helping at Nate's benefit was way out of her comfort zone. Nevertheless, she contacted the lady who was coordinating the event and asked if there was something she could do.

"I don't really know everyone, but I really want to help and I'd like to do something."

"Come on over and we'll find something for you to do," she was told.

Later, Brianna wrote: "I walked in and felt a little awkward because I didn't know anyone and I can be a little shy at times, and I also felt a little out of place. These were people who served at church and had real relationships with God and I did not. It was definitely out of my comfort zone, but I really wanted to be there. It was a huge step for me to try something new. I was amazed at how many people showed up, just for one person. Again, it spoke volumes about the kind of person [Nate] is.

"Here was this guy that just came out of a coma that was so gracious and thankful to everyone for praying for him and being there for him and actually apologizing for making everyone worry and sad for him, when most people probably would have been like, I can't believe this happened to me, my life is ruined. And he was so astonished that so many people came together and did all that stuff for him."

And so Brianna Hartman spent the afternoon at Nate's benefit, serving tea.

❊   ❊   ❊

Just as they were about to leave the benefit, Tammy spotted Brianna. "Come over here, Nate," she said. "I want you to meet someone."

They walked over to where Brianna was serving tea.

"This is Brianna," said Tammy. "She was one of your nurses at the hospital."

"Oh, hi," Nate said as he shook her hand. "T-t-t-thank you so much." Then Nate said something unexpected. "I *know* you. Can I give you a hug?"

At that moment, nobody—not even Nate—understood what he meant by "I know you," but it wouldn't be long before it became crystal clear. In the car as they were driving home from the benefit, Nate exclaimed, "Mom! That's my angel. That's the girl with the teeth and the eyes."

"What?" Tammy said. "That's the girl with the teeth and the eyes that you've been trying to figure out was real or not?"

"Yeah."

"You know what's even stranger, Nate? That's the girl that Dustin was trying to fix you up with before you fell, and you wouldn't have anything to do with it."

"No!" Nate said.

Right then, Nate pulled out his cell phone and called Dustin (aka surfguru who had now changed his El Ride name to DooDoo).

"D-d-d-do-do-do-doodoo? That's the girl you were trying to fix me up with? That was her? W-w-w-well h-h-hook it up, Dude!"

As they drove home, Tammy couldn't help being a little bit worried about Nate. For all they knew at that moment, Nate might never be able to date again. Now he wanted to meet this beautiful girl. But with his disability, his blue helmet, his stuttering, would she even be interested in him?

"God," Tammy prayed, "please let her be sensitive to his feelings. Let her be sweet and not hurt him."

Chapter 27

Brianna (2)

The Thursday following the benefit, Dustin and Jen invited Nate over to their house for dinner. Dustin, a gourmet chef, made fish tacos and they watched surf videos together.

"So, what do you think about Brianna?" Jen asked Nate.

"Who?"

"Brianna," Jen said. "Remember, you met her at the benefit?"

"Oh, yeah, yeah. She's really cool. She's really pretty, Dude. How did she get there? Did she know me or something like that?"

One lingering effect of Nate's injury was short-term memory loss, and so even though he had met Brianna only a few days before, he needed to be reminded of who she was.

"That was the girl we were telling you about, from the hospital," Dustin said. "That's the one I was trying to hook you up with. Remember, you met her at the benefit and you said that she was the girl with the teeth and the eyes."

Dustin and Jen had told Brianna that they were having Nate over and they invited her to stop by their apartment after she got off work. When she arrived, Nate walked over to her and gave her a big hug and stuttered out a greeting.

"Th-that's you, that's you. The girl with the teeth and the eyes. I thought you were an angel. You are, but you're real. I can hug you."

Sometime later, Brianna wrote down her reflections about that meeting:

"We ended up meeting at [Dustin and Jen's] house one night a few nights after the benefit. Nate was stuttering pretty badly, and he had lost a lot of weight and had half of his head caved in. Not exactly your ideal candidate for a potential relationship.

"I got his number from Dustin and called him the next day. I wanted to be able to tell him how he had touched my life, just to be able to thank him and also maybe be friends with him. I had a desire to have these kinds of people in my life at this point, people whom I could learn about the Lord from, that could show me a different way. That sounds very selfish, but I was also so interested to see how he would heal and progress."

First Date (Nate's Perspective)

The next day, Nate's phone rang.

"Nate? This is Brianna."

"W-who?"

"Remember? At the benefit the other day?"

"Oh, yeah," Nate answered, but he was still not sure. There had been so many people at the benefit, it was as if his brain was overloaded.

"Would you like to go talk somewhere?" she asked.

"Sure," said Nate. "Why don't we go get some ice cream or something?"

Brianna picked Nate up and they went out to a local ice cream shop. She couldn't help notice that people were staring at Nate, moving somewhat clumsily and wearing his blue helmet. At first she felt bad for him, but then she noticed that it didn't seem to bother him. When he had difficulty handling the cone—and managed to get ice cream all over himself—she laughed and asked him, "Would you like me to get a bowl to put that in?"

At that moment, Nate knew that Brianna was going to be a big part of his life, someone to help him. "At that point I wasn't asking for help," Nate said later. "But I knew that this [the recovery] was going to be a long term thing."

After Brianna got a bowl for Nate's ice cream, they sat and talked for hours, discussing everything from Nate's time in the Coast Guard to ministry. Nate perceived that Brianna was reaching out.

"When I took care of you, I've never had a patient like you. You touched my heart," Brianna said.

"How did you feel, looking at me in such a bad situation?" Nate asked.

"I was really worried," she said. "It could have been me. I saw this young guy, his dreams and life pretty much all over."

"So, I gotta ask you a question. You've got your own life going on. I cannot fathom why you would want to put up with someone who's so busted up right now."

"I've been a Christian all my life, but I never had a walk with the Lord."

At that moment, Nate realized something significant. As he put it, "I felt that my ministry was gone as far as serving and giving." But if his life and story was impacting Brianna, then perhaps he still had something to give.

When Brianna dropped Nate off at home, he said, "I'll be going to rehab in a few days. They tell me I'll be there six months, but I'll be out sooner than that."

"I'll call you a lot," Brianna said.

As he watched her drive away, Nate thought, "If somebody is willing to put up with all my speech problems and other issues, it can only get better."

First Date (Brianna's Perspective)

"I went and picked him up for what we now call our first date. He was so thin and had to wear a blue helmet and couldn't talk very well, so of course he attracted a lot of attention going out in public . . . . I was a little uncomfortable with people looking at him, but he was all smiles and didn't have a care in the world, so I just got over it.

"I shared with him that I had never known anyone like him, and I wanted him to know how he touched my life. I told him that I had always been a Christian, but not a Christ follower. I never talked about

God much with anyone, so it was a new experience for me, but I had to tell him.

"It has always been very difficult for me to talk to people about feelings and God, so I surprised myself at how easy it was to talk to him. I felt that I could be open with him, and I didn't feel that I would be judged at all. This was all a new experience for me . . . . I think I knew at that point that he was going to have a huge impact in my life, but I didn't quite know what that meant.

"At that point his future was so uncertain. There was a mountain in front of him and I had no idea how it was going to go, or why I had any right to be a part of it. We talked for several hours over ice cream, and he was so open about his life and experiences prior to his accident, and how he felt about all that he was going through. He was so positive and so sure that God would take care of him, and that everything would turn out okay.

"To have that attitude in the midst of where he was blew my mind. I was just so intrigued by him . . . . He made me feel like I could do this. I could change my life and let God take over and fix all the messes I had made. I wanted what Nate had. I wanted that quiet, easy confidence, that cloud of peace around him, that light that shone even through stutters and a helmet. I was amazed at his faith, in spite of the circumstances.

"I thought, wow, to be going through all this, and to have such unwavering faith. Who can do that? I want that. I want to know what it's like to live my life like that.

"From that day on, we talked every day."

Chapter 28

TLC

A bed opened up at TLC earlier than expected, and so after only about two weeks at home, Nate was on his way to Galveston. As he and his family looked back over the events of the past few years, they rejoiced at how God worked behind the scenes, providing for Nate's needs, even before his accident.

God had placed Nate in Galveston for the last two years of his Coast Guard enlistment because He knew Nate was going to be going back there to do his rehab. During the time Nate was stationed in Galveston he became involved in the Christian Surfers group and met many of his good friends: J. P., seabass, nip, jsh [Joey], Surfncpa, and others. Those friends gave him a strong support base in Galveston, which is why it was no big surprise that of the two rehab facilities in Texas that Nate could go to, one was the Transitional Learning Center (TLC) in Galveston. And TLC "just happened" to be the best choice for Nate's particular type of injury.

God had provided—again.

Located near the sea wall in Galveston's historic district, TLC would take Nate's rehab to the next level. At TIRR MH, because it is acute care, the rehab was limited in scope and sessions were short in duration—often about twenty minutes. At TLC, rehab would be Nate's full-time job. He would do rehab from nine to five, every weekday. Nate felt he was more than ready to meet the challenge. He knew there was a reason God didn't take him home when he fell. God had a call on Nate's life, to speak the truth about God and Jesus Christ into people's lives. If he was going to do that, he needed to get his speech back.

He also expected to make progress.

"God doesn't just meet our expectations," he told Tammy. "He exceeds them. If they said I'll be here for six months, I'll be out in three."

His resolve was strong. After Billy and Tammy had helped him get situated in his room and left to return to Victoria, Nate said to himself, "Time to get to work." He was nervous about being by himself, but he felt he was up to the challenge.

Nevertheless, his first week at TLC was not just challenging; it was frustrating.

He didn't get much sleep the first night because someone came into his room every hour and turned on the light to check on him and make sure he was safe.

"They don't know how far you've progressed," Nate said later.

Until they are tested and assessed, all new patients are treated alike at TLC, regardless of their current degree of recovery. And so, even though Nate had lived at home for two weeks and enjoyed a small degree of independence, he was now being watched carefully—and constantly.

Upon his arrival, Nate received a blue binder that contained his daily schedule, plus all the rules and guidelines he would have to follow while he was at TLC. One of the first pages in the notebook was a reminder of his accident.

"What Happened to Me?

"On June 4, 2007, I sustained a severe traumatic brain injury as a result of a fall from a ladder. I was transported to the hospital in Victoria, Texas. On June 28, 2007, I was transferred to TIRR in Houston, Texas

"On August 13, 2007, I was admitted to TLC to continue my rehabilitation. When I have completed my rehabilitation at TLC, I will live with my parents in Victoria, Texas."

Another page provided a quick summary of what Nate could expect.

"You will start out being closely supervised and then gain more freedom/independence as you progress. The degree and rate of progress is unique to each client."

Nate felt almost as if he were back in the military. He didn't know his limits, what he was and was not allowed to do. One thing was certain. Expectations were high. Under the heading "Behavior" in his notebook it read: "1. You are expected to be on time for all modules . . . . 2. When in a session, you are expected to participate and complete all assignments." Nate saw how literally this was enforced in one of his group sessions.

In one session, a young woman began to scream, "I've got to get out of here! Now! Now! Now! I can't be here. The walls are closing in. I've got to see my kids!"

She was gone the next day.

Nate felt sad for her. He realized that she was not only giving up on herself, but on her children, too. "If you can't take care of yourself," he thought, "how are you going to take care of your kids?" Nate resolved to work as hard as he could, so that he could complete his rehab successfully and go home.

No matter how difficult it got, he was not going to give up on himself.

❖   ❖   ❖

The program Nate was in had three levels, each involving progressive degrees of independence. The first involved constant supervision. At times Nate found the supervision frustrating because he had already been doing quite a few things on his own. Tammy asked for prayer in an El Ride post.

"Nate checked in to TLC in Galveston on Monday. He is trying to adjust. He is having a tough time with having to have someone watch him constantly . . . . We've all explained to him that this won't last long, but he's still a little frustrated with it . . . . Please continue to pray for Nate to recover quickly so he can get home. Also so that he can read again. He really misses that. Also, if you get a chance to visit him or give him a call on his cell phone from 5:00 p.m. to 8:00 p.m., I know it would really encourage him."

Tammy was correct. Nate's period of close supervision was very brief. In fact, in less than two weeks, he progressed to Level 2, still under supervision, but with more freedom. Shortly after that, he was promoted to Level 3, an "apartment" on the ground floor. At TLC, apartment living provided the greatest degree of independence. The goal was for Nate to cultivate the everyday skills he would need for living on his own.

Nate shared his apartment with a roommate who had suffered a head injury in a motor vehicle accident.

"I hate being here," he told Nate.

Nate's positive attitude spilled over. "Well," he said, "everyday's a good day when you're not in a coma. Gotta see the blessings through the pain."

His roommate was almost a year removed from his accident but still suffered from significant short-term memory loss, which made it difficult for Nate to have a conversation with him. Periodically, as they were talking, his roommate would say, "Oh, you know what happened to me, right?" and then explain how he was hurt all over again.

Even though Nate got frustrated at times, he understood what his roommate was going through. Nate had his own struggles with short term memory loss, although not as severe as his roommate's. Nevertheless, Nate found it difficult to pray. Before his accident, Nate would pray early in the morning, sometimes for a half-hour or more. Now, he sometimes got no further than, "Father, thank you for . . ." before he would have to start over.

"How do you pray when your memory's shot?" he often wondered.

And Nate not only wanted to pray, he longed to have a normal conversation. Even though he still stuttered, Nate was able to communicate where so many of the other patients were not. Whenever he could Nate would engage the therapists and other staff in conversations, just so he would have somebody to talk to.

Nate would also get on El Ride as much as possible, but his reading level was little more than first grade, and so often he was unable to read the posts. Nevertheless, he could recognize the various authors of the posts by their avatars.

Fortunately, Nate had several lifelines: His parents, his surfing buddies, and Brianna.

❖   ❖   ❖

Even though Nate was living over two-and-a-half hours away from Victoria, Tammy, Billy, and Brianna stayed in touch as much as they were able. TLC had tighter visiting hours than TIRR MH—Nate could have visitors only from five to eight p.m. on the weekdays. However, on alternating weekends, he was allowed to go home to Victoria with Tammy and Billy.

During the week, Tammy worked at a uniform store nearby in Sugar Land that her friend, Fran, owned, and then she would spend the night at Elissa's apartment in Houston. On weekends when Nate could go home, she would pick him up on Friday evening and take him back to Victoria with her. On the weekends where Nate had to stay in Galveston, Billy and Tammy would drive up and they would get a hotel room. Then they'd spend time with Nate there and take him out on a day pass. This was their routine for three and a half months.

During the week, when Billy and Tammy were unable to be there, Nate's surfing buddies would come by for visits and would take him out whenever they could. Reflecting on this later, Nate said, "When I was in the Coast Guard, I thought I was going to Galveston for them. Now, Galveston was there for me."

As for Brianna, she called Nate every night and sometimes they would talk for as much as two hours. One weekend she drove all the way to Galveston and they had lunch together on the seawall. At one point, he asked her, "Why would you come all the way down here to be with me?"

Another time, Nate broached a subject that had been on his mind for a while. "So, you wanna be my girlfriend?"

"You need to concentrate on getting well, not on having a relationship," she told him.

Nevertheless, on the weekends when he came home, they began to spend more and more time together. Nate admitted later, "About a month and a half in, I knew this was the person I wanted to spend my life with." And although Brianna was more cautious, she also knew that something special was developing.

"I talked to him on the phone every night for at least an hour or two," she wrote later. "I mostly just listened and it took him awhile to get out whatever it was he was trying to say. I learned what it means to be patient, to really listen to someone. Now I have a patience with him that could have only come from God, a patience that I don't have with many other people or things. I was excited to see how he would progress and where he would be in a year or two. He was so hardcore with his therapies and so determined to do the best he could do to overcome his disabilities. Our relationship grew and out of the worst circumstances, we became a couple.

"I still found it a little strange that my boyfriend had to wear a helmet and wasn't really normal, but I was so hooked."

❖   ❖   ❖

For several reasons, as the weeks passed, Nate's resolve grew. Partly, it was because he was around so many people who had sustained their injuries long before him, but who had not progressed as far in their recoveries as he had. Partly, it was a desire to get back home as soon as he could. But mostly, it was his realization that God had kept him alive for a purpose: to share his story. And as his resolve to make the most of his time in rehab grew, he began to make requests of his therapists.

In certain areas of his rehab, math for example, Nate was excelling. Where he really needed work was in speech therapy. At the beginning of his second month at TLC, he asked if he could double up on his speech therapy. Midway through the second month, he asked to triple up. He not only did three times as much speech therapy as required, but he asked for extra homework. For Nate, regaining his ability to speak and read were top priorities.

As he had predicted, Nate was ready to graduate from TLC in only about three and a half months. Nate was asked to prepare a five-minute graduation speech for the event, and he worked very hard to make it perfect. Before his accident, when Nate would teach or give a sermon, he always used notes or outlines. This time, he wanted to deliver his speech without notes and, most of all, without stuttering.

"Five minutes or less," he thought. "I can at least store a minute's worth of a speech."

Nate wrote down some thoughts and worked at memorizing them.

"It wasn't anything fancy," he said later, "I said that this place is a miracle place and thank you to all the therapists. And I'm looking forward to going home. This is a great place to get back to life. I couldn't have done it without them."

The speech was only about two minutes long, but the best part for Nate was that he didn't stutter. "When I first arrived at TLC, I stuttered badly, but when I walked out at graduation, I spoke slower—I'd trained my brain to slow down—and I didn't stutter.

After graduation was over, Brianna asked Tammy and Billy, "Would you mind if I drove him home?"

They agreed.

And so Nate loaded up his things in Brianna's car, and said goodbye to another temporary home.

Chapter 29

Back Home

After Nate graduated from TLC he moved back home with Billy and Tammy. He still had some rehab ahead of him, although it wouldn't begin until January. And this time it would be done outpatient, at Warm Springs Specialty Hospital in Victoria. He also faced more surgery. He still had a softball-sized hole in his skull, and a plate would need to be inserted before he could stop wearing his blue helmet. He was also going to need more surgery on his wrist. It had not healed properly and the muscles in his hand had atrophied. Although his hand would never be totally the way it was before the accident, Nate's orthopedic surgeon felt that by re-breaking his wrist and inserting a rod, they could free up some nerves that had been pinched when the bones in his wrist had fused incorrectly. But even more daunting than the surgical prospects was the question of where Nate's ministry should go from here. He knew God wanted him to share his story, and invitations to do that began to come in. In addition to speaking, Nate was eventually asked to take on the role of youth pastor at Parkway Church.

But the first priority was getting the hole in his head fixed.

❈   ❈   ❈

Nate was admitted to the hospital in Victoria early on Monday of Thanksgiving week for surgery to insert a plate in his skull. Although Nate was looking forward to not having to wear his helmet anymore, he was very nervous about the surgery, and questions raced through his mind.

Nate wondered, "Are they going to mess around with my brain again? Will I wake up? What if something happens and I go back to the way I was?"

Tammy, Billy, and Brianna prayed with Nate in pre-op. Because Brianna was a nurse, she was permitted to go with him into surgery, and she had planned to do so. But she eventually realized that she was too close to Nate now, and being in the OR while they operated on Nate was just too much. She elected to stay in the waiting room with Billy and Tammy.

As they waited for news about Nate's surgery, Tammy decided to talk to Brianna about her relationship with Nate. She had been concerned for a while, but hadn't said anything about it. Tammy wanted to be sure that Brianna genuinely cared for Nate and was not spending time with him because she felt sorry for him.[12]

"If you love Nate, and want to be in a relationship with him, that's okay," Tammy said. "But if you're here because you feel sorry for him, that's not going to work for either of you."

"That's not what this is about," Brianna replied. "It has nothing to do with feeling sorry for him. When he was in the ICU, I went down there because I wanted to see him. He had this sense of peace around him. I knew he was someone special. As I looked at him a thought popped into my mind. This is who you're going to marry. It was strange. Everybody was wondering if this kid was going to live, and here I am thinking this is who I'm going to spend the rest of my life with."

When Nate was out of recovery, Tammy, Billy, and Brianna were told they could go back to see him in the surgical ICU—the same place he was after his brain surgery. Unpleasant memories flooded through Tammy's mind as they approached the doors to the ICU. The thought of seeing her son unconscious in an ICU bed again was almost too much. She reached out and took Billy's hand.

---

[12] Author's Note: This conversation actually took place during a subsequent surgery (on Nate's wrist) but has been placed here in the interest of maintaining the flow of the story.

When the doors opened, there was Nate—in the exact same spot where he had been before. But instead of being unconscious, Nate was sitting up and smiling.

"Hey, what's up?" Nate said.

He had come through the surgery with no problems. A few days later, on the day before Thanksgiving, Nate went home, with no hole in his head and no more need for a helmet.

Setback

The Christmas holiday was an especially happy one for the Lytles. A little less than six months earlier, Nate had been lying in a hospital bed, not expected to live. Now, that bleak prognosis was a distant memory. Nate had not only recovered, but he had done so quicker and more completely than anyone had expected. In January, he would begin his outpatient rehab, mostly to address ongoing issues with his aphasia and apraxia. It looked like relatively smooth sailing for Nate from then on.

That would change dramatically a few days after Christmas.

Nate, Brianna, Tammy and Billy were about to leave the house to go visit one of Nate's friends. Tammy and Billy stood behind the couch where Nate and Brianna were sitting.

"Are y'all about ready to go?" Tammy asked.

Nate started to stand up, then a wave of dizziness hit him and he sat back down.

"Are you okay?" Tammy and Brianna asked together.

"Mom, I can't see," Nate said.

"What do you mean you can't see?

"I think I'm gonna be sick."

Tammy quickly retrieved an emesis basin left over from Nate's hospital stay and tried to hand it to him. Nate reached out but he couldn't grasp it.

"Do you feel like you're going to throw up or not?" Tammy asked.

"I don't know. I don't know," Nate replied.

Suddenly, Nate's right arm began twitching. Tammy put the emesis basin on the coffee table where Nate could reach it, but he couldn't reach out and take it.

"I can't," he said. Then he began to slur his words. Seconds later, Nate's head tilted back and his right arm and leg began to curl in. His mouth was now wide open and his tongue lolled to one side. A guttural moan escaped his lips. He began sliding off the couch.

"We've got to get him down on the floor, said Tammy"

Billy and Brianna were standing behind the couch.

"Call 911!" Tammy shouted.

While Billy went to call 911, Brianna went to help Tammy with Nate.

"Is he having a stroke or seizure or what?" Tammy asked.

"I don't know," Brianna said. "It could be a seizure. I don't know."

By this time Nate's arms and legs were curled up to his body, like those of a paralytic.

With Brianna taking care of Nate, and Billy also in the house, Tammy decided to go outside. She wanted to be out there to flag down the ambulance in case the driver had difficulty finding the house; she also couldn't stand the thought that Nate might be dying.

For the first time since Nate's injury, Tammy was on the verge of asking, "God, why?"

"I was so exhausted," Tammy said later. "I thought he was having a stroke, and I thought, 'I'm not going to sit here and watch my kid die. I can't do it. After all we'd been through.'"

Tammy, Billy, and Brianna followed the ambulance to the hospital and waited as the EMTs took him back to the trauma room. When the doctor came out, he told them that Nate had suffered a grand mal seizure. They would later learn that most people who have had open head injuries will have a seizure within the first six to eight months, but no one had prepared them in advance for that possibility.

Although the doctor started Nate on the anti-seizure drug Dilantin, it was not effective in controlling his seizures. It also made him sleepy, and so Nate and his family embarked on a long process of finding the right medication. After searching and praying, God led them to Dr. Brian Loftus in Houston, who tried a few more medications. He eventually settled on Keppra, an effective but very expensive anti-seizure drug. Again, God provided for Nate's needs in a marvelous way. Although Nate was able to get medications through the V.A., when he began having seizures, Keppra was not one of the approved drugs. Dr. Loftus tried several other medications first, with varying degrees of success. By the time he decided to try Nate on Keppra, the V.A. had approved it. Nate was now able to get the medication he needed—which normally cost over $300 per prescription—for only an eight-dollar co-pay.

When Nate was struggling to control his seizure disorder, for the first time since his accident, he became discouraged. He had been trying to serve as youth pastor, but the seizures so limited him that he didn't feel he should continue. He also decided to back away from speaking.

"How can I encourage people when I'm struggling myself?" he told Tammy.

But over time, and particularly once he was on Keppra, the seizures were brought under control and Nate was able to turn his focus back toward ministry. Nevertheless, he decided not to continue as youth pastor. He didn't need to be paid to work with the youth. He was more than happy to do that for free.

Proposal

Early in 2008, Nate decided it was time to propose to Brianna. He wanted it to be special, something they would both always remember.

And he came up with a plan that would make even the most romantic person envious.

Brianna's favorite color was purple, so Nate bought a glass jar and some little purple rocks. Then he painstakingly, crafted twenty five miniature envelopes, into which he put small, fortune-cookie-sized messages. Each message was something that Nate liked or appreciated about Brianna.

"Thank you for loving me the way you do," said one.

Another read, "Thank you for being so supportive."

He numbered the envelopes from one to twenty-five and with an atrophied wrist managed to tie a tiny purple bow on each one.

Beginning on Valentine's Day, he had Brianna open one envelope each night. He had scheduled the openings so that she would get the last envelope on their seven-month anniversary.

On March 9th, he cooked a special dinner for her, Chicken Alfredo. After dinner, he had Brianna open the final envelope.

The last note read, "I love you so much. Will you marry me?"

By the time Brianna had read the note, Nate was down on one knee, holding out a ring.

Brianna was delighted. "Yes, yes, of course I'll marry you."

Nate breathed a sigh of relief. "Oh, thank you, 'cause I didn't know."

Brianna laughed. "What do you mean you don't know?"

"Well, I'm still really jacked up."

Nate needn't have worried.

"I married Nate," Brianna wrote later, "because his life is a true example of what real love is. He lives by his faith and walks in God's love. He challenges me to be better. He doesn't settle for anything less than God's best and that is exactly what God gave me in him.

"He inspires people to be better. We were not meant to just coexist in this world but to live—with the living breathing Spirit of our Creator, and I might have missed out on that if God had not given me Nate to walk alongside. What an honor that I got to marry and get to spend my life with the best person I've ever known, my best friend and perfect mate that the Lord created just for me.

"What a blessing that I get to give and receive a love that has no bounds in my Father, and I get to share in this life with a man whom I love beyond what I thought was possible, and that He has perfectly intertwined those loves. What a precious gift from the Lord. To Him all the honor and glory and praise.

"Nate has taught me so much about love, about patience, about truly giving oneself up to the Lord, about the things in this life that really matter, about the person I want to be, about believing in myself because of who God created me to be in His eyes, about giving and selflessness, and most of all what it really means to have faith."

In March of 2009, Nate married his angel.

Full Circle

Late in May of 2008, almost a full year after Nate's injury, Tammy, Billy, Brianna, and Nate's grandfather, Papaw, took him down to the seawall. It was time to get back into the water. Nate was still in the process of getting his seizures under control, but he hadn't had one in several months. In any case, Nate had prayed about it and he was at peace with going back into the water.

A few months prior, he had undergone surgery to repair his damaged left wrist and still wore a brace, but he didn't worry about that either.

Just before his accident, Nate had decided that he would give up surfing for a year to devote his attention to building his relationship with God. After he was injured, his family and friends wondered if he would ever be able to surf again. But Nate knew he'd be back on his board within a year.

Mike Boyd, one of Nate's surfing buddies, met them at the beach. He promised Tammy that he would watch out for Nate and take good care of him. The plan was to just go a little way out into the water, to take things slow.

Nate was having none of that.

Before anyone realized it, Nate had paddled out past the end of the pier.

It wasn't pretty at first, but he was on a board. Back where he belonged.

God took away surfing from Nate for a year and then gave it back. But God gave him much more than surfing. He brought Nate full circle and gave him a ministry. Nate's passion has always been to speak the truth into people's lives.

God made him the object lesson.

"If even one person comes to Christ through all this," said Nate, "then it was all worth it."

Nate & Shawn at TIRR Memorial Hermann July 16 2007

Nate with the students, Devon (left), and Nathan (right),
promoting the PFN benefit in Victoria July 31 2007

Nate with friends home at Victoria wearing PFN shirts
July 31 2007

Nate with his mom, Tammy, July 31 2007

Nate meeting the neurosurgeon, Dr. Norvill,
for the first time August 1 2007

Nate with his parents, Billy and Tammy, speaking at the
PFN benefit August 5 2007

Nate with the surf crew at the PFN benifit August 5 2007

Nate on an outing with the TLC staff October 2007

Nate on an outing with other TLC clients and staff
November 2007

TLC graduation support from previous coast guard
co-workers, surfers, and family

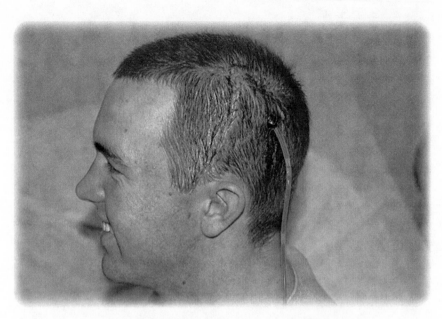

Nate after plate surgery November 21 2007

Nate surfing Hurricane Ike South Padre Island, TX
September 12 2008

Brianna and Nate at their wedding March 14 2009

Nate surfing Bob Hall Pier Corpus Christi, TX
September 17 2010

Nate surfing Bob Hall Pier Corpus Christi, TX January 9 2010

Nate recieving the Texas State Survivor of the Year award
Austin, TX April 16 2011

Nate speaking at the Brain Injury Association of Texas
statewide conference April 17 2011

Epilogue

A ten-year-old boy stood on the beach in Port Aransas. He had been born blind, but even though he couldn't see what was going on around him, his other senses were almost on overload.

The roar of crashing surf and seagulls' cries filled his ears. The air smelled of salt, and occasionally he felt a cool spray. Warm bubbly water from the Gulf of Mexico tickled his feet and his toes sank into the gritty sand.

He was attending his very first surf camp.

As he stood there, he sensed someone coming up to him.

"Hi, I'm Nate," a man's voice said. "You ready to catch some waves?"

"Uh-huh," the boy replied.

"You ever been to the beach?" Nate asked.

"Yeah," the boy said. "But I don't remember much."

"Well, this is a day you're not going to forget, man, because you're going to surf."

Nate, along with some other people, helped him walk out into the water and get on a board. He lay on his belly, feeling the water moving beneath the board. He could tell the board wanted to move too.

"Here comes one," said Nate. "Are you ready?"

The boy nodded.

Seconds later, he felt a surge, picking him up, propelling him forward like a rocket. It was exhilarating, like nothing he'd ever felt in his life. It was pure joy.

When he was back in shallow water, Nate and the others helped him do it all over again.

On his fourth try, the boy stood up.

He heard some voices behind him saying, "Look at these kids, dude! It's insane."

Yeah, it was. And he was loving every minute of it.

And Nate was right.

He would never forget this day.

Nate leading the young blind boy from the water Port
Aransas, TX August 12 2010

Watching a blind young lady finding peace and independence
on a surfboard Port Aransas, TX August 12 2010

Surf camp for the blind Port Aransas, TX July 12 2011

Surf camp for those with disabilities Port Aransas,
TX June 29 2009

Freedom Port Aransas, TX June 29 2009

All smiles Port Aransas, TX June 28 2010

All ages Port Aransas, TX June 28 2010

Nate sharing the joy with the little ones Port Aransas, TX
June 28 2010

Not so paralyzed Port Aransas, TX June 26 2011

Nate sharing the stoke with another young lady Port
Aransas, TX June 26 2011

Afterword

by Nate Lytle

No one is prepared for a traumatic brain injury (TBI). There are no easy ways to live with a brain injury and it is not easy to live with someone who has had a brain injury. Speaking for myself, I can only say that the power of prayer and the strength of Christ is what brought me this far.

While in the coma, my brain started working and comprehending. It's very weird because doctors say that I should have no recollection of the coma and other patients that have brain injuries remember little to nothing. I remember several things from the time I was in the coma. I remember the sixth week, shortly before I woke up, thinking that I must have been locked in a long dream that I couldn't wake up from. I remember thinking that the only way that I would wake up was by prayer. So I started praying that last week that God would just wake me up from this dream, and it worked.

Prayer is a tool that we can all use.

There are still days that I find more challenging than others. I still miss words while I type (I just missed four in the last paragraph), and I still have to take a nap daily. On days that I'm doing a lot, it shows in my conversations, and my short-term memory will never be perfect.

I'm not perfect . . . I wasn't 100 percent before my injury. It's good to be vulnerable. Even before I fell, I never wanted to be 100 percent. Being 100 percent means that I can do everything by myself, basically saying I do not need God.

I've just accepted who I am since the TBI. Because of the TBI, many doors have been opened, and I have met many amazing people I probably would never have met if none of this had happened. I pray and hope that this story has encouraged you to ask for help when needed. Life's too hard to live it alone, and with a TBI, it's pretty much impossible.

Falling and almost dying was the best thing that ever happened to me. I've never felt more loved. I feel like I never really asked a whole lot from people, just to listen and converse. Since I fell, being humbled to the point where I couldn't talk or walk put even a greater emphasis on people. While I was sleeping, people all over bore the load for me. When strangers are showering you and helping you go to the bathroom, any pride you had kind of goes out the window.

People are always saying that God is not big enough to take on our struggles, so we take on one hundred percent of the effort. One thing I do know is that God will always meet you half way if you ask and surrender your pride. You have to put in your fifty percent if you want God to honor your requests and that will be in His timing if/ when given.

I now understand that when I first fell, God put in the right people to bring me back to life; from Dr. Norvill (neurosurgeon) to Dr. McNeill (trauma) to therapists at the hospital, TIRR Memorial Hermann, TLC, and Warm Springs. He also provided friends for food, students for lively energy in the hospital, etc. God worked through everything and everybody! I was not competent at those times to do much for myself, so God provided the right things. Now that I have healed more, I'm able to make more logical decisions and do more cognitive thinking. If we would've written this book a year or three years ago, we would've missed too many miracles.

Think about a struggle you've had in your life, big or small. What do you do? Locate the problem, work through the problem (counseling, reading up on the issue, etc.), and finally you find a resolution to the issue and find peace. With a brain injury, though, it's a little bit harder. Even if you can recognize your struggle, how do you work through it when your memory is so shot and your brain direction is so backward that you can't even remember what you just told someone? Living with a brain injury is very challenging. It doesn't come and go. The struggle is ongoing.

Many people don't want to talk about the difficulties they face because it's too painful to look back at all you have gone through. I say, never forget. Embrace your past! If you forget your past, you'll never truly appreciate the present and how far you've come in your recovery and the future God has in store for you!

Try to live in that spot where God uses you best. Being forced to live there was an honor. I try to be there daily: that spot between a coma and an independent life. I would never want to go back to my previous life before the injury. I would have never met and shared life with the kind of people (brain injured patients and their families, etc.) I have recently, if I had not fallen.

Remember that your greatest misery is your greatest ministry.

—Nate Lytle, September 2011

Nate and Brianna now live in Corpus Christi, Texas.

Nate is an inspirational speaker and stays busy traveling and speaking to churches and groups, and sharing his story wherever he can. He also leads an ongoing support group at TIRR Memorial Hermann for families of people who have suffered traumatic brain injuries and visits brain-injury patients often.

Nate also conducts surf camps for the blind and disabled.

If you would be interested in having Nate speak to your church, group, or at your event, or you are interested in a surf camp, visit his Web site: www.natelytle.com

James H. Pence is a performance chalk artist, singer, speaker, published author, and ghostwriter. Jim has been called a "Renaissance man," but he prefers to be known simply as a follower of Jesus Christ and a storyteller. Jim is the author or co-author of nine books, including the recently-released The Encounter, a collaboration with bestselling author Stephen Arterburn. http://jamespence.com.

Appendix 1

More God

After Nate woke up from his coma with his difficultly of word finding and limited speech, anytime something happened that was obviously the hand of God, the easiest way he could explain himself to Tammy was by saying, "See, Mom? That's just more God." He decided early on that he would write a book about his journey and title it *More God*.

The authors hope that readers of this book may find encouragement as they review a few of the "God things" that happened in Nate Lytle's story:

- Nate was given fifteen minutes to live before being taken to emergency surgery. If everything had not gone exactly as it did (e.g., if Billy had waited for an ambulance or if Nate hadn't broken his wrist so badly that he was taken back to a trauma room), Nate probably would have died.
- The sign-in nurse at the ER was not present when Nate arrived, and so they were not told to wait in the waiting area. Even the shortest delay would probably have proved fatal.
- The CAT scan tech, Justin, lived across the street from the Lytles. He happened to come by at just the right time and expedited Nate's CAT scan.
- The neurosurgeon, Dr. Norvill, had an office across the street. There had been no neurosurgeon on call for three months at the hospital. Had Dr. McNeill not called Dr. Norvill and asked

him to come help out and Dr. Norvill not agreed to come, there would have been no surgery and Nate would have died. Because of the severity of Nate's injuries, there wouldn't have been time to CareFlight him into Houston.

- Nate's medical bills totaled nearly one million dollars, and he had no insurance. Every penny was paid by DARS, Social Security and generous donations from friends, family, and the community, and Nate has no debt from anything related to his accident.

- Dr. McNeill, the ER doctor, said that Nate survived a "non-survivable" event. Nate's brain had a mid-line shift of 1.7 centimeters. Dr. McNeill said that a shift of a couple millimeters is considered "grave." He also said Nate's CT scan showed signs of herniation which is usually fatal.

- Nate was not supposed to survive. If he did survive, the doctors said that he would never walk, talk, or communicate again because the part of his brain that was damaged controls those functions. Within days of his accident, Nate was responding. Within a few weeks, he was communicating. Within 42 days, he was walking and talking.

- Nate suffered massive trauma to the left side of his brain, yet has no trace of impairment on the right side of his body other than the loss of peripheral vision in his right eye.

- Nate had no insurance or funding, yet he was given a bed at TIRR Memorial Hermann, one of the best rehab facilities in the country for people with brain injuries.

- Nate's recovery was remarkable, particularly to people who deal with brain injury patients on a daily basis. One doctor said that they usually measure improvement by months in cases like Nate's. He improved radically in weeks.

- Even though he was at the bottom of a waiting list, Nate received major funding from DARS in a matter of weeks and at a time of the year when they don't normally even have money to distribute.

Appendix 2

Resources

BRAIN INJURY:

Glasgow & Rancho Los Amigos scales—http://www.waiting.com/
levelsofcoma.html

Brain Injury Association of America—www.biausa.org

Brain Injury Association of Texas—www.biatx.org

Brain Injury Forum—www.traumaticbraininjuryforum.com

Brain Injury Resource Center—www.headinjury.com

Texas Department of Assistive and Rehabilitative Services (DRS and
DADS programs)—www.dars.state.tx.us

The Institute for Rehabilitation and Research (TIRR Memorial
Hermann)—http://www.memorialhermann.org/locations/tirr

A Subsidiary of Post Acute Medical—http://www.warmsprings.org/
home

Transitional Learning Center (TLC)—http://tlcrehab.org

Betty Clooney Foundation—http://www.bcftbi.org

Centers for Disease Control and Prevention—http://www.cdc.gov/
TraumaticBrainInjury

General Resources—http://www.brainline.org/index.html

Information and Resources for People with Disabilities—http://www.
disaboom.com

SOCIAL NETWORKS / PATIENT RESOURCES:

Share Experiences, Meet Brain Injury People, Get Support and Information about Head Injuries—http://www.traumaticbraininjuryforum.com

The Social Network for Traumatic Brain Injury—http://www.wearetbi.org

CarePages websites are free patient blogs that connect friends and family during a health challenge—http://www.carepages.com

Connecting Family and Friends When Health Matters Most—http://www.caringbridge.org/partner/biausa

SURFING:

El Ride Texas Surfing Forum—http://www.elrideintl.net/main/forumv4/index.php

Texas Coastal Bend Chapter—http://surfridercoastalbend.org/coastalbend/Default.aspx

Christian Surfers U.S.—http://www.christiansurfers.com/index.php